Economics of the Caspian Oil and Gas Wealth

Euro-Asian Studies

General Editor: Christoph Bluth, Visiting Professor, Centre for Euro-Asian Studies, University of Reading, and Professor in International Studies, University of Leeds

The transition of the countries in Euro-Asia is one of the most important developments affecting the international system since the end of the Cold War. The development of market economies after decades of central planning, the formation of new states and national identities, the creation of new, democratic institutions of state and the reintegration into the world economy pose enormous challenges. Whilst some countries have progressed relatively well and are in the process of joining the European Union, others have experienced several economic and social dislocations, to the point of political disintegration and armed conflicts. The Centre for Euro-Asian Studies at the University of Reading is dedicated to the academic study of the political, economic, social and cultural aspects of this process. This series presents the most recent contributions from leading academics in the field. With an interdisciplinary focus, it seeks to provide a substantial, original and ongoing contribution to our understanding of the region which is of vital importance for academics and of high policy relevance for governments and businesses.

Titles include:

Yelena Kalyuzhnova
ECONOMICS OF THE CASPIAN OIL AND GAS WEALTH
Companies, Governments, Policies

Yelena Kalyuzhnova and Dov Lynch (*editors*)
THE EURO-ASIAN WORLD
A Period of Transition

Yelena Kalyuzhnova, Amy Myers Jaffe, Dov Lynch and Robin C. Sickles (*editors*)
ENERGY IN THE CASPIAN REGION
Present and Future

Yelena Kalyuzhnova and Wladimir Andreff (*editors*)
PRIVATISATION AND STRUCTURAL CHANGE IN TRANSITION ECONOMIES

Yelena Kalyuzhnova and Michael Taylor (*editors*)
TRANSITIONAL ECONOMIES
Banking, Finance, Institutions

Lúcio Vinhas de Souza and Bas van Aarle (*editors*)
THE EUROAREA AND THE NEW EU MEMBER STATES

Christoph H. Stefes
UNDERSTANDING POST-SOVIET TRANSITIONS
Corruption, Collusion and Clientelism

Christopher P.M. Waters (*editor*)
THE STATE OF LAW IN THE SOUTH CAUCASUS

Euro-Asian Studies
Series Standing Order ISBN 0–333–80114–8
(*outside North America only*)

You can receive future titles in this series as they are published by placing a standing order. Please contact your bookseller or, in case of difficulty, write to us at the address below with your name and address, the title of the series and the ISBN quoted above.

Customer Services Department, Macmillan Distribution Ltd, Houndmills, Basingstoke, Hampshire RG21 6XS, England

---

Economics of the Caspian Oil and Gas Wealth

Companies, Governments, Policies

Yelena Kalyuzhnova

Centre for
Euro-Asian Studies

First published 2008 by
PALGRAVE MACMILLAN
Houndmills, Basingstoke, Hampshire RG21 6XS and
175 Fifth Avenue, New York, N.Y. 10010
Companies and representatives throughout the world

PALGRAVE MACMILLAN is the global academic imprint of the Palgrave Macmillan division of St. Martin's Press, LLC and of Palgrave Macmillan Ltd. Macmillan® is a registered trademark in the United States, United Kingdom and other countries. Palgrave is a registered trademark in the European Union and other countries.

ISBN-13: 978-1-4039-8757-0   hardback
ISBN-10: 1-4039-8757-2   hardback

This book is printed on paper suitable for recycling and made from fully managed and sustained forest sources. Logging, pulping and manufacturing processes are expected to conform to the environmental regulations of the country of origin.

A catalogue record for this book is available from the British Library.

A catalog record for this book is available from the Library of Congress.

10   9   8   7   6   5   4   3   2   1
17   16   15   14   13   12   11   10   09   08

Printed and bound in Great Britain by
CPI Antony Rowe, Chippenham and Eastbourne

To the memory of my late grandparents and parents:
Alexandra and Nikolai, Galina and Grigorii

Contents

List of Tables, Figures, Boxes and Maps

Tables

Figures

Foreword

The writing of this book has been a crucial experience in my life. When I started it in 2005 I was very excited because the topic of Caspian oil and gas is particularly interesting and challenging. I felt privileged: having access to information on the region, and to the companies working there, knowing so many experts, academics and practitioners. But I never could have imagined that writing this book would also help me through a period of my life that was marked by the tragic death of my parents. In dedicating this book to them, as well as to my late grandparents, I am acknowledging a small part of the huge debt that I owe to them. It was a very difficult period, but throughout it I was blessed with the people who support me. I would like to thank Mikhail Kalyuzhnov, Yelena Kondrashova, Vladimir Amvrosyev, Vadim Chernykh and Botagoz Kulakbayeva for their friendship and understanding during this period.

I was fortunate to have the cooperation of many people in writing this book. All my requests for interviews with governments and companies were greeted favourably. I would like to thank Burren Energy, KazMunaiGaz, SOCAR (State Oil Company of Azerbaijan Republic) and Petrobras for giving me such valuable insights into their work. I am grateful to Terry Adams, Anton Artemyev, José Sergio Gabrielli, Atul Gupta, Anvar Gasimov, Malcolm Harrison, Kairat Kelimbetov, Julian Lee, Finian O'Sullivan, Jean-Yves Pitarakis, Richard Pomfret, Yurii Shokamanov, Marla Valdes and David Woodward for their interviews, helpful suggestions and encouragement.

I am indebted to John Gawthrop and Argus Media as well as to Paul Rawkins and FitchRatings for allowing me access to important information from their respective institutions with regard to the Caspian Sea region data.

My wonderful colleagues at the University of Reading were most generous with their time and suggestions. My special thanks go to Christoph Bluth, Mark Casson, Christian A. Nygaard, Jim Pemberton, Alina Spiru and Mike Utton. I am grateful to them for their endeavours, but all the remaining errors and mistakes remain my full responsibility.

I am especially grateful to Maxwell Watson for his talent in guiding me through the style and substance of the book: without his input this book would never have seen the light of day.

My special thanks goes to my friend and colleague Barbara Sofocli for her tremendous support at the final stage of completing this project.

I thank my PhD student Stela Cani for her technical support.

I am garteful to Linda Auld and Elizabeth Teague for their help and support with the copy-editing and proofreading for this book.

Finally, I would not have succeeded in writing this book, nor in going through the difficulties of my life, if Andrei had not been next to me – my main support, my only family.

Yelena Kalyuzhnova
Reading, UK

List of Abbreviations

ACG	Azeri, Chiraq and Guneshli (oil fields)
ADB	Asian Development Bank
AIOC	Azerbaijan International Operating Company
API	American Petroleum Institute
ARKS	Agency of the Republic of Kazakhstan on Statistics
bbl	barrels (of oil)
bcf	billion cubic feet
BH	'Bird in Hand' rule
bln	billion
BoP	balance of payments
BTC	Baku–Tbilisi–Ceyhan (pipeline)
CAPEX	capital expenditures
CEAS	Centre for Euro-Asian Studies
CEO	chief executive officer
CEP	Caspian Environment Programme
CFO	chief finance officer
CGES	Centre for Global Energy Studies
CIS	Commonwealth of Independent States
CITIC	China International Trust and Investment Company
CNCP	China National Petroleum Corporation
CPC	Caspian Pipeline Consortium
CPI	Corruption Perception Index
CTC	Caspian Training Center
CTR	Caspian Technical Resources
CTTC	Caspian Technological Training Centre
E&C	engineering and construction
E&P	exploration and production
EBRD	European Bank for Reconstruction and Development
EITI	Extractive Industries Transparency Initiative
EMV	expected monetary value
EPC	engineering procurement construction
EU	European Union
EVP	executive vice president
FDI	foreign direct investment
FEED	front end engineering design
FERF	Foreign Exchange Reserve Fund

FIC	Foreign Investors' Council
FPSA	Final Production Sharing Agreement
FSU	Former Soviet Union
FT	*Financial Times*
GC	Granger causality
GDP	gross national product
GOST	gosudarstvennyy standart
HR	human resources
HSE	Health and Safety Environment
IMF	International Monetary Fund
IOC	international oil company
IPE	International Petroleum Exchange
IRR	internal rate of return
ISO	International Standards Organization
JVA	joint venture agreement
KBTU	Kazakh British Technical University
KCO	Kazakhstan North Caspian Operating Company
KGM	KazGerMunai
KMG	KazMunaiGaz
KPA	Kazakhstan Petroleum Association
KPO	Karachaganak Petroleum Operating BV
KZT	Kazakh tenge (currency)
LCI	Local Content Indicator
LNG	liquefied natural gas
MDGs	Millennium Development Goals
mln	million
mmbtu	million British thermal units
mmscfd	million standard cubic feet per day
MoU	Memorandum of Understanding
mtpa	million tonnes per annum
NCCER	National Center for Construction Education and Research
NFRK	National Fund of the Republic of Kazakhstan
NGO	non-governmental organization
NOC	national oil company
NPV	net present value
OGDF	Oil and Gas Development Fund
OPEC	Organization of Petroleum Exporting Countries
OPEX	operating expenditures
OSCE	Organization for Security and Co-operation in Europe
OTP	operations training plant
PFD	Parsons Flour Daniels

PIH	Permanent Income Hypothesis
PSA	Production Sharing Agreement
PSC	Production Sharing Contract
RCA	regional comparative advantage
SFDOG	State Fund for the Development of the Oil and Gas Industry and Mineral Resources
SGI/SGP	Sour Gas Injection/Second Generation Project
SME	small and medium-sized enterprise
SOCAR	State Oil Company of the Azerbaijan Republic
SOE	state-owned enterprise
SOFAZ	State Oil Fund of the Azerbaijan Republic
SPPRED	State Programme of Poverty Reduction and Economic Development
tcf	trillion cubic feet
TCO	Tengizchevroil
VAR	vector autoregressive
VAT	value-added tax
WKO	Western Kazakhstan Oblast
WTO	World Trade Organization

Introduction

This book is a follow-up to *Energy in the Caspian Sea Region: Present and Future* (Kalyuzhnova et al., 2002), which dealt with different aspects – geological, political, religious – of energy issues in the Caspian Sea region. The current volume covers the same region, but concentrates on the economic issues of hydrocarbon wealth and relations between companies and governments which are in the end the most important influences on the exploration and production of any natural resource. This book thus tackles issues that have previously been given limited consideration in the literature, such as the role of the operating companies and the prudential management of hydrocarbon wealth in the Caspian Sea region. The challenge for governments in designing an optimal energy policy is also touched on in the book.

I have chosen to concentrate on three key oil-producing countries in the Caspian region, namely Azerbaijan, Kazakhstan and Turkmenistan. The Russian case is mentioned only briefly in the parts of the book where interesting analogies have emerged, because Russia has other substantial hydrocarbon resources outside the Caspian region which distort any comparison. Another littoral state, namely Iran, has been excluded from the analysis because at the time of writing Iran produces no hydrocarbons in the region.

This book is not an encyclopaedia of hydrocarbon development in the Caspian Basin, and therefore the choice of issues and case studies was made only on the basis of their special relevance in understanding the region. In particular, I attempted to analyse and understand the patterns of the behaviour of different types of players: oil majors, oil independents and national oil companies. I tried to capture the perceptions of the governments towards them, and the way in which national policies have evolved.

Through my professional experience I was fortunate to have first-hand knowledge in dealing with the governments of the region as well as an inside understanding of its economic realities, especially with regard to the role and activities of major companies in this area. This allowed me to set up and conduct interviews with representatives of governments and companies in the region. Interviews were held with close to 100 individuals in the years 2003–2007, primarily in oil companies such as Burren Energy, BP (British Petroleum), ChevronTexaco, KazMunaiGaz, SOCAR (State Oil Company of Azerbaijan Republic), etc., in ministries of energy, non-governmental organizations (NGOs) and in financial institutions. Some of the interviews were conducted under the 'Chatham House Rule', where I was entitled to use the information gained during the interviewing process, but without attributing it to the source, others interviewees are named in the book.

Part I (The Economics of Hydrocarbon Development) offers an overview of hydrocarbon development through the prism of economics. The central theme of this part is the impact of hydrocarbon resources on the economies and economic development of the Caspian countries. This is a subject of critical importance to the countries of the region, and for the study of the economics of transition and development. Previous work has been published on the impact of natural resources, especially hydrocarbons, on development; but so far no attempt has been made to study systematically the specific case of the Caspian region, using the economic data that are now available.

To explore more concretely the frame of reference of the economies of the Caspian region, the experience of their economic development during the last 15 years is considered. The economies of Azerbaijan, Kazakhstan and Turkmenistan represent examples of natural resource dependence, which have emerged recently, and all of them have set up resource funds during the past decade. In recent years the hydrocarbon sector in all these economies has played a crucial role in the recovery from the post-transition trough, and the attainment of a high rate of economic growth.

International and national statistics are drawn on for a comparative analysis of the caspian economies' dependence on oil and gas, and of the sustainability of economic growth in these countries. In addition, we aim to investigate to what extent the data support possible causal links between GDP (gross domestic product) and oil/gas production and consumption. In a resource-based economy, we expect such dynamic linkages to exist and play an important role.

Finally, the contribution that oil funds of the three economies can make to policy challenges facing Caspian resource-rich countries is discussed. The study reviews the potential role of such funds in the broader context of macroeconomic and energy policies – taking into account uncertainty about oil prices, the impact of institutional costs, and problems of organizational design. It then highlights the critical role of governance issues in three respects: defining transparently the goals of each fund; communicating these goals to build a constituency of public support; and ensuring the efficient and transparent management of the fund on an ongoing basis.

Part II (The Impact of the Operating Companies) examines in detail the relationships between companies operating in the Caspian Sea region and the respective governments. It starts from the description of the main oil and gas projects in the region and then analyses their direct and indirect impacts on the Caspian economies, spelling out the benefits as well as the costs and risks involved.

The analysis also brings out clearly the specifics of the relations between the Caspian governments and different types of operating companies involved in the projects and, in the case of Azerbaijan, the oil major BP; in Kazakhstan, the national oil company KazMunaiGaz; in Turkmenistan, the independent oil company, Burren Energy.

The concept of local content and its impact on oil and gas projects is tackled in the book from the point of view of companies and governments. It is understood that a hydrocarbon project of any size may have a significant impact on local communities. Priority of the policy agenda in all three countries (particular in Kazakhstan) is now given to deploying local content and assisting with local capacity-building in the oil and gas projects in the countries. The attitude and commitment of local management is crucial to finding the right balance. Practice shows that the wrong emphasis could easily damage the project. These issues are addressed in general terms with respect to the broader aspect of socio-economic impact and the specific issue of local content. The analysis draws on specific case studies from the Caspian Sea region economies to illustrate the points made.

Part III (Models and Policies for the Future) reviews issues of governmental policies with regard to production, revenues, public spending and overall development. The experience of investment in resource-dependent countries is distinctive because revenue from such resources is not hypothecated, even in a broad or implicit sense, to any set of government goals or categories of expenditure. The business or household sectors that pay taxes or duties broadly expect in return benefits in the form of national or personal security or economic, social or cultural services; but such reciprocity is not expected when the government exacts its dues from gifts of nature. It is a universal practice that because the resources available for exploitation are exhaustible, the government imposes a levy on such exploitation. Large sums are hence annually at the disposition of office-holders in national, and in some cases regional, governments without restrictions on their expenditure.

The details of oil taxation cases are presented for Azerbaijan and Kazakhstan in this part. It is well known that, in principle, 'taxing pure rents should not affect the efficiency of the industry being taxed or the economy at large' (Hannesson, 1998: ix). But in practice, Caspian realities have resulted in the opposite being true, because the approaches adopted in some cases have created undue uncertainties and risks. Some conclusions for the future are offered, based on analysis of current trends.

This concluding part of the book draws together a number of strands in the analysis to probe the nature of an optimal economic policy in the Caspian region: in other words, how to ensure that the economy is set on a sustainable development path. This is a complex process, which can occur in different ways and over varying periods.

In particular, any resource-rich country should take into account in its energy policy a number of key principles. These include protection of the environment as a public good, and the fostering of sustainable development and diversification in the local economy – which also involves many externalities. Another key area for progress in developing a sustainable and successful energy policy lies in transport links that ensure access to the international oil and gas market. Transport links, which again involve significant externalities, are discussed from the point of view of the relations between companies and governments involved in meeting this challenge. This part of the book also investigates the issue of preserving the terms of the PSAs (Production Sharing Agreements) over time, as an element of a credible and sustainable energy policy in resource-rich economies.

The final sections of the book are therefore devoted to the 'unresolved challenges' facing governments and companies today – issues of transportation, diversification and environmental protection, which need to be tackled systematically in order to ensure stable economic development in the region. We enquire how these key challenges can be tackled by Caspian governments at the present time, as they seek to develop viable national energy strategies. And against that backdrop we ask, more broadly, what the future holds for company–government cooperation in the Caspian region. These are the core questions that motivated the writing of this book.

Part I

The Economics of Caspian Hydrocarbon Development

1
Economic Development and Resource Dependence

In this chapter we consider the experience of three Caspian economies: Azerbaijan, Kazakhstan and Turkmenistan since independence.[1] We provide an overview of the economic setting to give a regional context for our economic analysis of companies–governments relations. We pay special attention to developmental differences and the role of hydrocarbons in their economies, as well as political-economy challenges with which the governments are currently faced.

1.1 Key similarities between the three Caspian economies

Azerbaijan, Kazakhstan and Turkmenistan represent examples of natural-resource-based economies. Commonly a resource-based economy is defined as one where natural resources account for 'more than 10 per cent of GDP and 40 per cent of exports' (Ahrend, 2006). As Table 1.1 shows, all three economies clearly conform to the above definition. However, we should stress that these data are based on a 'narrow' definition of the hydrocarbon sector: they understate the reality of the role of this sector in their national economies.

All the Caspian economies rely heavily on mineral wealth, and are highly dependent on it. A number of academic papers have analysed economic development in the Caspian Sea region since its independence (Pomfret, 1995, 2003, 2006; Kaser, 1997; Kalyuzhnova 2002). All of these highlight that the last decade has brought significant changes to the Caspian Sea region. The hydrocarbon sector in particular gave these economies a new shape. Kazakhstan and Azerbaijan became strategically important to world energy markets and thus attracted the largest share of FDI (foreign direct investment) in the region. (Figure 1.1)

---

[1] We do not consider Iran as a subject of our analysis. For the explanation, see Box 1.1.

Table 1.1   Average shares of contribution of the oil and gas sector in the Caspian economies to GDP and export, 2002–2007

Country	Share of oil and gas sector in GDP, %	Share of oil and gas sector in total export, %
Azerbaijan	42–50	83–90
Kazakhstan	15–18	50–65
Turkmenistan	35–55	55–76

Source: Column 1: Azerbaijan Asian Development Bank, *Key Indicators of Developing Asian and Pacific Countries* (2007); Kazakhstan National Bank of Kazakhstan, Turkmenistan Government of Turkmenistan and author's calculations. Column 2: Azerbaijan and Kazakhstan, IMF Country Report Nos 05/260 and 05/244 and author's calculations. Turkmenistan: state statistics and author's calculations.

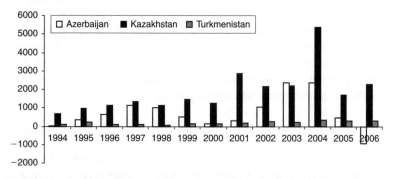

Figure 1.1   Caspian Sea region: foreign direct investments, 1994–2006, US$ mln
Source: EBRD (2006: 38); data for 2006 from IMF statistical database.

Box 1.1   Iran and its interests in the Caspian Sea region

The example of Iran is not developed in this book, although geographically Iran is one of the states that will be mentioned whenever we speak of the Caspian Sea region. The reasons for this deserve some discussion at the outset.

There is no question, of course, about Iran's enormous energy potential: 137.5 bln bbl of crude oil reserves, the second largest in the world. It is now producing around 4 mln bbl/day, but ought to be able to increase this figure significantly with adequate investment. In addition, Iran has an estimated 988.4 tcf (trillion cubic feet) of natural gas, about 16per cent of total world reserves and second only to those of Russia. Therefore, Iran is in a position to play a key role in the global energy security equation.

The demarcation of the Caspian Sea is still disputed, and Iran continues to claim a 20 per cent share of sea bed and sub-sea resources, while Azerbaijan, Russia and Kazakhstan have agreed offshore boundaries. On 15 and 16 October 2007, Iran hosted the second summit of the Caspian Sea countries, which included Azerbaijan, Iran, Kazakhstan, Russia and Turkmenistan. The meeting followed the 2002 Ashgabat summit aimed at achieving an agreement on the legal status of the Caspian Sea, and to define the littoral states' ownership of the sea's resources. However, the summit did not indicate a serious change in the countries' positions on this issue, thus failing to produce a final agreement on the legal status of the sea.

(*Source*: The Power and Interest News Report PINR, 'Iran Strengthens its Role in the Caspian Sea and Central Asian Regions', http://iranvajahan.net/cgi-bin/news-en.pl?1=en&y=2007&m=11&d=16&a=10)

Currently, Iran does not have oil and gas production in the Caspian Basin and, therefore, was excluded from this book. Taking into account the fact that the majority of Iran's oil and gas reserves are in the south and its population centres are in the north, it makes more sense to export the oil and gas in the south rather than pump it to the north and convert it to electricity. Therefore it makes economic sense to consider Iran as a potential consumer of oil and gas from other Caspian producers.

However, being a littoral state of the Caspian Sea, as well as a founder member of OPEC (Organization of Petroleum Exporting Countries), Iran will in future, no doubt, be a significant player in the region. In early 2000, Iran and the EU (European Union) signed a Memorandum of Understanding (MoU) on Energy Cooperation; Iran is perceived as an important East–West, North–South and West–East corridor for the transportation of energy carriers, and could contribute to the integration between the energy markets of the Caspian Sea region and those of the EU and Asia.

In 2004 Petróleo Brasileiro (Petrobras) signed a US$34 mln deal to drill in the Iranian part of the Caspian Sea (Tulson), and signed a second deal in 2006, taking the total value of the deal to US$37 mln (interview with CEO, José Sergio Gabrielli, 19 June 2007, London). In 2006 Iran's government-owned National Iranian Oil Company granted Petrobras a licence to explore a 3200-square-mile area of the Persian Gulf. The experience of Petrobras working in deep waters offshore was a crucial factor in securing this deal.

In addition, at the time of writing, the Iranian government is considering the Southern Caspian Exploration and Production Programme. Here the emphasis is on 3D seismic operations in the South of the Caspian Sea, where the water reaches depths of up to 2625 feet. According to Mahmoud Khaghani,[2] production is expected to start around 2008, although this appears very optimistic, since no discoveries have been announced and no drilling had been carried out by the middle of 2007 (interview with Mahmoud Khagani, 28 November 2006, Geneva). Energy demand in Iran is projected to increase between now and 2030 at an average annual rate of about 3 to 5 per cent. To increase Iranian oil production from 4.2 mln bbl/day in 2006 to 4.5 mln bbl/day in 2010 and to around 7 mln bbl/day in 2030, the estimated investment needed amounts to more than US$80 bln in 2006–2030. To increase Iran's natural gas production to 20.12 tcf by 2030, the country needs cumulative investment of US$100+ bln over the same period.

Nevertheless, while Iran has already managed to attract some investment for its oil and gas industry development, the form of contract (buy-back) that Iran has offered is not attractive to the industry. Investment has also been hampered by the political situation, especially US sanctions, which can be applied to any company investing significant amounts of money in Iranian oil and gas projects.

In recent years the hydrocarbon sector in these economies has played a crucial role in recovery from the post-transition trough, and attainment of a high rate of economic growth. From 2000 a steady increase in GDP was recorded in all three economies, at rates that varied between 7 and 30 per cent annually (see Table 1.2.)

Economic growth remains very strong in Kazakhstan, even if it has recently slowed somewhat as a result of stress in the financial sector and the impact of this on the construction industry. The year 2007 marked the eighth consecutive year of real GDP growth in excess of 7 per cent. Sharp increases in oil prices in the early 2000s and subsequently the growth in non-oil revenues allowed for a further substantial

---

[2] Director general for Caspian Sea and CIS Oil and Gas Affairs and deputy petroleum minister for international affairs of the I.R. Iran, Ministry of Petroleum.

Table 1.2   Growth rate of per capita GDP, % per year

	2002	2003	2004	2005	2006	2007	2008	Per capita GNP, $, 2005
Central Asia	7.7	7.8	8.8	10.0	11.4	9.4	9.1	
Azerbaijan	7.3	9.6	9.4	25.2	30.6	22.2	15.7	1240
Kazakhstan	9.6	8.7	9.0	8.3	9.7	7.9	8.9	2930
Turkmenistan	10.1	7.6	11.1	8.1	7.6	–	–	–

* Projections.
Source: Asian Development Outlook 2007.

Table 1.3   Kazakhstan and Azerbaijan: oil and oil products in total export, %, 2002–2005

Country	2002	2003	2004	2005*
Azerbaijan	89	86	83	90
Kazakhstan	50	53	55	61

* IMF staff projections.
Source: IMF Country Report Nos 05/260 and 05/244.

expansion in budgetary expenditures and, parallel to this, a sizeable increase in the overall fiscal surplus.

Azerbaijan is in a similar situation, with a GDP growth rate of 31 per cent in 2006. At the time of writing, the country expects production to peak in 2010 (assuming no new oil and gas reserves will be discovered). The main challenge for Azerbaijan in this respect is to ensure the sustainability of the growth of the non-oil and gas sectors of the economy, and poverty alleviation.

The Turkmen economy is continuing to grow at 20 per cent (based on government statistics); however, according to ADB's estimation, this figure is likely to be 9 per cent in 2006. Again, as in two previous cases this growth is accounted for by increased gas prices (which were successfully renegotiated with Russia) and export volumes.

In general, all three economies continue to grow strongly as a result of rising oil exports funded by foreign direct investment. All of them, indeed, have a high export concentration in mineral resources in the past and at the time of writing (see Figure 1.2, Tables 1.1, 1.3). Table 1.1 in particular depicts the high (and somewhat increasing) rate of dependence on oil and oil-related products in these countries. This, however, makes their economies particularly vulnerable to fluctuations in world

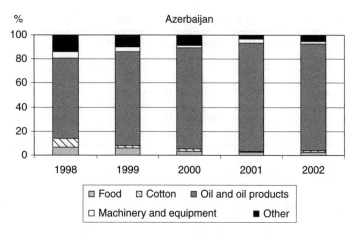

Source: Azerbaijan National Bank, State Statistical Committee.

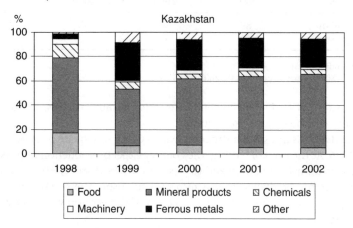

Source: Agency on Statistics of the Republic of Kazakhstan.

Figure 1.2   Azerbaijan, Kazakhstan and Turkmenistan: principal exports, %, 1998–2003

commodity prices. In addition, it leads to a concentration in specific markets which again highlights a significant dependence on external factors – the 1998 Russian financial crisis being one of the major examples.

What are the advantages and disadvantages of resource-based economies? Table 1.4 attempts to summarize the main pros and cons. 'Economic theory suggests that increased natural resource rents and the foreign exchange obtained from resource exports should raise investment and

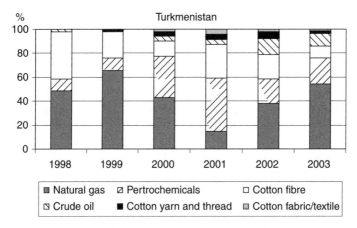

Source: Asian Development Bank (ADB), Key Indicators 2006 (www.adb.org/statistics)

Figure 1.2 (Continued)

Table 1.4 Advantages and disadvantages of resource-rich economies

Advantages	Disadvantages
Natural resource rent	Concentration on resource sector of the economy at the expense of others
Increase of employment	Rise of employment only in resource and resource-related sectors
Increase of investment	Rise of investment mainly in resource sector
Boost a country's capacity to import capital goods	More possibilities for rent-seeking behaviour
Acceleration of economic growth	Unable to sustain economic growth

boost a country's capacity to import capital goods, so that if the rents are efficiently invested they will accelerate economic growth' (Auty, 2006: 4).

Although this is only theory, we can see how the resource-based economies are benefiting from their resource wealth. Examples include the UK, Saudi Arabia, Norway, Canada, the USA, etc. Since the early 1950s researchers have attempted to evaluate the positive role of natural resources in the development of a country (Viner, 1952; Lewis, 1955): 'The possession of a sizable and diversified natural resource endowment is a major advantage to any country embarking upon a period of rapid economic growth' (N. Ginsburg, cited in Higgins 1968: 222). Similar views were also expressed by Balassa (1980), Krueger (1980) and Drake (1972).

However, alongside prosperity and a good potential for economic growth there is also uncertainty and fragility. Socio-political factors can also affect the development of these economies. Political interference or the inability of the government in question to sustain a balanced economic policy can lead to a concentration of benefits (investment, employment, etc.) only in the resource sector, and all this results in the longer term in the inability to sustain the country's economic growth.

All this was highlighted in the literature, which argued that the international commodity market could make a resource-rich country very vulnerable and resource exports could be a real disadvantage; resource abundance could increase the probability of negative economic growth, inflation, high unemployment, low savings as well as affect other political and social factors, namely corruption, poverty, and decline in human development (Prebisch, 1950; Leite and Weidmann, 1999; Sarraf and Jiwanji, 2001; Isham et al., 2002; Eifert et al., 2003; Bannon and Collier, 2003; Sala-i-Martin and Subramanian, 2003; Davis et al., 2003; etc.). These points were illustrated by comparative cross-country studies, although the selection of countries could be the subject of some debate, and there is some contrary evidence which suggests that natural resources could have neutral, and in some cases positive, effects, on economies as well as on countries' social indicators (Davis, 1995; Smith, 2004).

There are certain views about resource-based economies that have taken on a life of their own and an almost mythical status, at times independent of balanced analysis. These deserve objective examination.

The first of these 'myths' concerns primary product dependence, growth and inequality. There is some empirical evidence to suggest that countries with a large share of primary exports in GNP have bad growth and high inequality records, especially if the quality of institutions and the rule of law are bad (van der Ploeg, 2006), for example that these countries by definition will have low levels of know-how. To date the existing literature has discussed the experiences of successful cases of the USA, Chile and Brazil (e.g. Wright and Czelusta, 2004).

A second myth is related to the supposed inefficiency of the economy if property rights belong to the state. One of the arguments here is about high transaction costs which, according to the Coase theorem, create obstacles to bargaining, and as a result prevent efficient outcomes. From our point of view well-defined property rights with the proper institutional support (effective institutions) would appear a real step forward in improving efficiency. Mehlum et al. found that 'when institutions are bad, resource abundance is a growth curse; when institutions are good, resource abundance is a blessing' (Mehlum et al., 2006: 1127).

The academic literature tends to focus on the macroeconomic implications of countries' natural resource wealth – such as revenue volatility, changes in the terms of trade and 'Dutch Disease' (Atuy, 2006; Corden and Neary, 1982). At first glance the task of the Azeri, Kazakhstani and Turkmen governments on the macroeconomic and structural front is relatively similar: strengthening domestic institutions to encourage investment, building human and physical capital, and providing adequate and sustainable social protection mechanisms.

There are clearly potential challenges ahead, namely, rising inflation (for all countries), banks' risk management of their loan portfolios and funding base (especially for Kazakhstan), diversification of the economy (for all countries), and through this enhancing competitiveness of the non-oil and -gas sectors of the economy. In addition, fiscal and monetary policy coordination would have paramount importance in enhancing sustainable growth. The fundamental question will be how to sustain this growth. As resource-based economies, what should these three countries do, and under what conditions, in order to sustain their current growth performance?

1.2 A causality-based analysis of the three Caspian economies

In this section we aim to investigate to what extent causal links between GDP and oil/gas production as well as GDP and oil/gas consumption are supported by the data. In a resource-based economy, we expect such dynamic linkages to exist and play an important role (see for instance Fatai et al., 2004). Previous research in this area concentrated solely on the causal links between energy consumption and economic growth, with energy defined in a broad sense, and typically reached conflicting results. Empirical findings seem to vary from bi-directional and unidirectional causality between energy consumption and growth (Masih and Masih, 1996; Asafiu-Adjaye, 2000; Chang et al., 2001) to no causality at all (Cheng, 1997; 1999).

Our empirical methodology involves testing for Granger causality (GC) between the above variables within a vector autoregressive (VAR) framework. Due to the econometric problems induced by the presence of non-stationary variables and the potential presence of co-integrating relationships, our implementation follows the methodology developed in Toda and Yamamoto (1995). For each country of interest, we estimate a VAR in levels, specifying its optimal lag length, say L, using the AIC model selection criterion. The Granger causality test is subsequently implemented within the overfitted VAR(L + 1) model. We consider the following specification:

$$Y_{it} = \gamma_{1i} + \sum_{j=1}^{L} \lambda_{1ij} Y_{it-j} + \sum_{j=1}^{L} \lambda_{2ij} X_{it-j} + \upsilon_{1it} \tag{1.1}$$

$$X_{it} = \gamma_{2i} + \sum_{j=1}^{L} \lambda_{3ij} X_{it-j} + \sum_{j=1}^{L} \lambda_{4ij} Y_{it-j} + \upsilon_{2it} \tag{1.2}$$

where Y_{it} is the GDP of country i in year t; X_{it} is oil/gas production or oil/gas consumption, L is the number of lags of the VAR, γ and λ are parameters to be estimated and υ_{it} are random disturbance terms. Once equations (1.1) and (1.2) have been estimated, Granger causality tests simply involve testing joint zero restrictions on the parameters of the above VAR so as to assess whether past values of variable X say, are significantly predicted by variable Y and vice versa.

Empirical results

We investigate the presence of causal relationships between GDP and oil/gas production and GDP and oil/gas consumption across the three Caspian economies of Azerbaijan, Kazakhstan and Turkmenistan. Our data series spans the period 1990–2006. We use the GDP index (1980=100) to measure national output. Oil/gas production and consumption are also measured in index form (OILC, GASC, OILP, GASP). Table 1.5 presents the p-values corresponding to the null hypothesis of no Granger causality. A small p-value indicates a rejection of the null and to the finding of causality.

We first note that there is no systematic pattern of causality or no- causality across the three economies, with the exception of causal

Table 1.5 Granger's causality test results: p-values for the null of no Granger causality

Casual relationship	Azerbaijan	Kazakhstan	Turkmenistan
OILC→GDP	0.8081	0.7883	**0.0039**
GDP→OILC	0.7364	**0.0002**	**0**
OILP→GDP	0.6217	0.175	**0.0032**
GDP→OILP	**0.0167**	**0.0253**	0.5046
GASC→GDP	0.1949	**0.019**	**0**
GDP→GASC	**0.0572**	0.0831	**0.0001**
GASP→GDP	**0.026**	0.4736	0.3072
GDP→GASP	0.1388	0.1541	0.4556

links between GDP and gas consumption. For Azerbaijan our results strongly point to causal links between GDP and oil and gas production and GDP, while the remaining pairs are mostly statistically insignificant. Looking at Kazakhstan, the results strongly support the presence of causal linkages from GDP to oil consumption, oil production and gas consumption, as well as from gas consumption to GDP. Finally, looking at Turkmenistan, we document strong causal links between oil consumption, oil production, gas consumption and GDP, as well as between GDP and oil/gas consumption.

Overall, and as expected, the above results show the importance of energy consumption for GDP growth in all three Caspian economies.

1.3   Key developmental differences

There is a striking difference in income level between these three countries. According to the World Bank classification, all of them belong to the *Lower Middle Income* country group; however, there are major differences between them in terms of income level. To a certain extent this explains the behaviour of the decision-makers.

From my personal observations, during the last four years the Kazakhstani government has appeared more willing to pass on the benefits of the oil boom to the population than in the earlier years of transition. This can be explained in part by a pre-emptive effort to defuse potential popular discontent. However, the gradual changes in governmental thinking and operations, and the country's substantial fiscal resources, could also explain this change in behaviour.

In the case of Azerbaijan, by contrast, the government is faced with the problems of a low level of GDP per capita, limited fiscal resources and administrative capacity, a substantial informal sector and a high incidence of poverty (Dobronogov, 2003). According to a recent survey, 49 per cent of the population is living below the absolute poverty line (approximately US$ 25.8 per capita/month) and 17 per cent of the population lives in extreme poverty (approximately US$ 15.5 per capita/month) (State Statistics Committee, Household Budget Survey, 2001). However, 'as a result of rapid economic growth [due to high oil prices] and increased social spending, poverty declined to 40.2 per cent in 2004 from 49 per cent in 2001' (IMF Country Report No. 05/260, July 2005: 5). Still, there is a long way to go with regard to poverty alleviation in the country, reflected in the current three-year State Programme of Poverty Reduction and Economic Development (SPPRED).

Turkmenistan represents a challenge for scholars with regard to the analysis of recent trends of development. In the absence of any statistics from the government, the assessment of the development is *ad hoc*. To date Turkmenistan remains a strongly socialist country, with the state social protection systems providing the population with the basic consumer goods and utilities on a free basis or employing a principle of soft budget constraints (soft subsidies). The post-Niyazov government is expected to take more steps in the direction of external liberalization, reducing the degree of state control and relaxing the plan indicators in industry and agriculture.

The pattern of public expenditure in part reflects these different levels of development. Moreover, there are significant differences in the labour market, reflecting historical circumstances. Azerbaijan has to look after people who were displaced from their own towns within the territory of Azerbaijan following the dispute between Azerbaijan and Armenia in 1989 – and among whom poverty is endemic. Moreover, real unemployment is significantly higher than the officially recorded level (which puts the unemployment rate at around 1.3–1.5 per cent of the labour force in 2003) (from interviews with international financial institutions, 2006–2007).

In Kazakhstan, by contrast, there is no comparable problem of displaced persons. The unemployment rate is falling. Moreover, incomes are cushioned by extensive under-employment in the economy, especially in industrial enterprises which still need to be restructured. Real wages are rising strongly – resulting in an improvement in average living standards.

In Turkmenistan the unemployment factor is likely to be very significant, as many school graduates are unable to find appropriate jobs, due to lack of opportunities as well as required skills and the seasonal nature of jobs in rural areas (where 60 per cent of total population lives).

In sum, the economies of these three oil-rich economies differ significantly, with Kazakhstan being somewhat richer and more advanced in transition but with a mixed performance regarding social indicators (see Table 1.6). Both Kazakhstan and Azerbaijan are expected to triple their income per capita by 2007 based on their oil and gas exports.

It is important to avoid the vulnerability to oil price declines that has caused adversity in the past for countries such as Venezuela in the period after the oil booms in the 1970s and early 1980s. The governments should without doubt look at the possibility to diversify industrial production and to foster competitiveness of the economies, but based on

Table 1.6 Key socio-economic indicators for Azerbaijan, Kazakhstan and Turkmenistan, 2006

	Azerbaijan	Kazakhstan	Turkmenistan
1. Minerals as % of exports	79.5[a] (87.8[b])	76.4[c]	82.6[b]
2. Cotton fibre as % of exports	1.07[c]	0.8	4.4[b]
3. GNI per capita, ATLAS method (current US$)	1240	2940	–
4. EBRD transition indicator	3–	3	1+
5. GDP index (1989=100)[e]	119.8	122.8	131
6. Capital formation as % of GDP	38	27	23
7. Government consumption as % of GDP	6.0	11.4	12.7
8. Private sector as % of GDP[e]	60	65	25
9. External debt as % of GDP	20.3	69.4[d]	28.4

[a] First half of 2004.
[b] Full year 2003.
[c] ADB (2006) and author calculations.
[d] IMF (2006: 21).
[e] Full year 2006.
Source: 2003 data in rows 1, 2 and 7 from ADB 'Key indicators of Developing Asian and Pacific countries', 2005: www.adb.org/statistics/default.asp; 2004 data from IMF (Country Report Nos 05/18 and 05/239); rows 4 and 8 EBRD (2006: Table 1.1) (arithmetical average of nine indicators graded 1 to 4+); row 5 UNECE (Economic Survey of Europe, No. 1, 2005: Appendix Table B.1); rows 3 and 6 http://devdata.worldbank.org/data-query/; row 9 EBRD, *Transition Report Update, 2005*: 29, 49 and 73).

the specifics and needs of the Azeri and Kazakhstani economies (e.g. recently risen inflation in Azerbaijan). Partly as a result, the demand on the oil funds will differ as well, reflecting the different priorities and initiatives by their governments. The management of oil revenue may require pursuing reform agendas that are markedly different. In each case the economics of the challenge are undeniably complex – and ultimately require finely balanced political judgements. Nonetheless, an examination of the way their respective oil funds operate suggests interesting parallels in terms of the steps needed to ensure that these institutions are fully effective in these two very different economic contexts.[3]

After seven years of significant growth, it would be reasonable to expect that living conditions in all three economies would improve. However, in reality this process is developing slowly and in some places (Turkmenistan in particular) it has stagnated. In terms of GDP per capita,[4] Kazakhstan leads with US$3460. To set the stage for later discussion of the industry's impact and of development challenges, it is useful at this point to explore the experience with (and perceptions of) living standards in these three economies. This analysis will benefit from some previously unavailable survey data as well as interviews in the region.

The recession of the early 1990s was not kind to the population of these countries, but provided ample opportunities for access to privileges, positions acquired during the old time (members of the Communist Party, technocrats). While all income groups experienced a decline in real household incomes, those at the bottom suffered the most. As we can see from Table 1.9, the Human Development Index shows the places of these three countries in the world ranking, putting Kazakhstan at place 79, then Azerbaijan (99) and Turkmenistan (105). Accordingly the indicator of the distribution of family income (Gini coefficient) depicts the changing environment. The observed deterioration of income distribution in post-Soviet countries was very fast and, the Gini coefficient doubled its value from the pre-transition level. 'The increase in income inequality in Kazakhstan was relatively moderate but Turkmenistan saw the value of its Gini coefficient rise from 26.4 in 1988 to 40.8 in 1998.' (Bandara et al., 2004: 122). However, the situation in Kazakhstan has improved throughout the 2000s (see Table 1.7).

By 2005 the share of the population with income lower than the value of the subsistence level was one-third of that in 2001. Quite positive results have been achieved with regard to the poverty gap and poverty acuteness.[5]

Most of the emphasis in this chapter is on material indicators of progress, such as income per capita. However, overall well-being clearly depends on a wider range of influences, and recently economists have started to pay more attention to non-material indicators (Layard, 2005; Eggers et al., 2006; Namazie and Sanfey, 2001) that affect overall human happiness or well-being.

---

[3] For a full discussion of the impact of development priorities of investment needs, see Chapter 2.

[4] In current US$.

[5] Unfortunately, we do not possess comparable figures for Azerbaijan and Turkmenistan.

Table 1.7 Main indicators of inequality of income distribution in Kazakhstan

	2001	2002	2003	2004	2005
Share of population with income lower than value of subsistence level*	28.4	24.2	19.8	16.1	9.8
Share of population with income lower than cost of food basket*	11.7	8.9	6.3	4.3	1.6
Poverty gap*	7.8	6.1	4.6	3.3	1.7
Poverty acuteness*	3.1	2.2	1.6	1	0.5
Income ratio of highest 10% to lowest 10%, times	8.8	8.1	7.4	6.8	6.8
Gini index by 10% groups of population	0.339	0.328	0.315	0.305	0.304

* Data are based on the income equivalence scale.
Source: *Statistical Yearbook of Kazakhstan, 2006.*

In the literature there are very few studies related to this subject in the Caspian Sea region. One of them estimates the determinants of well-being for three years – 1996, 2001 and 2006 – in Kazakhstan (Kalyuzhnova and Kambhampati, 2008). Using household-level data, the authors analyse the impact of macroeconomic performance as well as personal, household and regional factors on individual well-being. The results indicate that the income of the individual and the size of the house that he lives in are highly significant in all three years. The final finding is related to the impact of regional unemployment on well-being. The last is a good example to capture the swing in mood and perception of the population in relation to the progress of transition in 1996 (when unemployment was a relatively new concept for the Kazakhstani economy, and regional unemployment reduced the life satisfaction of both those who were employed and those who were unemployed. By 2001, regional unemployment was beginning to have a positive impact on the life satisfaction of the unemployed because it was being interpreted as a systemic failure rather than an individual one. By 2006 this had once again changed, so that those who continued to be employed despite high regional unemployment had higher life satisfaction.

An interesting overall lesson can be learned from the Kazakhstani experience by Turkmenistan, which is in a very preliminary stage of transition. The more advanced the progress of transition, the more profound the dissatisfaction from the shock of the reforms.[6] Box 1.2 shows

---

[6] However, the EBRD's study on life in transition confirmed that more people declared themselves to be satisfied with life than dissatisfied (EBRD, 2007).

that the memories of the 'good old times' can sometimes prevent realistic evaluation of the economic improvements of the current time.

Box 1.2   Assessment of well-being by Kazakhstani citizens

Interesting inferences could be drawn from the CEAS Household Survey (2006) of the well-being by the population, commissioned by the Centre for Euro-Asian Studies (UK) and carried out by the Agency of the Republic of Kazakhstan on Statistics (ARKS) on 640 households across all the regions. The survey was designed to be nationally representative.

The sampling methodology was designed to make our sample inter-regionally representative. In order to achieve this, a two-step sampling procedure was employed to select the individuals to be included in the sample. The first step was for the regional branches of ARKS to identify the unit considered for selection in the next step of sampling, namely districts, towns, villages, etc. The probability of selection was proportional to size, where the measure of size was identified as population in this particular region (*oblast*). The second step in sampling consisted of selecting individuals within each sampling unit. Here the main purpose was to balance the survey in terms of gender, education and ethnicity. However, every sampling unit had a freedom of randomness entered into the selection process. A questionnaire was then administered to the individuals selected in this way. The questionnaire asked questions relating to the individual's characteristics – type of work, ethnicity, marital status, education levels etc. Most of the questions were 'closed' questions in which individuals were given options between which they could choose. However, there were a number of open-ended questions that were useful for individuals to make more nuanced responses.

In assessing the impact of the economic reforms (*Do you think the reforms have helped Kazakhstan?*), 90.7 per cent of respondents think that reforms did help the country and only 9 per cent are deny their positive impact. Similar answers are related to the impact of the reforms on the life of people of Kazakhstan,[7] where 81.8 per cent

---

[7] The precise question is: *Do you think the reforms have helped people of Kazakhstan more generally?*

of respondents think that the reforms helped people and only 17.9 per cent state that they cannot see this positive impact.

However, the picture is different when the respondents were asked to evaluate whether or not the reforms helped them personally.[8] A total of 56.8 per cent of the population think that the reforms helped them, although 42.6 per cent think that personally they did not benefit much from the reforms.

While 86.2 per cent of respondents stated that they were happier 20 years ago, only 46.4 per cent remarked that they were happier ten years ago (Table 1.8.)

Table 1.8   Were you satisfied 10 and 20 years ago? (based on 2006)

	10 years before, %	20 years before, %
Yes	46.4	86.2
No	53.3	13.7

This table an easily be explained by the fact that in 1996 the newly independent Kazakhstan was going through a severe recession and an economic crisis occasioned by transition. The majority of the population was still undergoing the process of adaptation to the new conditions (privatization, changes in the labour market, etc.) and finding their new place in the economic system. The nostalgic thoughts about the period of 20 years ago can be explained by sociological and emotional points of view, as well as the age factor (the age brackets 31–40 and 41–50).

The respondents were asked to name (by their own choice) the main reasons for being less happy than 20 years ago. A striking similarity in their answers was evident. Four main categories emerged, namely: (1) more troubles now (23.9 per cent of total respondents' answers); (2) more stability in the past (19.7 per cent); (3) easier to find a job and low prices in the past (11.2 per cent); (4) everything was cheaper and available (10.2 per cent). We have analysed these answers by looking at the respondents' age group; see Table 1.9.

As we can see, the age brackets 20–30 and 31–40 highlight their unhappiness due to having more difficulties now (24.4 per cent and 47 per cent interviewed people of this age group), whereas

---

[8] The precise question is: *Do you think the reforms have helped you?*

Table 1.9   Summary of the four most frequent reasons for being happy 20 years ago, by age group

Respondent age	More difficulties now, %	Easy to find a job and low prices in the past, %	More stability in the past, %	Everything was cheap & available
20–30	24.4	0	4.0	6
31–40	47.0	14.3	21.4	32
41–50	19.3	46.4	34.7	30
51–60	5.0	28.6	35.7	24
61–70	2.0	8.9	2.0	4.0
71–80	0.8	1.8	2.0	4.0

Note: Total number of respondents 498.

46.4 per cent of the 51–60 age group found it easier to find a job and low prices in 1986. In addition, 34.7 per cent and 35.7 per cent of age groups 41–50 and 51–60 respectively remembered more stability in the past.

Another approach to capture the views of economic development by the populations is to look at perceptions of the reforms. In Azerbaijan a sociological survey[9] was conducted for the years 2004, 2005 and 2006, with financial support from the Friedrich Ebert Foundation, Germany. The survey included questions regarding the socio-economic situation in Azerbaijan, the living standard and incomes of the population, changes in views on life, and attitudes to actual problems. Based on the results of the survey, one of the main conclusions is that the overall situation in Azerbaijan is regarded as stable (see Figure 1.3).

It is evident from the answers that the positive feelings about living in Azerbaijan are dominant. The dynamics of these three years (2004–2006) demonstrates a significant reduction in the number of respondents characterizing their feeling about life in Azerbaijan by the word 'fear'. At the same time one can observe an evident growth in the number of those who noted 'progress'. However, it should be noted that this poll was carried out before the significant rise in prices of electricity and public utilities, and does not take into account the negative public reaction. The proportion of participants in the polls that expressed either 'confidence' or 'disappointment' remains at the level of 11 per cent. These are

[9] The project was carried out by «PULS-R» Sociological Service.

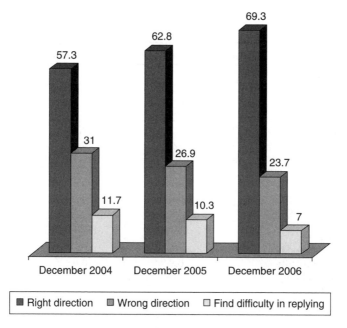

Figure 1.3   Respondents' opinion regarding social and political development in Azerbaijan
Source: *Azerbaijan in 2006, Sociological monitoring*, Baku, 2007.

outsiders who did not experience economic growth in the country (Table 1.10).

There are no comparable surveys available with regard to Turkmenistan. During my visits to Turkmenistan I attempted to conduct various interviews instead. Around 50 interviewees were chosen on the basis of a quota sampling, where the population was first divided into sub-groups (as in the case of Kazahstan) according to their age (see Table 1.9). A potential problem is that these samples may be biased and I realize that the conclusions presented below might be controversial. To the question *'How is life in Turkmenistan?'*, the majority of respondents answered that it is difficult [economic situation], but better than to have a civil war in the country. (The political propaganda of a stable state without regional conflicts was put as a priority in the early 1990s, when the Chechen and Tajik conflicts took place in the Former Soviet Union – FSU.) This impact of indoctrination is evident across all the groups of the population. An interesting peculiarity was noticed in the 18–25 age group: a lack of awareness of different life styles. This generation grew up under the Orwellian style of leadership of the late President

Table 1.10   Which of the words stated below reflect your personal feelings about living in Azerbaijan more precisely?*

	December 2004		December 2005		December 2006	
	Quantity	%	Quantity	%	Quantity	%
1. Fear	61	6.1	65	6.5	31	3.1
2. Hope	582	58.2	595	59.5	581	58.1
3. Uncertainty	197	19.7	174	17.4	148	14.8
4. Despair	106	10.6	122	12.2	108	10.8
5. Confidence	295	29.5	341	34.1	389	38.9
6. Disappointment	118	11.8	152	15.2	118	11.8
7. Progress	87	8.7	53	5.3	108	10.8
8. All the above-mentioned	2	0.2	7	0.7	10	1.0
9. None of the above-mentioned	5	0.5	4	0.4	5	0.5
10. Find difficulty in replying/ refuse to answer	9	0.9	6	0.6	8	0.8

* No more than two answers accepted.
Source: *Azerbaijan in 2006, Sociological monitoring*, Baku, 2007.

Niyazov, with replacement of formal education of students by the 400-page *Rukhnama* (the book, 'inspired by God', that President Niyazov wrote and published in 2001, describing it as the 'core of all my political, economic and life targets'). Graduations depended on a student's ability to answer questions on the *Rukhnama*. The president cut mandatory schooling from ten years to nine, reduced the number of students allowed into universities, and banned all Soviet-era textbooks, without printing new ones to replace them. He left the *Rukhnama* as the dominant teaching tool for future generations. The national culture and spiritual values were quickly replaced with the ideas and theses of the book *Rukhnama*.

The teaching of humanities subjects has been replaced by the study of the *Rukhnama*, and therefore it is no surprise that in their answers the age 18–25 group demonstrated a lack of knowledge of world culture or universal values.

A very small group of respondents in the age group 35–45 were critical of the phenomenon of Turkmenistan's corruption, flunkeyism and repression. They explained that the president and the state controlled the economy and people through the mechanisms of corruption and repression. Some members of the government are afraid to lose what they have illegitimately gained. The state machine has collected compromising information on almost all former government officials, which is keeping them under control. In addition, the free exit from the country was restricted, unless permission was granted.

Features of flunkeyism and repression were found during the interviews across the groups, but especially with the older generation (age group 50–63). The respondents were unwilling to give their opinion on economic or social issues, stating that the president knows where to lead the country. This established the fact that flunkeyism had reached the level of national politics in Turkmenistan. In professional life no one could freely express their opinions. This right belonged exclusively to President Niyazov. The consequence is fear and repression. There is some patchy evidence of people who attempted to criticize the government during the Nyazov era having been imprisoned. The only figure given by the respondents was their salary (which varied from US$40 to US$100).

As Table 1.11 shows, poverty remains an issue in Azerbaijan and Turkmenistan, and to a lesser extent in Kazakhstan (where, according to the estimations of the international agencies, poverty has been in decline since the late 1990s, with 25 per cent of the population living below the poverty line). Reduction of poverty is a major challenge for Azerbaijan.

According to the 2003 Household Budget Survey (HBS), close to 3.7 million people, or about 44.7 per cent of the total population, lived in poverty in 2003, consuming less than AZM 178,850 ($36.50) per capita per month. Among these, a group of 800,000 persons, or 9.6 per cent of the total population, lived in extreme poverty with monthly consumption below AZM 124,137 ($25.50 per month). (ADB, 2005a: 1)

In Turkmenistan there is a system of guaranteed distribution of gas and water to households, as well as administrative (subsidized) pricing of basic consumer goods (e.g. salt); however, all this cannot make it easy for a great number of impoverished people. My estimate of the level of poverty in Turkmenistan is around 58 per cent in 2006.

Another indicator that requires attention when one speaks of the impact of economic development is the inequalities of income and disparities in regional development. Over the past 15 years, the distribution of income in the Caspian region has changed significantly. Recent controversies over excessive pay in the oil and gas sector while the rest of the economy enjoys relatively modest average pay have intensified the debate on income disparity in the region. Everything is relative: Kazakhstan is richer and more prosperous than Azerbaijan and Turkmenistan, but still has a regional disparity in income distribution. The economic

Table 1.11 Poverty indicators in the Caspian Sea region

Country	GDP per capita, US$	GDP per capita US$ at PPP	Human Development Index (rank out of 177 countries), 2004	Human Development Index (HDI) value	Share of population living below the poverty line, %	Household income or consumption by percentage share		Distribution of family income – Gini Index
						lowest 10%	highest 10%	
Azerbaijan	1500	7500[f]	99	0.736	44.7[c]	2.8	27.8[a]	36.5[c]
Kazakhstan	3460	9400[g]	79	0.774	19	3.3	26.5	31.5[d]
Turkmenistan	1060	8500[f]	105	0.724	58[f]	2.6	31.7[b]	40.8[b]

[a] Data for 1995; [b] data 1998; [c] 2001; [d] 2003; [e] 2004; [f] 2006; [g] 2007.
Sources: Economist Intelligence Unit; World Bank; UNDP; World Factbook.

environment at the beginning of the 2000s was very favourable to the oil and gas sector of these economies. The concentration of income and wealth has increased sharply recently in Kazakhstan and Azerbaijan as rising oil prices and rapid economic growth generously rewarded those at the top of the income pyramid.

1.4 The impact of oil and gas wealth on the national economy

The importance of the oil and gas industry should not be overlooked in terms of its indirect effects on the rest of the economy (non-hydrocarbon sector), in particular the impact of the oil and gas industry on the exchange rate. In the Netherlands, following the discovery and exploitation of natural gas reserves, the country experienced pressures on the exchange rate as well as a significant expansion of Dutch domestic demand relative to its domestic supply potential. This phenomenon is called 'Dutch Disease', and the literature contains a number of discussions on whether or not the Caspian Sea region countries are already suffering from it (Kalyuzhnova, 2002, 2005; Kaser, 2003; Kutan and Wyzan, 2005; Rosenberg and Saavalainen, 1998).

So far, the experience in the Caspian Sea region seems to require some corrections of the traditional model of Dutch Disease, at least as it applies to transition economies. The development of the oil and gas industry in the newly independent states of Azerbaijan, Kazakhstan and Turkmenistan took place at the same time as the transition from a centrally planned economy to a market-oriented structure has been progressing. In the initial stages the equilibrium real exchange rate persisted due to lack of productivity gains; however, in the course of the years it started to appreciate more and more as economies began to liberalize.

The development of the hydrocarbon sector in these countries was followed by capital inflows (domestic and foreign), a surge of domestic demand and stronger exchange rate appreciation. For example, the increasing value of the Kazakhstani hydrocarbon sector increased the value of the tenge relative to the US dollar due to a surge of inflows related to FDI and exports, and borrowing by the private sector. Over 2004, the tenge appreciated in real terms by 15.3 per cent against the US dollar, and by 2.9 per cent on an average annual basis in 2005; however, tighter market conditions in the final months of 2005 resulted in a 2.2 per cent depreciation on an end-of-year basis. Due to oil-related revenues, real appreciation continued in 2006. The real effective exchange rate appreciated by 5.9 per cent year on year, eroding the price competitiveness of domestic producers.

Therefore, as part of the initiative to raise the competitiveness of the economy, the Kazakhstani government has introduced a variety of tax incentives, which should improve the non-hydrocarbon sector.

Although high world oil prices in recent years had a beneficial impact on growth and fiscal performance in Azerbaijan, they also had an impact on the exchange rate. The National Bank of Azerbaijan was faced with the challenge of tightening monetary policy by lifting the discount rate by 50 basis points to 9.5 per cent in 2006. In addition, the National Bank of Azerbaijan also had to absorb the excess petrodollars by purchasing over US$1 bln on the foreign exchange market. Nevertheless, the manat appreciated by 5.4 per cent in 2006.

The Turkmen government has not released inflation figures for 2004–2006. According to the ADB, 'at end-December 2004, the official exchange rate was pegged at TMM5,200/$1 (as it has been since 17 April 1998), but the parallel market rate rose to TMM24,500/$1 from TMM20,000/$1 in 2003, due to a scarcity of foreign exchange' (ADB, 2005b: 49–50). This led to significant price increases for most imported goods.

Overall, the danger for all three economies is an excessive loss of competitiveness and, as a consequence, stagnation of the economy and its erosion in the long run. The so-called 'spending effect' occurs when the excess of revenues from natural resources creates rising demand (and thus inflation) in other sectors in the economy. Therefore it is important not only to have a governmental policy on oil production and revenue collection, but also on spending the oil wealth.

1.5   Political-economy challenges of three Caspian economies

At the time of writing, the challenge which all three Caspian economies are facing is how to sustain economic growth. As the figures above demonstrated, Azerbaijan, Kazakhstan and Turkmenistan share two specific features: high mineral export dependence – all three countries on oil, Kazakhstan on other minerals and Turkmenistan on gas – and a high ratio of investment to GDP. 'The interdependency is clear: mineral earnings sustain the high rate of capital formation, but that investment is required to sustain the exploitation of natural resources and to diversify the capital stock into other branches of production and the formation of human capital' (Kalyuzhnova and Kaser, 2006: 168).

Currently, a fundamental question relevant for all three Caspian countries, as resource-based economies, is whether, and under what conditions, they will be able to sustain their current growth performance. It is true that the development paths will differ in all three cases, with Azerbaijan facing a rapid period of depletion of its oil reserves and finding a new niche in its industrial development. In the coming years Kazakhstani governmental policy will probably need to concentrate more on non-materialistic goals, including health and well-being, and not only on supporting/ sustaining economic growth, whereas Turkmenistan still remains at the initial stage of transition and is likely to experience a shock due to the reforms.

In the medium to long term the overall challenge for all three economies, if the countries want to sustain growth at the present high level, is to increase export value. As Table 1.12 demonstrates, imports account for a significant share of consumer goods (e.g. in Azerbaijan – 54 per cent of GDP). This could be explained by the fact that domestic industries which produced these consumer goods either cannot sustain a high level of competition from aboard or are non-existent.

If we continue to analyse the substance of the advantages in the Caspian industries, it is clear that the regional comparative advantage (RCA) consists of natural resources (including hydrocarbon) and energy-intensive basic manufactures in all three Caspian economies (as we can see from Table 1.12). The use of energy in production or manufacturing is quite significant (somewhat higher in Kazakhstan than in Azerbaijan and Turkmenistan). It is a fact that energy intensities of transition countries have historically been very high compared with those of other industrialized economies (Cornillie and Fankhauser, 2002), and it is possible to conclude that the three Caspian economies still carry the legacy of the previous period.

As we can see from Table 1.12, all three economies are energy-exporting rather -importing nations, with the RCA in oil and oil products increasing in Kazakhstan to 61 per cent and to 90 per cent in Azerbaijan. There are

Table 1.12   Income, imports, energy use and energy import in Caspian region, 2005

Country	Gross national income, ATLAS method at current US$	Import of goods and services (% of GDP)	Energy use (kg of oil equivalent per capital)[a]	Energy import, net (% of energy use)[a]
Azerbaijan	10 399 253 504	54	1559	−55
Kazakhstan	44 604 497 920	45	3551	−116
Turkmenistan	....	48	3265	−274

[a] Full year 2004.

Source: World Development Indicators database. http://devdata.worldbank.org

ultimately two potential challenges here, one of which is related to the fact that all the talented labour force in the country is concentrated in the resource sector (with the happy exception of Kazakhstan, where there are other sectors, e.g. banking and real estate which are attracting capable labour forces). The only comfort is that the mineral sector is not labour intensive and can absorb only a certain level of the labour force. In resource-rich economies, the link between the share of natural resources in exports is associated with potential corruption. The latter makes economic growth slower in the long term (Larsson, 2006; Mauro, 1995). 'Natural resource-abundant countries constitute both growth losers and growth winners, and the main difference between the success cases and the cases of failure lies in the quality of institutions.' (Mehlum et al., 2006). Therefore, in order to prevent corruption, corruption-resilient structure/institutions are required. One of the instruments of such precaution could be the establishment of resource funds (see Chapter 2), which should possess a fair share of the resource rent.

Another aspect could be development of other (non-raw-material) sectors of the economy – economic diversification. The rationale here is two-fold: a more diversified economic structure is desirable because it will secure the economic stability of the country and its economic growth. In addition, it will reduce corruption and rent-seeking behaviour directed towards the resource sector, providing a more complex structure of the economic functioning of the country as well as more opportunities for the population to engage in business. A pattern of development based on a broader range of sectors should also help achieve greater regional development and spread the benefits of economic growth more widely among the population. Obviously for the three Caspian countries there is a very long way to go as far as this is concerned. One universal generalization can be made for all of them. Caspian governments should be very realistic about what their diversification programmes can and cannot achieve.

In Chapter 7 we shall discuss at length the main steps of macroeconomic policies for diversification. However, one remark should be made here: what works in one country might not work in another. Obviously the three Caspian economies are not an exception in this regard. Even though their challenges seem to be similar, solutions should be tailored individually.

1.6 The role of the state: setting the stage

The countries of the Caspian are confronted with a bewildering array of problems on their transition to stable independent states. The term 'transition' was initially used to denote a path of development from a central command economy and a communist regime to a free market economy and a liberal democracy. However, the endpoints of transition in the former Soviet space are no longer certain as the level of economic reform varies substantially from country to country, and Communist rule has been supplanted by personality cults and authoritarian governments with varying degrees of repressiveness (Kalyuzhnova and Lynch, 2000). Moreover, intraregional cooperation is quite weak despite the magnitude of the shared social, economic and security problems. Indeed, the region has been plagued by a multitude of armed conflicts with varying degrees of severity (Lynch, 2000).

Political factors clearly play a critical role in all aspects of state policy. The literature suggests that the type of political system has a significant impact on the distribution and spending of hydrocarbon revenues, and ultimately on economic sustainability (Auty, 2003; Eifert et al., 2003; Lal, 1995). Understanding where the Caspian countries stand in this respect will, possibly, provide insights into the policy options available to the governments.

The Soviet Union encompassed a large number of different nationalities and ethnic and linguistic groups, representing an enormous range of cultural, tribal and religious diversity. The disintegration of the Soviet state into 15 separate states on the basis of the republican boundaries of the Soviet period corresponded to the boundaries of a multitude of ethnic groupings. Although the Soviet Union was dissolved peacefully, the states that emerged were to some extent inherently unstable because they did not represent natural units that could easily develop their identities as nation-states. Consequently the region harboured very significant potential for conflict (Gleason, 1997).

The leaders of the Central Asian countries were those of the final years of the Soviet era, and from this point of view the transition was quite smooth. This was not the case in all countries in the Caspian region. In Azerbaijan the old Soviet bureaucrat Haidar Aliyev came to power in a coup, whereas Georgia was embroiled in a civil conflict until former Soviet Foreign Minister Shevardnadze established himself, only to be eventually turned out of office by an 'orange revolution'. Consequently the style of governance continued to be authoritarian, without the trappings of communist ideology, which in any case had been less pervasive in the southern regions of the Soviet Union.

There is much evidence that the authoritarian style of governance is itself a source of instability as there are no mechanisms for resolving political, economic or ethnic grievances, and political opposition movements are severely restricted and have (in most cases) no hope of attaining or sharing power. Indeed, the transfer of power is an issue that most governments have not addressed. But the severe social and economic dislocation in the period of transition, combined with large-scale rent-seeking by the political elite and the neglect of the basic needs of the population, has created significant potential for discontent, of which extreme Islamic movements are the most dangerous expression. Moreover, governments in the region have not put in place suitable policies to deal with the interests of the various ethnic groupings, choosing largely to support the interests of the majority. This creates conditions for separatism, irredentism and ethnic strife. This is evident in the conflict between Georgia and Abkhazia, Azerbaijan and Armenia, the civil war in Tajikistan and the low-level conflict in the Ferghana Valley. Internal instability is therefore likely to remain a major factor of the security environment of the region for decades to come.

Caspian region countries have been struck by a dramatic deterioration of economic conditions since 1992. These include an economic recession, a drastic decrease of per capita income, a rise in levels of indebtedness, a continuous depreciation of national currencies, an unemployment boom, the development of an unofficial economy, drag trafficking, etc. The whole situation has been aggravated by certain government policies, leading to a predation logic that rules these economies and is crucially related to the high share of primary exports (such as oil and gas), high level of corruption, development of the narcotics trade and high unemployment. There were varying efforts to reform the economy, privatize industry and agriculture, and attract foreign direct investment. The densely integrated nature of the Soviet economy meant that the industrial capacities that the newly independent states inherited were not suitable for their own needs or for the development of a national economy. States that were involved in significant conflict (such as Armenia, Azerbaijan, Georgia and Tajikistan) inevitably fared worse (Pomfret, 1995).

Hydrocarbon resources in the Caspian states offer significant opportunities to reverse the economic decline, but also complicate economic policy-making and the redistribution of economic wealth across ethnic and social groups. The literature on resource-rich economies demonstrates quite irrefutably that oil and gas revenues, which are unpredictable and based on exhaustible resources, can create significant problems of economic management.

The potential of conflict and instability in the region arises from the weakness of states, the lack of fully formed national identities that encompass all ethnic groups, and emerging power imbalances. The borders between the states in the Caspian region remain porous, and the spread of terrorism and transnational crime, especially the narcotics trade, is hard to interdict. In order to assess the potential of conflict, some of the key states are examined below.

Kazakhstan

Under the leadership of Nursultan Nazarbayev, a former member of the Soviet Politburo, Kazakhstan was the last Soviet republic to formally declare its independence in 1991. The Central Asian states were not involved in or consulted about the dissolution of the Soviet Union, and generally opposed it. Kazakhstan was assiduous in supporting a successor organization to the Soviet Union, an endeavour that did not meet with success. Kazakhstan was quick to embark on reformist measures such as price liberalization and privatization, but macroeconomic stabilization came much later, after the country left the rouble zone in November 1993. Consequently Kazakhstan experienced a period of hyperinflation (Kalyuzhnova, 1998). Like other Central Asian states, Kazakhstan adopted the formal procedures of democracy such as elections of the president and parliament, but in reality Nazarbayev became an autocratic ruler who concentrated political power in his office and blatantly rigged elections, partly by eliminating powerful rival candidates on specious pretexts. In the mid-1990s privatization shifted from being based on a voucher scheme to asset sales, as a result of which by the end of 1996 many of the most valuable state enterprises had been sold. Rent-seeking was endemic, involving the entire political elite, including especially the presidential family. From the mid-1990s the elite focused on oil and gas development as the principal source of wealth generation, but initially it was hamstrung by the low level of oil prices and Russian control over export routes. The dispute of the legal status of the Caspian Sea was another instrument that Russia used in order to limit Kazakhstan's role as competitor in the export of hydrocarbon resources. The financial crisis in Russia in August 1998 had a serious impact on the economy of Kazakhstan. Overall the economic performance of Kazakhstan in the 1990s was rather dismal. However, from 1999 onwards, following a currency devaluation, an increase in proven oil reserves and an upturn in oil prices, Kazakhstan experienced dramatic economic growth starting in 2000 and continuing as the oil price topped US$60/bbl in 2005. This has provided a significant opportunity for Kazakhstan to develop its infrastructure and the atrophying sectors of its economy in order to create sustained growth. However, it remains unclear whether the country can deal with the rent-seeking and corruption, and responsibly invest its oil windfalls as political reform remains elusive.

Kazakhstan national security policy was developed in a peculiar strategic and military situation. The newly independent state found itself in between two nuclear powers, Russia and China, but in a relatively benign environment without a major external threat. The principal threat to national security originated from two sources: Russia's hegemonic ambitions with regard to the former Soviet space; and the problems of internal stability. These two issues were linked by the geography and ethnic composition of the country. The large Russian population concentrated in the north of the country (37.8 per cent of the population in 1989; 32 per cent in 2006) (Olcot, 2002) created the potential risk that Kazakhstan could split in two, or that Russia might intervene in order to safeguard the interests of its citizens. This situation was part of the motivation for the decision to move the capital from Almaty in the South to Astana (previously called Akmola) in the north.

The loss of Soviet military assets following independence meant that Russia essentially became the guarantor of Kazakhastan's security against external aggression, which was a paradoxical state of affairs given that Russia at the same time posed the greatest threat to the sovereignty of the country. Nazarbayev acknowledged that Kazakhstan had to strive for the largest possible degree of independence. In 1992 Kazakhstan signed the CIS Collective Security Treaty (the Tashkent Treaty), but this treaty did not establish a viable collective security regime in the former Soviet space. This was due to the imbalance of forces in Russia's favour and the absence of an institutional mechanism that would give it legitimacy. Russia intervened in those conflicts in which it chose to involve itself, in a manner that lacked impartiality. Thus Russian intervention could be a source of insecurity as well as security for Central Asian states. This situation was tolerated by the Kazakh government because it did not have the resources for an alternative policy and there was no external threat to the survival of the state. The principal security risk that preoccupied Nazarbayev was the stability of the country and its economy. Kazakhstan was not seriously threatened by overspill of conflict from other areas, such as Tajikistan or the Ferghana Valley. Potential points of conflict with China related to the risk of uncontrolled immigration from China, the demarcation of the border between the two countries, and the Uighur rebels who were committing terrorist actions in Xinjiang province from bases in Kazakhstan. But these problems were largely resolved. The border demarcation resulted in an adjustment in China's favour, and immigration from China into the empty steppe of Kazakhstan never reached serious proportions. China and Kazakhstan developed a security partnership through the Shanghai Security Organization and have a common strategic interest in the exploitation of Caspian energy resources in which China has acquired a significant stake.

Overall, the assessment is that the authoritarian government is relatively benign and has delivered more in terms of economic prosperity than other Central Asian countries. In terms of the classification above, Kazakhstan could be described as a reformist autocracy.

In summary, Kazakhstan is not a major source of potential conflict in the region for the foreseeable future. It will not be involved in serious disputes with its neighbours, and the oil revenue has resulted in economic growth that limits popular discontent.

Azerbaijan

Azerbaijan is of crucial concern with regard to the security dilemmas in the Caspian region because of its large offshore hydrocarbon reserves and its role in one of the major conflicts in the region. In the final years of the Soviet Union, Azerbaijan underwent major social upheavals as the first ethnic conflict in what is now described as the former Soviet space, and the anti-Soviet Azerbaijan Popular Front was formed. In January 1990 Soviet troops intervened in Baku to stop anti-Armenian pogroms. The conflict in the region of Nagorno-Karabakh started in 1988 when the Armenian majority in this province voted to unite with neighbouring Armenia and sought to overturn Stalin's 1921 edict which had incorporated Nagorno-Karabakh in the Azerbaijani Soviet Socialist Republic. After the Soviet Union was dissolved in 1991, the conflict over Nagorno-Karabakh escalated to the level of a full-scale war as the Armenians in the region voted to establish an independent state. Armenian separatists took control of much the enclave, which led to the overthrow of the neo-Communist leader of Azerbaijan, Ayaz Mutalibov, and his replacement by Abulfaz Elchibey of the Azerbaijan Popular Front. Elchibey won presidential elections in 1992 due to his control over the state apparatus. He launched a campaign against the Armenians, which resulted in 40 per cent of the enclave returning to Azeri control, but renewed fighting in 1993 reversed the situation to some extent. Moreover, the Armenians occupied Kelbajar, an Azeri district located between Nagorno-Karabakh and Armenia. Armenia had provided weapons and other support to the Armenian rebels, and by December 1993 regular Armenian troops were involved in the fighting. The fighting ended in 1994 with Nagorno-Karabakh and several Azerbaijani regions under

Armenian control. Nagorno-Karabakh has become an independent auton-
omous region closely linked with Armenia (using the same currency).
Elchibey was ousted in June 1993 by a rebellion led by Surat Husseinov,
who paved the way for the old Communist leader from Azerbaijan, Haidar
Aliyev, to come back into power. Aliyev won presidential elections in
August 1993 with 98.9 per cent of the votes. During the following years,
Aliyev succeeded in gaining control over all the means of coercion and
economic resources of the country, essentially suppressing political opposition and in particular the Azerbaijan Popular Front. But Aliyev was
unable to deliver an acceptable resolution of the Nagorno-Karabakh conflict or a significant improvement in the standard of living. Between
1990 and 1996 GDP declined by 42 per cent. Rent-seeking became pervasive as in another newly independent states, with a newly wealthy elite
that supported the regime in order to maintain its position. Foreign investment in oil exploration and production brought about a partial recovery of
the economy, although the fall in the oil price in 1998 hit Azerbaijan hard.
Foreign investment in non-oil industries is considered to be high risk. Oil
production declined significantly after the dissolution of the Soviet Union
due to the general decline of the country and the ageing infrastructure, but
as a result of US$1.8 bln being invested between 1994 and 1998 oil produc-
tion grew again, reaching a level of 107.75 mln bbl. Onshore and offshore
operations are controlled by the State Oil Corporation of the Azerbaijan
Republic (Dekmejian and Simonian, 2003).

Azerbaijan remains a 'reformist autocratic state' under the leadership of
Aliyev's son Ilham Aliyev. The blatant manipulation of elections and the
failure to deliver on economic development means that there is a latent
potential for unrest. Azerbaijan continues in a tense relationship with
Russia. Both Russia and Iran supported Armenia, but Russia still has
interests in Azerbaijan, and the stalemate in Karabakh may serve Russia's
efforts to obtain more leverage. Azerbaijan joined the Tashkent Collective
Security Treaty but withdrew in 1999. Nevertheless, it still has some military cooperation with Russia, such as joint exercises in the Caspian Sea.
Despite the lack of progress towards democracy, the USA has a significant
strategic interest in relations with Baku. Not only is there major Western
involvement in Azerbaijan's oil industry, but the BTC (Baku–Tbilisi–
Ceyhan) pipeline has provided a major transport route, bypassing
Russia. Azerbaijan has also established close relations with Western institutions, such as NATO, the EU (it was invited to join the Council of
Europe in 2001) and the pan-European OSCE (Organization for Security
and Co-operation in Europe). Thus Azerbaijan has been successful in
limiting Russian influence, although the fact that 25 per cent of its

population works in Russia means that it depends critically on the inflow of funds earned in the Russian Federation. There is no doubt that there exists a potential for major security problems, primarily due to the radicalization of youth with regard to Nagorno-Karabakh and the threat of a return to violence which could have an impact on oil production and country risk assessments.

In Kazakhstan and Azerbaijan there is a social consensus regarding development and impact on non-oil traded sectors, which involves institutional and economic implications, namely policy stability, some degree of transparency, a drive for competitiveness and low transaction costs (particularly in Kazakhstan's case), a strong constituency for stabilization and fiscal restraint, expenditure smoothing, stabilization (creation of resource funds), state investment complementary to the competitive private sector, as well as an active exchange rate management to limit any outbreak of Dutch Disease.

Turkmenistan

The case of Turkmenistan is different in two important respects: first, Turkmenistan successfully adopted a strategy of strategic isolation which limited Russian and other external influences, insulated the country from the political conflicts elsewhere in the former Soviet Union and adjacent regions. At the same time Saparmurat Niyazov, previously the first secretary of the Turkmen Communist Party, adopted a totalitarian leadership style and achieved a high degree of internal stability (albeit without legitimacy) that survived his sudden death from a heart attack in 2006. This means that Turkmenistan is rightly classified as a 'predatory autocracy'. It is characterized by a failure of consensus-building, a lack of transparency, corruption and rent-seeking. Consequently, in Turkmenistan we find the risk of an unsustainable long-term spending trajectory and little economic diversification. The efficiency of the policy is clearly affected by the influence of the authoritarian means of decision-making.

Since the beginning of transition, the oil and gas industry in the Caspian region has undertaken an impressive expansion programme in all three states – Kazakhstan, Azerbaijan and Turkmenistan – although not without its own 'local' specifics. The enthusiasm of the earlier period (the beginning of the 1990s) was replaced by more mature governmental views in 2005–2007. Table 1.13 illustrates the dynamics of the Caspian reality. As we can see from this table, Kazakhstan is an obvious leader, indicated by production of 1.5 mln bbl/day in 2007, whereas Turkmenistan is producing 200 000 bbl/day.

Table 1.13   Daily production by countries, thous. bbl/day

Country	1995	2007
Azerbaijan	183	900
Kazakhstan	440	1500
Turkmenistan	93	200

Source: CGES.

Growth, expectations etc. were 'corrected', among other things, by the technical availability, costs and transport routes as well as by issues of governmental policies on which we concentrate here. Any governmental policy with regard to the oil and gas sector aims to improve the overall prosperity in the country. Obviously the three Caspian countries are not exceptions in this regard.

Let us now analyse the evolving role and interests of the state in the hydrocarbon industry. This we will consider not from a company perspective – or even that of a national company – but in terms of national political and economic goals and development objectives.

The over-arching goal of any resource-rich country's government, assuming some degree of democratic accountability or vision, will be to maximize the benefits for the whole nation from oil and gas wealth. The route through which the government will operate is a hydrocarbon agency/ministry. Its primary role is, or should be, managing the country's hydrocarbon industry to the long-term benefit of the nation. It is of course debatable what is 'long term' and who and how 'true benefit to the entire nation' are defined – and this needs to be seen in the light of governmental statements, manifesto and programmes on the development of the hydrocarbon resources.[10]

Any national petroleum policy should be based on the following principles: sound economics and environmental practices, as well as best legal practices and technologies. Therefore, any resource-rich country's government will build its relations with investors (foreign or domestic) based on the primary aim of the host government, namely to ensure economic benefits for the country.

The political environment in which governments have been pursuing these goals has evolved over time. On the one hand, governments have built up their financial resources and experience. They feel better placed

[10] In later chapters we shall consider the programmes that exist to date in the Caspian region countries.

to press their strategic interests *vis-à-vis* industry. On the other hand, companies have become less aggressively concerned to start new projects. In the recent past, getting the Caspian oil and gas projects into international oil companies' approved capital portfolios has proved challenging (although this could evolve over the medium term in light of demand and supply factors in global markets). Specifically, a number of projects may have turned out to be 'commercial' but not 'competitive'.

Foreign investors who desire a 'commercial' rate of return are important to consider as investment partners – and in a wider sense as sponsors – for the Caspian region. Big projects attract multiple partners who can more easily mitigate and diversify risk than any one company (even major): there is safety in numbers. And the last few years demonstrate that government assurances of fiscal certainty and/or incentives can greatly reduce risks and ensure that a project is 'competitive'. Nonetheless, the reverse has also been seen. There have been cases of tension surrounding changes in tax regimes or local content regulations – as well as a number of cases where the foreign firms have been accused of tax avoidance (*Argus FSU*, 11 August 2000).

An example of tensions in the commercial environment has been seen in Kazakhstan, since the beginning of 2004, where there have been major changes in the legal regime applicable to the petroleum industry. A first set of amendments to the Tax Code came into effect from 1 January 2004, and a further set was adopted to become effective from 1 January 2005. On 8 December 2004 amendments to the Petroleum Law and Subsurface Law became effective. And finally, a new Production Sharing Agreement Law (applicable to the Caspian and Aral Seas) is soon to be adopted. These changes will have a substantial impact on the petroleum industry in the future. They reflect the government's policies with respect to increased participation of the national oil company (in production); greater attention to the use and development of local content and 'high technologies' (a topic developed further in Chapter 5); a change in government (tax) take; and increased regulation and oversight.

Through their experience in relations with Caspian region governments, investors have come to identify three prime areas of concern. These are, first, that fiscal arrangements can be changed *ex post*; second, that changes in the petroleum and tax regime may well prove discriminatory *vis-à-vis* some companies (due to size and financial capability, degree of foreign ownership, or tenure and past success in the host country); and, third, that income tax structure and scheduled payments to the host government may not prove credible in the contracting company's home country. In these respects, it is not only the sharing of economic gains that has changed in the past few years; it is also the level of policy-related risk.

Meanwhile, perceptions and approaches have shifted on the company side towards greater caution about taking on new risks in the region. This has underscored the need for governments to foster a new stability in the balance of interests and influence in the region. In a period when the world oil industry perceived a state of over-supply (a decade ago), the major multinational oil companies changed their posture. From aggressors seeking to acquire new places to explore, they became reluctant suitors, as can be clearly seen in the Caspian region at the time of writing. Moreover, throughout the last decade, contracting service companies have been changing their aspirations with regard to the status of the region. If at the beginning of 1990s an integrated multinational oil company had to concern itself with 'finding a home' in the Caspian region (e.g. see *Argus FSU*, 28 February 1997), now the financial objective of the contracting company in the Caspian has become one of balancing geological, political and fiscal risk against the economic parameters of prospective returns on out-of-pocket investment achieved in a quick and orderly manner.[11]

In this setting, some mitigation of risk by government became essential to foster continued hydrocarbon development, and this included the emergence of greater stability and a sense of legitimacy as regards government–company relations. There are several routes to this, which are complementary – and their implications extend beyond the hydrocarbon sector to the broader question of national development strategy, including security of contracts and positive relations with the international financing agencies. One fundamental route is through the creation of more predictable governance in terms of the contractual environment. A second is, more broadly, the creation of a favourable business environment. And a third possible route is through direct involvement via such economic risk-sharing mechanisms as debt guarantees, low interest rate bond financing and low-price protection.

As discussed earlier, in the early 1990s the Caspian governments were not ready for these obligations. Only later, when economic recovery took place after 2000, did local ownership add incremental value. That provided an opportunity to bridge the gap between 'commercial' and 'competitive' projects. One response was tactical: to begin making overtures to smaller companies in the hope of achieving their nation's

---

[11] Based on various of interviews with industry players in the Caspian region.

petroleum objectives – in particular, the crucial need for know-how, new capital and opening up of new markets. An example of this is Nations Energy (Canada), which developed the Karazhnbash field in Mangistau region, before being bought by CITIC (China International Trust and Investment Company) in 2006. But a broader and more strategic response was to shift towards a more stable environment and a greater sense of legitimacy in government relations with larger companies.

Consequently, the last few years have seen some degree of government response on the fundamental governance issues. It is helpful to consider first how governance issues directly affect national economy, which is the topic of Chapter 2.

2

The Management of Hydrocarbon Wealth: National Oil Funds[12]

2.1 Introduction

Oil revenues offer important opportunities to enhance economic development. But they are also volatile, unpredictable and ultimately exhaustible; and they can thus greatly complicate economic management. In the Caspian region, the starting assumption must be that resource endowment is potentially a 'blessing' that can help overcome transition disruptions. But the lesson of experience elsewhere is that fulfilling this promise – and avoiding the risk of natural resources becoming a 'curse' – is crucially dependent on policies, including a commitment to enhanced policy transparency.

The recent literature on resource-rich economies supports the view that oil and gas revenues can pose problems for policy-makers, and highlights the possibility that natural resource endowment can be an economic curse rather than a blessing (Auty, 2006; Auty and Mikesell, 1998; Gylfason, 2001; Kalyuzhnova and Kaser, 2006; Sachs and Warner, 2001, etc.). In a range of cases, economic performance has indeed appeared to suffer rather than benefit from the impact of natural resource endowment (Gylfason and Zoega, 2003; Paldam, 1997).

As a consequence, the international community, including notably international financial institutions, has become growingly concerned about the effectiveness with which natural resource revenues are used, and in particular how they can help foster long-run economic and social

---

[12] This chapter is based on a revised version of the paper by Y. Kalyuzhnova, 'Overcoming the curse of hydrocarbon: goals and governance in the oil funds of Kazakhstan and Azerbaijan', *Comparative Economic Studies*, Vol. 48, No. 4, December 2006; 583–613.

development. This latter concern is part of a wider topic: the political economy of resource-driven growth.

The governments of resource-rich countries face the challenge of devising policies that can channel effectively 'income transfers to governments and the inflow of foreign exchange from foreign investments' (Kalyuzhnova, 2002: 79). To tackle this challenge, many oil-producing countries are setting up national oil funds. Such funds have become fashionable in the wake of recent high and volatile oil prices, and with new discoveries of hydrocarbon deposits.

National oil funds have different titles, goals and rules, but they share the underlying objective of helping governments deal with the problems created by large and variable revenues from the energy sector. In the Caspian region, such funds have been established in Azerbaijan (1999) and Kazakhstan (2000). The funds in these countries operate as both a *stabilization* and a *savings* fund (see Table 2.1). In Turkmenistan, the State Fund for the Development of the Oil and Gas Industry and Mineral Resources (SFDOG) was set up in 1996. This complements a larger fund, the Foreign Exchange Reserve Fund (FERF) at Deutsche Bank, which derives its financing from a range of sources.

In light of emerging experience with such funds, there is a need to explore under what circumstances they can become part of a policy solution – rather than ending up as a part of the problem.[13] The core question is whether oil funds, generically, are a panacea for the so-called 'paradox of plenty'; whether their effectiveness depends on specific operating conditions and rules; or whether, more pessimistically, they deliver results only in national circumstances that are in any case particularly benign.

In this context, the literature identifies oil funds as a tool that may help in addressing two specific problems associated with oil revenues: the unpredictability and volatility of world market prices, and the concern to save part of the revenues for future generations (the 'Permanent Income Hypothesis' – PIH: ECON, 2002; Davis et al., 2001,; 2003; Fasano, 2000; Gelb, 1985; Karl, 1997). In this context, oil funds may serve as a form of 'commitment mechanism', thus substituting for the IMF commitment mechanism. A further problem could in principle also be mitigated by oil funds: the 'Dutch Disease'.

---

[13] In addition, a 50 per cent tax on foreign exchange receipts from gas exports was introduced in 1997 (IMF, 1999, 14 and 28).

Table 2.1 Comparison of rules for accumulation and use of the national funds of Azerbaijan and Kazakhstan

Azerbaijan	
Use of the fund	Profit gained from the fund's deposits placed in credit organizations with a high rating is mainly used for investment purposes. The fund's resources are used according to directions (programmes) confirmed each year by decrees of the president of the Azerbaijani Republic. For the country's socio-economic progress, the fund's resources can be used for solving national problems, and constructing and reconstructing infrastructure facilities of strategic importance.
Management of the fund	The executive director carries out operational management of the fund's activities. He/she is appointed by the president of the Azerbaijani Republic. The executive director of the fund: • organizes the current work of the fund and manages it; • prepares proposals on the main directions (programme) of spending the fund's resources and submits them for approval to the president of the Azerbaijani Republic, along with the opinion of the Supervisory Council; • prepares an annual report about the fund's activities and submits it to the president of the Azerbaijani Republic, along with the opinion of the Supervisory Council; • prepares a draft estimate of expenses on the management of the fund (including expenses on personnel) and submits it for approval to the president of the Azerbaijani Republic; • ensures the preparation of materials on the basis of instructions from the president of the Azerbaijani Republic; • appoints employees of the fund's administration to positions established by the law and dismisses them, and applies measures of encouragement and reprimand with regard to them; • ensures the necessary conditions for the auditor appointed by the president of the Azerbaijani Republic to conduct audits; • publishes in the press the auditor's opinion reflecting the fund's annual activities;

- prepares analytical certificates on the fund's activities and submits them to the president of the Azerbaijani Republic and the Supervisory Council; implements other authorities in accordance with the legislation of the Azerbaijani Republic and this statute.

With the aim of ensuring general supervision over the fund's activities, the Supervisory Council is formed from representatives of relevant state bodies and public organizations, as well as other people.

The president of the Azerbaijani Republic confirms members of the Supervisory Council.

The Supervisory Council examines and expresses its opinion regarding the main directions (programme) of using the fund's resources, its annual report (together with the auditor's opinion attached to it) and balance, as well as the draft estimate of the fund's annual expenses on the basis of the executive director's representation.

The Supervisory Council holds its sessions when necessary, but no less than once a quarter. The Supervisory Council can hold extraordinary sessions at the initiative of the executive director or half the members of the Supervisory Council.

The members of the Supervisory Council carry out their activities on a public basis (without payment).

Report & Accountability	The oil fund is subordinated directly to the president and is accountable to him. The fund carries out accounting procedures and statistic reports as established by the law. The annual financial activities of the fund have to be inspected and confirmed by an independent auditor appointed by the president of the Azerbaijani Republic.
Kazakhstan	
Use of the fund	The fund may be used: • to execute its stabilization function – in the form of receipts from the fund to the republican and local budgets to compensate for losses to be determined as the difference between approved and actual amounts of tax and other mandatory payments receipts; • in the form of targeted transfers of the fund to the republican and local budgets for the purposes defined by the Kazakhstani president; • to cover expenses connected with management of the fund and annual external audit conducted.

(Continued)

Table 2.1 (Continued)

Azerbaijan	
Management of the Fund	The president of the Republic of Kazakhstan: 1) establishes a Management Council of the national fund; 2) Issues directives that are binding on the Council, the government and the National Bank with regard to issues relating to the fund; 3) exercises other authorities stipulated in the rules of the fund. With regard to management of the fund, the Kazakhstani government exercises the following powers: 1) develops and approves rules for the compilation of reporting documents and the order for accumulation and use of the fund; 2) develops together with the National Bank and approves a schedule for the submission of informational materials and financial reporting on activities associated with the management of the fund; 3) provides for the submission of a report on the accumulation and use of the fund to the president and information on activities related to the formulating and use of the fund for the parliament; 4) ensures that an annual audit of the fund is carried out; 5) ensures that accounting is carried out for the formulating and use of the fund; and 6) exercises other powers stipulated by the rules. The National Bank exercises fiduciary management of the fund on the basis of a fiduciary management agreement concluded between the National Bank and the government. A consultative and deliberative body (the Council) is created under the Kazakhstani president for the purpose of implementing the powers of the president with regard to management of the fund. The main task of the Council is to provide assistance and develop recommendations for the president with regard to issues the use of the fund.
Report & Account-ability	Each year, by 1 February of the year following the reporting year, the government together with the National Bank have to compile an annual report on accumulation and use of the fund. By 1 April of the year following the reporting year, the government should submit, for the approval of the president, the annual report on accumulation and use of the fund together with the results from external audit.

2.2   Key features of funds in the Caspian region

In Azerbaijan, President Aliyev signed decree N240 'On setting up the State Oil Fund of the Azerbaijani Republic' (SOFAZ) on 29 December 1999, to govern the collection of oil revenue and bonuses. The oil fund is directly accountable to the Azeri president, who appoints the executive director and confirms members of the Supervisory Council. Samir Sharifov was appointed by the president as the first general manger of the fund.

According to the presidential decree, SOCAR received authorization to ensure the transfer of funds to a special oil fund account in the National Bank of Azerbaijan. Initially, according to SOCAR's President Aliyev, US$270 964 652 of Azeri oil revenues and bonuses provided by the foreign companies were transferred to the oil fund account. The largest part of this amount was made up of revenues from the sale of 7.09 mln bbl of oil produced from the Chirag field.

SOFAZ receives all revenues associated with the 'new oil fields'. These fields are those included in the 1994 'Contract of the Century' (Aliyev, 1997: 9). It receives and records proceeds from the state's share of oil sales, royalties, pipeline fees, rental fees, bonus payments and interest income. Most of the revenues presently come from the first and only operational consortium at the Azeri, Chiraq and Guneshli (ACG) oil fields, the source for the Baku–Tbilisi–Ceyhan (BTC) oil pipeline (see SOFAZ press release, 16 April 2003).

In Kazakhstan, the oil fund (the National Fund of the Republic of Kazakhstan – NFRK) was established in August 2000. Legal aspects were defined by Presidential Decree N402, of 23 August. The NFRK is run by a special Management Council, formed by President Nazarbayev. The governing body includes the president of the country, the prime minister, the heads of the two chambers of parliament, the National Bank chairman and the finance minister. The fund is managed by the National Bank of Kazakhstan and is overseen by a governing board chaired by the president of Kazakhstan. Information on the fund's revenues and expenditure, and the audit result are published in the local press. The fund is subject to an annual independent audit.

The NFRK invests in liquid foreign equities, and will be capitalized by corporate income taxes, VAT, royalties, bonuses and Kazakhstan's revenues from production sharing agreements (PSAs). The fund has a long-term investment function (75%) and a smaller stabilization function (25 per cent).

The origins of Turkmenistan's FERF (the Foreign Exchange Reserve Fund) go back to 1989 when the Turkmen authorities gained a general licence from the Soviet Central Bank which allowed them to manage foreign currency at the Turkmen commercial bank. After the collapse of the Soviet Union, by 1992, the money was moved to Vnesheconombank of Turkmenistan and later to the Central Bank of Turkmenistan. Since 1995 money has been deposit in the Deutsche Bank under the direct and total control of the late President Niyazov.

2.3 Economic context

The rules governing the accumulation and use of resources in oil funds differ widely. A comparison is provided in Table 2.1. The differing features of the funds must be understood, in part, in light of the economic situation of each country, which results in varying priorities. As an illustration, it is useful to compare the rules governing the national funds of Kazakhstan, Turkmenistan and Azerbaijan, which are strikingly different.

First, governments and the international agencies consider the estimated life of hydrocarbon deposits as a decisive argument for or against placing the funds' investment portfolio abroad, whence income will be accrued on the PIH. The scale and pace of exhaustion of reserves, of course, differ across countries.

- In Kazakhstan, the IMF had originally estimated the year 2045 as the date when the hydrocarbon resources would be exhausted. However, this projection did not take account of then unproven reserves. Recent exploration in Kazakhstan has led to the discovery of the Kashagan field in the Caspian Sea. This alone is believed to hold nearly 40 bln bbl of oil reserves. Estimates of how long countries will remain significant producers of oil need to take into account anticipated future discoveries set against future rates of production. These production rates are based on extraction and transport costs at the contemporary and projected world price. Kazakhstan's proven reserves may well amount to 18 bln bbl (including Kashagan's proven reserves).
- In Azerbaijan, ACG will be producing – albeit at a declining rate towards the end of the period – for another 30–40 years. BP's production profile, as an indication, shows a rapid fall. However, the government's receipts will be higher in that period, due to the structure of its production sharing agreement (PSA). Shakh Deniz will most likely be on stream for another 50 years – peaking at around 2015–2020 and depending on the evolution of gas markets. It can, of course, be questioned whether national oil funds in practice continue to operate for such a long period.

- In Turkmenistan, long-term oil and gas production forecasts have recorded political aspirations, rather than an interpretation of geology. Nevertheless, the country's large gas reserves and relatively undeveloped oil and gas resources mean that it should remain a very significant producer of gas and a relatively small, but increasingly important, producer of oil for several decades to come.

Second, investment ratios in these economies are high, and external financing has been drawn on to differing degrees in achieving this. Azerbaijan and Turkmenistan in particular have a very high share of capital formation in GDP (Table 1.6). Both countries, as well as Kazakhstan, exhibit ratios well above those of other transition economies. That Kazakhstan has drawn heavily abroad for its capital finance may be inferred, in part, from its high ratio of external debt to GDP – in 2004 this was 68.9 per cent. This high ratio compares with levels of only 28.4 per cent in Turkmenistan and 20.3 per cent in Azerbaijan. At that time, the moratorium on disbursements from the 'oil funds' was in force, and hence these governments were not achieving their high investment rates through the use of these funds. But the steady fall in the Turkmen ratio for external debt (from 101.7 per cent of GDP in 1999 through 78.6 per cent in 2001 to 34.8 per cent in 2003) suggests that drawings on the oil funds may have been substituting for external borrowing. With the expenditure moratoria lapsing in 2005 and the Turkmen fund under no such mandatory constraint, the question arises whether it is more rational to borrow money from international organizations or capital markets, with the ensuing service costs (which could come from the 'oil funds') or to invest the 'oil money' in domestic development.

2.4 Mapping goals on to national priorities

This economic context helps one to understand the differing designs of oil funds, and again the contrast between the three countries will serve to make this point clear. In Kazakhstan, the national fund is designed to save resources for future generations, and avoid undue pressure on the domestic economy – and added on to this is a stabilization function. President Nazarbayev made clear at the outset that resources would not be spent on covering current expenses, but would accumulate in the NFRK for future generations, as well as for the contingency of economic recession. Stabilization by the NFRK is achieved by means of 'reference prices' for gas, oil and four metals (chrome, zinc, lead and copper). The nine largest oil companies and three from the metals sector are subject to transfers based on the reference price. When the targets are exceeded, surplus tax payments are transferred to the NFRK. On the other hand, if market prices are below the reference prices, the fund provides revenue to the government. The stabilization portfolio must constitute at least 20 per cent of NFRK assets.

With the Kazakhstan budget in a strong position, and oil prices rising in the recent past, this strategy has proved entirely workable. During the first five years of its existence the NFRK has accumulated extra payments made to the republic's budget from major companies operating in the raw materials (oil and gas) sector. In 2003 the fund began accumulating proceeds from the sale of state property. The fund's reserves currently exceed US$14.5 bln (see Figure 2.1).

The underlying situation in Azerbaijan is different. At the time of writing, the economy requires substantial investment for economic development. The state budget does not have the means to meet this demand. Therefore the Azeri government is in the situation of borrowing resources from the international economic organizations, sometimes with conditions viewed as unfavourable for the country. There is the difficult question of how far it makes sense to borrow money from international economic organizations for the country's economic needs and to pay the debt back later with interest (which would come from the oil fund) or, alternatively, to spend oil money now directly on the development of the national economy. Part of the answer depends on the cost of official borrowing – which is in part on concessional terms. But there is also the question of whether the rate of return on

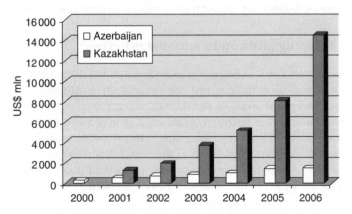

Figure 2.1   Funds of the SOFAZ and the NFRK, 2000–2006, US$ mln
Source: SOFAZ and NFRK annual reports.

the international investments of the fund is higher than would be achieved – subject to capacity constraints – by investing infrastructure and other reform needs in the domestic economy.

The differing roles and objectives of national governments are reflected in the investment strategy of the funds. From its conception the investment strategy of the NFRK was based on the rules governing the foreign exchange reserves of the National Bank of Kazakhstan: eligible assets were low-risk interest-bearing securities (AA– grade or better). According to the FitchRatings agency,

> the NFRK offers a good degree of fiscal and balance of payments support, but as its assets are still not especially large, this support is finite. Assets should rise more rapidly during the coming years, in part related to the timing of additional oil production, although the authorities might wish to revisit the question of the trigger price to ensure regular and reliable inflows into the Fund. (FitchRatings, 2003: 12).

Of course, a prudent strategy of investing resources in high-quality external assets could be compatible with a more diversified portfolio approach in the future.[14]

In Azerbaijan, by contrast, the oil fund has a strong commitment to the financing of investment in the state oil company's (SOCAR) share of the equity investment in Baku–Ceyhan. This, clearly, is not a liquid, market-based and diversified investment – rather the opposite. However, in this particular situation, when Azerbaijan needs an alternative route for its oil export and where the future economic prosperity is highly dependent on the implementation of this project, the investment may be strategically prudent. Moreover, this is not consistent with the 'Bird in Hand rule (BH),[15] which was adopted by SOFAZ. In contrast, to date Kazakhstan has been very cautious on this front and has been praised by the IMF (see IMF, 2004: 73).

---

[14] It is important to note that at present the management of the fund could envisage a longer-term investment horizon and a broader diversification. Although investments in equity instruments involve a higher risk of exposure to short-term fluctuations in market value compared to bonds, historically they have provided a better average return. Whether risk-adjusted returns are higher depends on the adjustment one makes for risk and the investor's risk-aversion. Generally only the richest countries (e.g. Kuwait) invest any more than a very small proportion of their assets in equities.

[15] For the definition of BH see IMF (2004: 50–51).

A radical question to pose in light of these differing national circumstances would be whether it was optimal to create SOFAZ in Azerbaijan. In particular, was it realistic or relevant to think of channelling resources to a savings-oriented fund, when domestic development priorities were pressing?

Without doubt, the issues to be weighed in deciding on the creation of an oil fund are quite complex. The answer will require many factors to be taken into account. The economy needs investment in order to diversify the economy, the investments could only come from hydrocarbon development and therefore savings into the oil fund could be problematic. Azeri President Aliyev has already adopted a long-term oil revenues management strategy for 2005–2025. This strategy focuses on hydrocarbon resource depletion and maintenance of macroeconomic stability with the expected growth of oil revenues.

Current efforts to diversify the Azeri economy have remained weak and structural reforms have stalled. The privatization programme is still subject to procrastination and resistance. The economy overall is highly exposed to oil price fluctuations despite the fact that the country's external balance sheet has been substantially improved and public finances are strengthening on the back of rising oil revenues.

An alternative approach to the issue in Azerbaijan would be to think in terms of transparency and governance. What better example of this than the question of how best to use the Azeri fund, given domestic development needs? The arguments may be finely balanced. The governance challenge, in assessing the policy issues, is to set out clearly the present goals of the fund, and a transparent critique of the rates of return on different strategies. This would facilitate a public debate on the appropriate use of the fund, in this situation – which differs markedly from that in many oil-rich economies.

Again, if the conclusion in Azerbaijan were to channel more resources to domestic development, then this would need to be done in a transparent way. It could be done by diverting more resources to the budget for public investment. Or it might be effected by creating a development bank capitalized by the oil fund to issue loans and credits outside the oil sector. This might assist in stimulating development of the non-oil sector of the Azerbaijani economy at a time when financial resources are short, as well as securing an economic return for the fund when the loans are repaid. However, dedicating resources to domestic investors would not smooth the economic impact of oil revenues or mitigate the impact of the Dutch Disease.

FERF received 50 per cent of hard currency gas revenues and 30 per cent of all oil and cotton revenues as a tax.[16] The value of this fund is estimated at around US$2 bln. According to Global Witness, from the 2001 contract all gas revenues from 2002 to 2006 were supposed to be paid into this account in Frankfurt.[17] Very little is known about how the deceased president managed them. One fact known for sure is that Niyazov 'invested' them into a personality cult replete with extravagant palaces and golden statues of himself.

To summarize, examining the current operations of SOFAZ, NFRK and FERF in general, one difference in philosophy is already to be found in practice:

• In both cases (SOFAZ and NFRK) it was planned that the funds would not be touched for the first five years of their existence, but an exception has been made in the Azeri case, given the need to support citizens forced from their historic places of settlement, to build housing for refugees from the Fuzilin and Agdam regions and to administer the fund.

There are, again, marked differences between the three countries in terms of investment targets. NFRK invests only abroad. In Azerbaijan, by contrast, the government is using the oil fund to finance the state oil company's (SOCAR) share of the equity investment in Baku–Ceyhan, which amounts to approximately US$170 mln. In the Azeri case the argument is often advanced that without BTC SOFAZ would simply not exist (Mann, 2003). However, using Azeri oil fund money to help displaced persons and to invest in BTC may be desirable, but it suggests that the oil fund is treated as a special government budget for exceptional spending rather than for stabilization or investing for when the oil runs out. In Turkmenistan, the use of FERF went to sponsoring the cult of the late President Niyazov.

2.5 Future challenges for oil funds[18]

The challenge ahead for the economies of Azerbaijan, Kazakhstan and Turkmenistan is clear: to ensure that the current economic progress,

[16] From 2005 and 2006 Global Witness interviews with budget experts.
[17] From this it is possible to conclude that no money from the gas trade went into the Turkmen budget.
[18] Kalyuzhnova (2006) provides a general brief overview of the major oil funds of Alberta or Norway.

initiated by the seed capital of hydrocarbon development, proves stable and sustained. The experience to date of resource-rich countries in operating oil funds demonstrates empirically that these are no panacea for the 'paradox of plenty'. Moreover, the path of oil prices over time does not encourage a view that funds can be designed to achieve an optimal smoothing of income or assurance of intertemporal equity.

To the extent that oil funds serve a useful purpose, this is at once a more modest and more ambitious goal. Modest, because a realistic goal is to achieve some degree of pragmatically based smoothing and intertemporal redistribution, with no pretence of optimality. Ambitious, because the value of oil funds can lie in reinforcing the transparency, implementation and credibility of key fiscal rules – thus addressing at source a number of the institutional weaknesses that may lie behind the poor performance of many resource-rich economies.

As Glennester and Yongseokh (2003) showed, transparency is correlated with improvements in investment and growth performance. Azerbaijan and Kazakhstan are already known as countries with a low level of transparency, and opportunities for fraud and corruption (see Transparency International's Corruption Perception Index). Without doubt both countries need to improve their disclosure of negative practices.

What is true for the economy at large is all the more true for the resources concentrated in the oil funds. Transparency in the management of oil revenues is essential to prevent a few interest groups from appropriating oil resources, by allowing a democratic debate and avoiding corruption and waste of public resources. Part of this initiative is to increase transparency with respect to revenues by those host-country governments. Resource revenue transparency has been advocated by international financial institutions, including the IMF. Transparency is expected to focus initially on that of the general government, but because of the special needs of transition economies it should be extended to relevant stakeholders (including companies investing in the sector and financial and strategic investors supporting lending).

Four dimensions of transparency deserve particular attention in this connection: a clear definition of goals and rules-based operations; the public availability of information; the adequacy of internal accounting and auditing of the funds; and arrangements for the appointment of officials and managers. Experience in Azerbaijan and Kazakhstan is considered briefly below in light of these priorities, illustrating that transparency is a significant issue for both funds. In the Turkmen case even minimal accountability and openness would be considered a major step forward.

Definition of goals

In Kazakhstan and Azerbaijan, the main objective for the management of NFRK and SOFAZ, respectively, is defined as the investment of capital in such a way that the international purchasing power of the funds is maximized, taking into account an acceptable level of risk. 'Following also IMF guidelines, the investment portfolio of the "oil funds" is best placed abroad. In sum, both domestic electorate and the international community should have confidence that the funds are well-managed, transparent, and used for the purposes set out by law' (Kalyuzhnova et al., 2004: 16).

In Turkmenistan, the choice of capital projects to be financed by the two 'oil funds'[19] may already be scrutinized because it was not subject to five-year moratorium. However, the attribution of funds to any particular capital scheme (and the cost) is conjectural in the absence of published accounts. Three major projects have been completed during the lifetime of the funds: the presidential palace and a large statue of former President Turkmenbashi (Niyazov) in the capital and a vast mosque at Gypchak, the president's birthplace; a mosque at Geok Depe to commemorate the 1881 battle there, completed in 1995, would not have been paid for by the fund.

Investment in such non-tradables is costly in foreign exchange – for three of the projects, the main contractor was the French firm Bouygues – and does not diversify the Turkmen economy towards non-energy exports. The lavish stud and horse-racing establishment near Ashgabat is an export-earner, from bloodstock sales of the famous Akalteke horses. In the absence of accounts, it is unclear if current expenditure is also involved, but the country displays a substantial share of government consumption in GDP – as shown in Chapter 1, that share is the highest of the three economies.

OGDF and FERF were under the personal control of the late President Niyazov. This leads to absence of public accountability and clear rules of functioning.

> Little has been published about either fund but it appears that FERF expenditure is substantially for public projects (discussed below), whereas OGDF is more industry-oriented, investing in the main five state-owned enterprises in the hydrocarbon sector, but also financing the reconstruction of Ashgabat airport. (IMF, 1999, pp. 28–9) (Kalyuzhnova and Kaser, 2006: 173)

---

[19] FERF ('official' oil fund) and Oil and Gas Development Fund (OGDF).

According to Freedom House data, in 2004 public sector workers were owed nearly US$290 mln in back wages. At that time the late President Niyazov had blamed his subordinates for the accumulation of wage arrears. However, an alternative explanation of the shortfalls in a state budget could be the constant diversion of substantial revenues from the hydrocarbon and cotton sector to a special presidential fund. My estimations are that by December 2006 the fund was worth at least 80 per cent of the country's GDP.

Rules-based operations

As to whether the funds are rules-based, in a mechanical sense this is broadly satisfied (see Table 2.1). However, in the case of Azerbaijan, the rules have proved susceptible of interpretation that dilutes some of the value of the fund, through deployment of resources for priority domestic needs. In Kazakhstan, much of the legislation and administrative infrastructure was borrowed from Norway's oil fund. However, more precise implementation of Norway's model based on a non-oil deficit target rule could be a way to enhance the transparency of the NFRK. Broader recommendations for Kazakhstan to increase its degree of transparency include consolidation of the treasury reports and better integration of all fiscal costs and risks associated with extra budgeting operations (including the NFRK itself).

Recently, in order to establish a long-term strategy for the use and accumulation of oil revenues, the rules governing the NFRK have been redesigned. Under the current system, fiscal payments from identified companies in the natural resources sector are subject to transfer to the NFRK. In 2004 the number of companies was reduced and the transfer of their fiscal payments is calculated on the basis of a reference oil price. However, the main criticism of the original reference price (US$19/bbl), which was established a long time before the oil boom, is that this does not reflect the true situation. The original rules for placing resources in the NFRK allowed the government to deplete the balance if prices were to fall significantly below the reference price. The practical difficulty here was that the rules were not applied rigorously, due to the fact that the definitions of oil income and oil enterprises could be interpreted differently and easily changed, depending on the intention to save less or more than the rule currently commits the government to.

Overall, even if at first sight the rules look quite straightforward, practice has demonstrated that the reality was a complex one, with many computations, etc. The Kazakhstani authorities intend to fully integrate the NFRK with the budget, and to devise a rule to guide the use of oil revenue, possibly by linking the non-oil fiscal deficit to the amount of development spending. All central government oil revenue will accrue to the NFRK, from 2007 onwards, and will flow into the fund via the budget. Some funds will then be released back to the budget to finance development spending. There is an intention to set clear limits on how much can be spent in any one year. In addition, for the three-year periods, ceilings will be determined. These changes aim to strike a balance between meeting current development needs and providing a savings cushion for future generations. The NFRK used to include 'excess' revenues not only from the oil sector but also from other sectors such as metals. As of mid-2006, all taxes collected from oil companies accrue to the fund (see Box 2.1).

Box 2.1   New rules of NFRK

From July 2006 changes took place in the NFRK's rules. The new mid-term strategy with a formalized method for the balanced budget is outlined below:

$$E = G_{NO} + G_O + D, \tag{2.1}$$

where

E = national budget expenditures

G_{NO} = non-oil sector revenue

G_O = guaranteed transfer from the fund estimated based on the average volume of expenditures for budgetary development programmes for a certain period

D = net public borrowings, for which the annual average value limit for a five-year period is set the level of 1% of GDP for the respective year.

$$GO = A + bNFRK_{t-1}\, e, \tag{2.2}$$

where

A = constant approved by law and set in tenge

b = coefficient equal to the average level of investment income for a certain period

$NFRK_{t-1}$ = assets of the NFRK as of the beginning of a financial year

e = tenge rate against the reference currency of the fund.

So, as can be seen from equation (2.2), the main concern is constant A, which is set by the parliament. Although 'by selecting various parameters for the rule' there is a hope that the selection will be driven by 'how much of the volatility in prices and quantities will be transferred to the economy via the fiscal framework' (World Bank, 2005: 35), the main concern remains: how independent and based on an economic rather than a political rationale this process could be.

Two more general considerations are also relevant:

- It is arguable that the principles of operation should be formally enshrined in legislation, to guarantee reliable functioning of the oil fund over the long term. Legitimacy and permanence would be improved by having the oil funds set up by the parliaments of the republics, rather than presidential decrees.
- Issues of implementation matter. The relevant question in each case is not just the principles agreed at the outset, but the question of how transparent the implementation is likely to be.[20]

Public availability of information

In terms of public availability of information, until now the population of both countries has been largely unaware of the existence of oil funds.[21] But the citizens of Kazakhstan and Azerbaijan should have a primary voice in their country's development since they will face the economic, environmental, human rights and social impacts of hydrocarbon development. By involving them in the process, the problem of corporate and governmental accountability could be partially solved. The citizens need to know how much income was taken from the fund, on what grounds, and how that money was spent.

The question of awareness about the existence of the oil fund in Kazakhstan comes from the 2006 Survey of Households commissioned

---

[20] In April 2003, Kazakh National Bank Chairman Marchenko endorsed President Nazarbayev's decision to divert over US$1 bln from a secret account into the NFRK, telling journalists that 'this was the right decision from the economic point of view', although it may have been flawed from a political or legal perspective (Reuters and Interfax-Kazakhstan, BBC Monitoring International Reports, 2003). The Kazakhstani officials claim that almost US$880 mln of the US$1 bln deposited five years ago in Swiss bank accounts was used to pay off pension arrears and support the national budget. Marchenko refused to reveal how much money the government still has in foreign bank accounts on the grounds that it is a state secret.

[21] Author's interviews with a number of citizen of Kazakhstan and Azerbaijan in 2002–2003.

by the Centre for Euro-Asian Studies (UK) and carried out by the Agency of the Republic of Kazakhstan on Statistics (ARKS). It is based on 640 households across all the regions and is designed to be nationally representative.[22]

The survey also included questions relating to individual well-being (as discussed in Chapter 1).[23] The questions related to life satisfaction as well as the impact that the reforms have had on individual perceptions of their well-being, which allows us to draw a clear picture and links individual well-being to the existence of oil funds.

From the question *'Do you know about the existence of the National Fund of Republic of Kazakhstan?'* we learnt that 45 per cent of the Kazakhstani population do not have any idea about NFRK. Through the regional analysis we found out that the majority of lack of awareness is concentrated in the regions of Mangistau (11 per cent), Karaganda (9.7 per cent), North Kazakhstan (9.4 per cent) and Kostanai (7.6 per cent). An unexpectedly high percentage of lack of awareness was recorded in the two capitals (Astana city, 6.3 per cent, Almaty city, 6.9 per cent). In contrast, Southern Kazakhstan has the highest awareness among all regions, where only 1 per cent of the population do not know about the NFRK.

In analysing the educational level of the population (Figure 2.2) that is not aware of the existence of the NFRK, we found that the largest

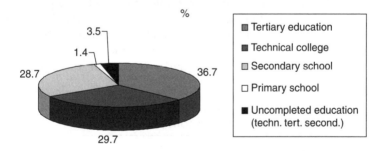

Figure 2.2 Percentage of Kazakhstani population, by educational level, who are not aware of the existence of the NFRK
Source: Calculated from the CEAS Survey's data.

---

[22] For the methodology of the survey, see Chapter 1.

[23] It includes information on income, expenditures, the nature and quality of housing, and other household characteristics such as number and age of household members, labour force status, educational attainment, health status, etc. across all the regions of Kazakhstan.

percentage (36.7 per cent) of people with tertiary education are not aware, which disproves the common belief that level of education is correlated with engagement in public life.

However, from the analysis by respondents' professions we discovered that those most knowledgeable about the existence of the NFRK are economists (15.6 per cent), teachers (14.3 per cent), oil and gas engineers (10.7 per cent), and accountants (8.4 per cent).

The respondents who were aware of the existence of the NFRK were asked *'To what extent does the National Fund of the Republic of Kazakhstan influence your standard of living?'* The results of the summary statistics are presented in Table 2.2. Overall a very small percentage of people think that the NFRK has a significant impact on their well-being (13.8 per cent).

In a broader context of assessing the oil wealth of the country, the respondents were asked how from their point of view the oil money should be spent.[24] From the six possible answers (health care, economy, oil and gas, agriculture, welfare and population), of which they could choose more than one, the most popular answers were 'health care' (17.4 per cent), 'welfare' and 'economy' (16.4 per cent and 16.2 per cent respectively) as well as 'population' (15.5 per cent). This proved that the population thinks about the present and perceives oil wealth as a blessing of today rather than of tomorrow. For example, the answer 'oil and gas sector' received the support of only 0.5 per cent of the population.

In the Akmola region, respondents wanted to put oil money into the economy (37.5 per cent of the total of respondents' answers). The populations of Almaty city (40 per cent of the total of respondents' answers) as well as Eastern Kazakhstan (30 per cent of the total respondents' answers) have similar views. With regard to health care, the population

Table 2.2 Summary statistics of the perceptions of the NFRK influence on the population's standards of living

Answer	%
High	13.8
None	37.8
Don't know	48.4
Total	100

[24] The actual question in the survey was: *'What do you think oil money should be distributed for?'*

of Almatinskaya, Kostanai and Kyzyl-Orda regions (all around 30 per cent of the total of respondents' answers for the region) strongly supported this option. The respondents from the Mangistau region in particular wanted to distribute oil money among the population (57.5 per cent of the total of respondents' answers). The respondents from the agricultural regions of Kyzyl–Orda and Southern Kazakhstan strongly supported the investment of oil money into agriculture, with 25 per cent and 44.1 per cent of respondents, respectively, favouring this.

Accounting and auditing

In terms of adaptation of best practice in accounting and auditing, both funds report quarterly in the press on the total amounts of assets, inflows received, expenditures, and interest earned by the funds. The funds have their own websites. This obvious transparency in both cases is the main argument used by the executive directors of the funds in debates on the subject.

Since their existence, external audits of both funds have been conducted (by Ernst & Young); the last one is under way. Although the NFRK has a website, it gives information only on the total national fund assets, broken down by portfolio. Commentators have criticized this point and claim that it demonstrates a greater lack of transparency compared to Azerbaijan.

An annual audit of the funds is *prima facie* evidence of transparency, but it is only the tip of the iceberg as regards high standards of governance. It is encouraging that in both Kazakhstan and Azerbaijan increasing emphasis is being laid at present on the transparency and efficiency of investment processes in the funds. This should ensure compliance with the rules under which the funds were set up and diversification of investment projects within the areas of the funds' operations.

Appointment of officials and managers

An analysis of the Azeri and Kazakhstani oil funds highlights some structural weaknesses. In both cases the funds have been characterized as representative and participatory. The rule is that the president approves all the members of the board and all of them are government officials. On 15 May 2006, by the Decree of the President of the Republic of Azerbaijan, Shahmar Movsumov was appointed executive director of SOFAZ. This strong control by the executive branch has enabled uses of the fund that are contrary to its purposes. The official explanation for this is that the society is relatively immature, and by allowing other people (for example the parliament) to decide the strategy for using oil funds, control over the oil wealth will be lost. If transparency of the oil funds of the two countries is to be established in a credible manner, the structure of the fund management needs to become more representative and less dominated by government. Only through such a structure can the high level of political influence be overcome. In Azerbaijan, at the time of writing, SOFAZ is in the process of selecting foreign managers for the placement of its assets in foreign banks.

By 2003 Kazakhstan had saved 63 per cent of its oil windfall in the NFRK, which by all standards demonstrates a remarkably prudent fiscal stance and gives rise to cautious optimism for the future.

Very little is known about FERF and OGDF since the death of President Niyazov in December 2006, however, none of the international financial institutions relaxed their concerns over these funds. The EBRD refused to fund private investments in the production and export of oil and gas that is connected to the FERF (see EBRD, 2006).

Further steps

The establishment of the oil funds is itself a major change in fiscal practice, but as both of the funds were required to accumulate funds for five years without spending them (except for emergency spending on refugees and financing the BTC pipeline in Azerbaijan), the degree to which the stabilization function (as distinct from accumulation) is effective has yet to be demonstrated. Indeed, the present market context of high oil prices is providing some test of whether the existence of the funds will result in greater fiscal restraint.

A long period is needed to determine the real impact of the funds. But the emphasis in this chapter, in the meantime, is on the core importance in these countries of continuing to enhance governance and transparency of the oil funds in order to maximize chances of success. Inevitably this limits government discretion in disposing of the mineral wealth of the nation. It is, however, essential to build public support for the funds, and to leverage their economic impact through a strong influence on market expectations.

By establishing periodic auditing and analysis of management performance, it is possible to ensure the sustainability and efficiency of the management revenue. The fund's assets should be placed abroad (to provide protection from the populist ideas of helping the local economy by taking investments from the fund) and greater diversification of the assets portfolio is required (as was demonstrated in case of the NFRK). To date it is difficult to confirm whether SOFAZ, SFDOG and

NFRK have gained public support. The public is hardly aware that such funds exist.

In its recommendations the EBRD stressed

> transformation of the FERF into a transparent fund, with some proportion of it saved for future generations. Critical to the operation of such a fund (similar funds exist in Azerbaijan and Kazakhstan) would be proper accounting of all financial flows, as well as the requirement to disclose operations publicly. Discretionary spending from the FERF outside an annual unified budget would need to be restricted. (EBRD, 2006: 26)

The governments of Kazakhstan and Azerbaijan discussed the need to have a long-term vision and determination in pursuing their policies of management of the oil revenues, which should contribute to sustainable development. Among these goals, greater confidence in the transparent management of oil funds, and greater public understanding of their objectives and operations, are essential in order to safeguard their sustainability and efficiency. In these respects, there is a long way to go for SOFAZ, SFDOG and NFRK.

Part II

The Impact of the Operating Companies

3
Major Oil and Gas Projects

3.1 Historical context

The first period of development of the Caspian region oil industry by foreign companies took place in the early years of the twentieth century, when Azerbaijan was the world's largest oil producer (McKay, 1984). Around 320 companies were involved in the Russian oil industry before World War I.[25] That war, however, shook the relatively well-developed Russian oil industry to its foundations. By the end of the tsarist era, Baku had become a point of international conflict, with the oil industry at its epicentre.

The next phase in the region's history was marked by the decision of the Council of People's Commissars to nationalize the entire Russian hydrocarbon industry, with complete expropriation of property from the former owners. The main feature of the Soviet period was thus the absence of individual ownership in oil fields, plants and transportation systems.

The state-owned Soviet oil industry that was thus created in the Caspian region consisted of eight major groups: Azneft, Grozneft, Krasnodarneft, Kuybyshevneft, Molotovneft, Bashneft, Kazakhstanneft and Sredasneft. The state was concerned to become independent from the West in drilling and production techniques. It was thus a major priority of the Soviet government to increase the capacity of the hydrocarbon sector and the volumes of production, as it sought to recover from the effects on the industry of Word War I (Nazaroff, 1941).

World War II gave a boost to the oil industries of the Caspian Sea republics as a result of the high demand for fuel for military purposes.

---

[25] Three very important groups should be mentioned here: the Nobel group, the Russian General Oil Corporation and the Royal Dutch Shell group.

In fact, World War II was a time of industrialization for some republics. In Kazakhstan, for example, new branches such as ferrous metals, machine-building and the oil industry were created. These changes were due not only to the impact of the war, but also to the fact that the USSR's government was seeking to pursue a complex development strategy for the Soviet Union as a whole (the USSR's labour specialization regions), with less regard to the balanced development of individual republican economies (Kalyuzhnova et al., 2004).

During the 1950s and 1960s, the focus of the Soviet hydrocarbon sector began to shift away from the Caspian Sea region, following oil and gas discoveries first in the Volga–Urals Basin and then in Western Siberia (Lydolph and Shabad, 1960). One of the specific features of that period was the opening up of a substantial gap between productive capacity and consumption levels of refined products in the Caspian region. In 1971–1975 Soviet Caspian Sea republics were explicitly faced with this problem. By the end of 1975, the local refining sector could satisfy less than 25 per cent of demand in these areas. In response to the directive to locate refining capacity close to consumption centres, processing capacity in Ukraine, Belorussia, Turkmenistan and Kazakhstan was increased, which became a problem later during the transition period.

During this period, the USSR established itself as a leading producer, consumer and exporter of oil and gas. At the end of the 1980s, according to the Centre for Global Energy Studies,[26] it accounted for nearly 20 per cent of the world's output of liquid fuels and 15 per cent of the world's oil consumption. At the same time its net exports of oil were 14.5 per cent of the volume traded worldwide.

Nonetheless, the growing economic difficulties of the Soviet economy started clearly to emerge, and to affect the hydrocarbon sector, around this time. This could be seen in the decline in oil production at the end of 1980s; the inability to raise investment resources for the development of new oil and gas fields with high unit costs; and, as a consequence, a continuing decline in the rate of exploratory drilling. The technical characteristics of the Soviet oil industry also indicated some key problems, namely: an increase in the number of inactive wells; a drop in the number of meters drilled; ageing equipment;[27] constant failures of supply chains to fulfil contractual obligations (due to the chronic

---

[26] CGES, *Oil in Fifteen Volumes*, Vol. 10, *The Former Soviet Union*. London: CGES, 2006.

[27] At the end of 1990, only 4 per cent of the machinery and equipment used in the industry met world standards requirements. (CGES, 2006: 18).

shortage of materials, spare parts, etc.); and rising production costs due to a general move to mechanized means of oil extraction as the number of free-flowing wells fell.

The refining sector was also suffering. With the costs of primary production constantly rising in the 1980s, the possibilities to invest in upgrading refineries were quite slim (Kalyuzhnov et al., 2001: 133–68). Another serious problem which the Soviet oil and gas industry was facing concerned transportation routes. This problem was to become a very hot topic for discussions in the transition period, providing a major source of concern for foreign oil and gas investors (see Lee, 1996; Soligo and Jaffe, 2001).

Immediately after the dissolution of the Soviet Union, Western oil firms started to look seriously at Caspian oil reserves as an alternative to Middle Eastern crude oil (Effimoff, 2000). The first challenges were associated with the decline of the local economies, the rapid rise of corruption, and the difficult investment climate in the region. Every Caspian state had its own problems, as well as unequal and uncertain shares of regional oil and gas reserves. In the 1990s there was no official source of information on the proven/probable reserves in the Caspian Basin (and in particular no breakdown in terms of the respective Caspian states).

According to data by Lev Churilov, the Soviet minister of oil and gas, the USSR's oil reserves were estimated at 172.26 bln bbl, with the Caspian republics accounting for 20.52 bln bbl (12 per cent) and Russia for 148.07 bln bbl (86 per cent).[28] Other estimates suggested that the Caspian reserves might be in excess of 40 bln bbl of oil.[29] 'The remaining liquids potential of the six major basins in the region could be more than 160 bln bbl. In addition to crude oil, it is estimated that there is undiscovered potential for over 200 bbl of oil equivalent of natural gas.' (Hamilton, 1995: 113). However, Terry Adams has confirmed that this exaggerated level of reserves was being used for political purposes in Washington DC to obtain congressional support for Clinton's foreign policy initiatives in the Caspian and Caucasus (interview with Terry Adams, founding president, AIOC, 25 August 2007, Reading).

The new and impressive estimates that were emerging with regard to Caspian reserves did not go unquestioned. Some authors were convinced that

> the Caspian Basin does not pose a major challenge to the supremacy of the Arab Arab Gulf as a pivotal supplier of oil to world markets, ... with

[0] Neftyanoe Khozyiastvo, No. 9, 1991. Moscow.
[0] 1 tonne of oil is approximately 7.33 bbl.

a long-term production that would contribute roughly 3 per cent to future global oil supply, the Caspian will never be a strategic alternative to the Arab Gulf and that it is destined to play a supporting role rather than a deciding one in supplying the world oil markets in the future. (Salameh, 2002: 33)

Nevertheless, time showed that the Caspian reserves were larger than previously assumed (see Table 3.1).

Meanwhile, the level of depletion in the Middle East (the main global producer with the lowest costs of production) had increased, and its oil production capacity has stagnated for 20 years. The Middle East felt the threat of competition and was even prepared (e.g. Saudi Arabia and Kuwait) to start negotiations to open their oil and gas sectors to foreign investors in order to remove those investors who might otherwise look to the Caspian region. By the 1990s it was clear that Caspian energy assets might be able to reduce consumers' dependence on Middle Eastern oil. The decision of Middle Eastern producers not to allow international oil companies to exploit their resources, and the potential availability of promising reserves in the Caspian region, influenced the international oil companies in favour of major investments to the Caspian.

By 2005, moreover, the difference between the cost of oil production and the sales price had reached a huge figure and allowed to the oil producers to enjoy extraordinary profits, and this still in a period before markets saw the tight supply situation of 2006, the warnings of a possible terrorist attack in Saudi Arabia, or worries over Iran's resumption of its nuclear programme push oil prices to levels – breaching US$75/bbl – at which comparative production costs would become irrelevant (Table 3.2). This means that the country could make its profit elsewhere.

Table 3.1   Proven oil and gas reserves in the Caspian Sea region

Country	Oil reserves, bbl	Gas reserves, tcf
Azerbaijan	7	48.36
Kazakhstan	39.6	105.9
Russia*	0.2 (total 74.4)	5.65 (total 1688)
Turkmenistan	0.5	102.37
Uzbekistan	0.6	16.24

Note: *The first figures show the Russian share in the Caspian; figures in parentheses give total Russian oil and gas reserves.
Sources: BP, *Quantifying energy* (2006); BP *Statistical Review of World Energy* (2007). Data for Russia are estimates of Lukoil for the Northern Caspian.

Table 3.2 Costs of production by different produces

Producer region	Crude oil operational costs, US$/bbl
Saudi Arabia	3
Caspian Sea region	10–14
North Sea	10–12

Source: Author's calculations.

There is no doubt, in this connection, that in conditions of spiralling competition, the concern to control resources can bring companies to new areas and make them ready to compromise in their relations with countries. Indeed, history demonstrates that there are cases where, in order to meet commercial objectives, companies and oil-rich governments breach their previous 'red lines' and back up dictatorial governments, civil violence, etc. (Yergin, 1992; Sampson, 1975)

As companies braced themselves for the development of the Caspian region, they faced a varied and potentially costly endeavour. The hydrocarbon resources known in 1990s (Kazakhstan, 15.66 bln bbl; Azerbaijan, 3.44 bln bbl and Turkmenistan, 1.54 bln bbl) were uneven and noncomparable. Exploiting them would require different types and scales of projects, and different types of operating companies.

Indeed, the last ten years have brought to the Caspian region its own pattern of development and specifics, as international oil companies began to announced large-scale projects.

> Between 1994 and 1998, 26 companies from 13 countries signed Production Sharing Contracts (PSCs) in Azerbaijan. Kazakhstan could tell a similar story, but the structure of its oil industry is very different. (Nanay, 2000: 112)

In Kazakhstan this era would be characterized as a predominant era of oil majors (Chevron, Texaco, Eni, Exxon, Mobil, Shell, BP, BG). In Azerbaijan the situation is similar with a single major player – BP. In Turkmenistan the initial involvement of Mobil and Monument has evolved in favour of other oil companies (Burren Energy, Dragon Oil and Petronas). Country resources, companies and projects display a wide variety across the region.

In May 2007, at the summit in Turkmenbashi (Turkmenistan), President Nazarbayev again demonstrated his principle of 'divide and conquer', when instead of looking West, he sealed a deal with the Russian and the Turkmen presidents for a new pipeline to be built along the coast of the Caspian Sea to transmit additional Kazakh and Turkmen natural gas exports north into Russia. Such a step would clearly disappoint and frustrate US Vice President Dick Cheney's efforts to 'convert' Kazakhstan to US economic and political interests. However, some experts take the view that this agreement actually ensures that the gas will be delivered to the West, rather than to China, albeit through Russia, rather than across the Caspian Sea and the Caucasus (interview with Julian Lee, 21 August 2007, London).

3.2   National experience

To understand better the strategic issues facing states and companies, it is helpful at this point to discuss some key features of the three main countries – Kazakhstan, Ajerbaijan and Turkmenistan – and the way that the hydrocarbon sector has developed in them. Individual companies are part of this story, but the perspective in this chapter will be national. In Chapter 4, we shall present a detailed analysis of the records of international energy companies in the Caspian region, explaining the strong and weak sides of their performance; and in Chapter 5 we shall have the opportunity to complete this picture by looking at the challenges of different exploitation and operating strategies from the perspective of both governments and companies.

It is Kazakhstan that in many ways dominates the energy development experience of the region. However, the picture would not be complete without including the oil and gas projects in other countries of the region,[30] where the hydrocarbon industry is having a significant impact on economic development. An overview of major oil developments is presented in Table 3.3. With rising world oil prices, the Caspian oil sector is expected to increase exports to around 3 mln bbl/day by 2008. The Caspian Pipeline Consortium (CPC), which links Kazakhstan's oil fields to the Russian ports on the Black Sea (see Map 3.1), intends to add 0.5 mln bbl/day by 2006–2008, although at this stage of the development this figure looks very unlikely given Russia's opposition to expansion.

Neither Russia nor Iran is considered here. Russia is an important player in the Caspian Sea region, but mainly as a transit state, although it may become a significant regional oil producer in the future from discoveries in its sector of the Caspian Sea. Iran, of course, may turn out to be a significant Caspian producer in the future (see Box 1.1). There are

---

[30] For instance, Lukoil recently discovered a field of 5 bln bbl of proven reserves in the Russian part of the Caspian shelf.

Table 3.3   Major oil development projects by companies' involvement

Project	Oil reserves, bbl	Company (license-holders)	Country
Tengiz	6–9 bln recoverable	Tengizchevroil (TCO) 100%: Chevron 50%, ExxonMobil 25%, KazMunaiGaz 20%, LukArco 5%	Kazakhstan
Kashagan	7–9 mln recoverable	Agip Kazakhstan North Caspian Operating Co. (Agip KCO) 100%: Eni 18.52%, Shell 18.52%, ExxonMobil 18.52%, Total 18.52%, ConocoPhillips 9.26%, KazMunaiGaz 8.33%, Inpex 8.33%*	Kazakhstan
Kurmangazy	Estimated 7.33 bln	KazMunaiGaz 25%, Total 25%, Rosneft 50%	Kazakhstan
Karachaganak	Estimated 2 bln recoverbale	BG (32.5%), Agip (32.5%) ChevronTexaco (20%), Lukoil (15%)	Kazakhstan
Azeri–Chirag–Guneshli (ACG)	5.4 bln	Azerbaijan International Operating Co. (AIOC) 100%: BP 34.1%, Chevron 10.27%, SOCAR 10%, Inpex 10%, Statoil 8.56%, ExxonMobil 8%, TRAO	Azerbaijan
Araz–Alov–Sharg	6.6 bln	BP 15%, ExxonMobil 15%, Statoil 15%, EnCana 5%, TRAO 10%, SOCAR 40%	Azerbaijan
Khvalynskoye	264 mln crude, 125 mln condensate	Caspian Oil & Gas Co. 100%: Lukoil 50%, KazMunaiGaz 50%	Russia
Tsentralnoye	521 mln of oil equivalent	KazMunaiGaz 50%, TsentrKaspNeftegaz 50%: Lukoil 50%, Gazprom 50%	Russia
Cheleken (Livanov, Lam, Zhdanov)	645 mln	Dragon Oil 50% Turkmenneft 50%	Turkmenistan

Source: *Oil and Gas Journal*, 13 June 2005: 36. CGES.
* All figures correct prior January 2008.

indeed suggestions that Iran has sizeable hydrocarbon reserves in the Caspian Sea, although the development of these reserves remains to be seen (Townsend and Rushworth, 2001). The government has not done any significant exploration of the Caspian Sea, and does not

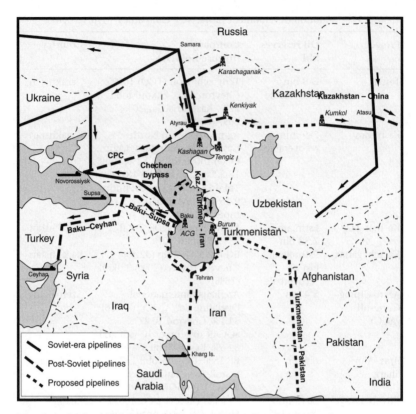

Map 3.1   Major oil fields and pipelines in the Caspian Sea region
Source: Courtesy of Julian Lee, CGES.

have any proven reserves there. Until agreement on the territoriality of the waters of the southern part of the Caspian Sea is achieved[31], this will remain a theoretical, rather than practical, topic. So the region has not played a significant role in Iran's economic development.

Kazakhstan

The key Kazakhstani projects are significant not only for the country but for the Caspian region as a whole. The first major involvement of a foreign company in the region was Chevron in the Kazakh Socialist Republic, through the development of the Tengiz oil field. This is the main

---

[31] Ownership of the south Caspian fields is a continuing source of dispute between Azerbaijan and Iran.

Box 3.1 Oily Rocks

Neft Dashlari (Neftanye Kamni) or Oily Rocks are located between Absheron and Turkmenbashi (Turkmenistan). This is a range of underwater mountains and in a few places they rise high enough to create small islets which are 28 miles offshore. Since 1949 the field was commercially developed to extract oil. I had the privilege of visiting Neft Dashlari by special invitation from SOCAR by helicopter from Artyom Island (26 April 2007). Neft Dashlari is a unique offshore development, built entirely on stilts, and is right in the middle of the Caspian Sea. This 'town' is very real. It has its own infrastructure, including a power station (with a capacity of 48 MW), which is of paramount importance, and also proper roads with signs. It has traces of the past glory of the Soviet era in the form of nine-storey apartment blocks (at the time of its establishment they were proudly featured on a 1971, 4-kopeyek Soviet stamp); a monument of the 'Xmas tree' where the first oil was pumped out; murals of cosmonauts; and the legacy of environmental negligence. Around the town in the sea are many old metal constructions: these are no longer in use for producing oil, but – as I was told by the management of Neft Dashlari – they are 'too expensive to dispose of'.

What was difficult to impress on the management is a sense of responsibility for the environment in Western understanding. Throughout the interview it became clear that health and safety issues are unknown concepts here: 'We have a health centre and all our workers are healthy'. The concept of environmental management is not very well understood or developed. For example, in May 1999 a tragic accident killed one and injured two people. The workers were performing repair work on an oil platform when they fell into the Caspian Sea because of faulty and outdated equipment.

Overall, the facility is poorly maintained at the time of writing, and there are around 2000 men working on 14-day shifts. In recent years SOCAR has invested some money into refurbishment of accommodation and into the health centre. However, not very much is being invested in equipment and production. 'We know that only 124.61 mln bbl of oil has been left here, so why invest?' (from the interview with the management of the Neft Dashlari,

26 April 2007). As a result, 600 wells are inoperative or inaccessible. Nevertheless, the site, despite its imperfections and dilapidation, still produces significant crude oil output of Azeri oil, giving a crucial contribution to the state budget. According to SOCAR, Neft Dashlari produced 6 597 000 and 6 025 260 bbl of oil in 2006 and 2005 respectively, with a daily output of roughly 14 800 bbl. Gas production is also important, with production for 2006 and 2005 reaching 1.87 bcf (billion cubic feet). In Soviet times, when Azerbaijan was the main oil producer in the USSR, the oil production figure is estimated to have been 180 000 bbl/day.

Caspian project, with estimated recoverable reserves of 7–9 bln bbl, one of the largest fields in the world. Original negotiations started in the late 1980s, when the Soviet Union was so desperate for hard currency that it was willing to enter into arrangements to allow international companies to extract its resources on almost any terms and conditions. At the outset, therefore, Chevron was negotiating an oil and gas consortium joint venture[32] at Tengiz with Moscow directly.

However, after the first visit to Atyrau, the management of the region (*oblast*) expressed its disappointment that the leaders of the Kazakh Socialist Republic were not involved in negotiations. This tactical mistake was quickly corrected by the plan to create a joint venture – a route very fashionable that time in other spheres of the economic life (Dunn, 1987).

The joint venture was finally formed in 1993. At the time of writing, the project is being managed by Tengizchevroil (TCO), a Chevron-led consortium. The major partners in Tengizchevroil are ChevronTexaco (with 50 per cent ownership), ExxonMobil (25 per cent), the national oil company KazMunaiGaz (20 per cent) and LukArco (5 per cent). In 2006, after a US$3 bln project expansion, the TCO consortium produced 450 000 bbl (72 000 m^3) per day, or one-third of Kazakhstan's daily production. According to ChevronTexaco, Tengiz could potentially produce 700 000 bbl (111 000 m^3) per day by the end of 2010. Oil from the Tengiz field is primarily routed to an export terminal close to the port of Novorosiysk through he Caspian Pipeline Consortium (CPC) pipeline, which

---

[32] However, the unfair conditions of this venture were highlighted in a confidential memo by Y. Gaidar to M. Gorbachev in 1990 and other options including PSAs options were described there, (interview with source C).

remains a major concern for TCO due to the fact that negotiations for the CPC are proving difficult. This was reflected in the rating (by FitchRatings) of the TCO as BBB– despite its very strong current financial performance.

The sour gas injection/second generation project (SGI/SGP) is on its way, although the project was not contracted on a fixed price turnkey basis, and further cost deviations are still possible (FitchRatings, 2006). Originally the deadline was April 2007. However, increased output from sour gas injection is now expected in 4Q 2007, with the second generation project anticipated six months after that (2Q 2008). The delay is attributed to a labour dispute in 2005. In addition, the delay may have something to do with the slow pace of contractual negotiations with Azerbaijan over cross-Caspian deliveries for onward shipment through BTC (interview with Julian Lee, senior energy analyst, CGES, 11 May 2007).

The possibility of expanding of TCO production, after the SGI project comes to completion, might be explored further. At the time of writing, this potential project is named the 'Future Growth Project'. It will be based on the outcome of the SGI project as well as the results of the negotiations over transport routes.

Another major project, although it may not be technically classified as 'Caspian', is the Karachaganak project, based on the Karachaganak gas-condensate field in the northwest region of Kazakhstan. This is one of the world's largest oil and gas condensate fields. It covers an area of over 69 190 acres and holds more than 8.79 bln bbl of oil and condensate and over 47.65 tcf of gas. The field was discovered in 1979, and production started in 1984. In 1992 the Kazakhstani government began negotiating a PSA with Eni and the BG Group, and a 40-year final PSA was signed in November 1997.[33] In 1999 construction work began by a consortium of four international partners – British company BG Group (which leads the consortium) and Eni of Italy, each with a 32.5 per cent interest, Chevron of the USA with 20 per cent, and Lukoil of Russia with 15 per cent. Currently with net investments over US$2.1 bln, the Karachaganak field produces over 0.25 mln bbl of liquids, with the capacity to inject over 700 mmscfd (million standard cubic feet per day) and sell over 700 mmscfd of gas.

At the time of writing, phases I and II of development of the Karachaganak field are completed, which has doubled annual production. Karachaganak's next major development involves the construction of additional facilities for liquids stabilization and is expected on-stream

---

[33] ChevronTexaco and Lukoil join the international consortium.

by 2009. By 2008, Karachaganak Petroleum Operating (KPO) aim to sanction a new gas development phase (commonly known as the Gas Project or Phase III). This is a massive, multi-billion-dollar project, involving some 120 new wells and increased gas injection. It will very significantly boost gas sales and liquids production.

In 2038, when the field is returned to the people of Kazakhstan, it will be capable of producing for at least another 50 years. Currently Karachaganak has two major export routes: the Atyrau – Samara Pipeline (2 mtpa) and the CPC pipeline 7 mtpa. New pipeline infrastructure will be important, and strategic options to east and west are currently under consideration. The challenges and opportunities that the project is facing at the moment are: access to multiple markets (particularly with resistance to the expansion of the CPC pipeline from the Russian Federation); stability of the operating environment; defining policy frameworks; and partnerships with developers.

Tengiz and Karachaganak were both based on Soviet-era discoveries. The Kashagan field is the first major offshore discovery (11.3 bln bbl of proven reserves) since Kazakhstan's indepenedence.[34] It is located in the northern part of the Caspian Sea close to Atyrau. The North Caspian Sea PSA consists of seven companies: ENI (18.52 per cent), Shell (18.52 per cent), Total (18.52 per cent), ExxonMobil (18.52 per cent), Conoco-Phillips (9.26 per cent), KazMunaiGaz (8.33 per cent) and Inpex (8.33 per cent).[35] Eni is the operator, on behalf of the North Caspian Sea PSA.

Technically, environmentally, politically and economically Kashagan is a highly complicated project, due to its location, geological features, size and importance for Kazakhstan and global oil supply. Indeed, every kind of delay has been experienced from the beginning of development.

The initial plan to start production in 2005 was derailed, and a new timetable was adopted which highlighted 2008 as a starting year of production, with an initial output rate of 75 000 bbl/day. However, even this date is likely to be missed and the first oil from the 11.3 bln bbl Kashagan project in the Kazakh sector of the Caspian is now expected to flow in 2010–11, due to the technical complexity of the project. Observers expect Kazakhstan to fine the partners for any further delay. They paid a fine of around US$150 mln in 2004 for delaying start-up from 2005 to 2008 (*Argus FSU*, 27 February 2004). In addition to this

---

[34] The Kashagan field was first discovered in 2000 while drilling an exploration well.

[35] Originally the group included BG Group (16.67 per cent) instead of KazMunai-Gaz; however, BG Group sold their stake in the field to the partners in 2004.

delay, the Kazakhstani government proposed a Kashagan PSA change (*Argus, FSU,* 23 June 2006). According to these changes the stake of KazMunaiGaz will be transferred to a new subsidiary – KMG Kashagan.[36]

Kazakhstan has entered into a number of other projects with foreign oil companies, including projects to develop the Kumkol group of fields in the South Turgay Basin and the Karazhanbas field in Mangistau region, among others.

Azerbaijan

Azerbaijan could be considered an example of exaggerating Caspian reserves. The link between Azerbaijan and oil had already been made in the nineteenth century, when Azerbaijan was a front-runner in the world oil and gas industry. The recent discovery rate has been disappointing, and the country has failed to resurrect the 'past glory' of the early twentieth century. A process of steady depletion has been evident in Azerbaijan since the 1940s (see Box 3.1).[37] However, it had been predicted by SOCAR technocrats before the collapse of the Soviet Union.

Despite this, the offshore prospects near Baku raised much interest and high expectations when the country reopened to foreign investors in the 1990s. These prospects (wrongly referred to as 'fields') potentially offered clear advantages in terms of production cost (less than US$2/bbl) and quality of oil in relation to the whole Caspian region.

As in the case of Kazakhstan, negotiations between Azerbaijan and international oil companies date back to the Soviet period. As discussed in Chapter 1, at the beginning of the 1990s the Caspian republics still lacked the financial and technical resources to develop their mineral wealth. Azerbaijan was no exception, and this is why in 1991 the Azeri government announced a tender for their hydrocarbon projects. BP, in alliance with Statoil, Amoco, Unocal and other oil majors participated (Bagirov, 1996). At that time, the PSA was the only form of contract suitable for the young Caspian states. 'It was the way the state was able to retain the ownership of the resource. Azerbaijan and the other Caspian states were able to achieve their oil and gas development goals in a way that they could sell politically and publicly' (interview with David Woodward, former president, BP Azerbaijan, 22 March 2007).

The outcome was the signing, in September 1994, of a contract between a BP-led consortium and SOCAR. This 30-year production sharing deal was called the 'Contract of the Century', with expected

---

[36] For the full story on Kashagan, see Chapter 7.
[37] Last peak of Azeri oil.

production of 700 000 bbl/day. British Prime Minister John Major, in his letter to the president of Azerbaijan, remarked 'The signature of the agreement between Azerbaijan and consortium of western oil companies, headed by BP, marks the start of a new phase in relations between our two countries' (Major, 18 September 1994, quoted in Major, 1997). Production is now expected to exceed 1 mln bbl/day.

The contract covered the development of the Azeri, Chirag and deep-water portion of the Guneshli offshore oil fields with estimated reserves of 5.4 bln bbl (see Table 3.3). Participating companies include: BP, 34.1 per cent; Chevron, 10.27 per cent; SOCAR, 10 per cent; Inpex, 10 per cent; Statoil, 8.56 per cent; ExxonMobil, 8 per cent; TPAO, 6.8 per cent; Devon Energy, 5.6 per cent; Itochu, 3.92 per cent; Delta/Hess, 2.75 per cent; together forming the Azerbaijan International Operating Company (AIOC). As Nanay remarked in the late 1990s, AIOC 'has the only project in Azerbaijan with proven reserves' (Nanay, 2000: 122). However, 2005 was a turning point for the project with the BTC pipeline started to operate over the course of the year and in 2006 AIOC's production reached 470 000 bbl/day.

Taking account of the risks involved, as well as its potential future impact, this agreement appears significant for Azerbaijan in both political and economic terms. This is so even though some experts consider the contract less beneficial to Azerbaijan than the previous version (before June 1993) in certain respects (Bagirov, 1996). The government had high hopes of Azerbaijan's oil potential in rebuilding the shattered

Table 3.4 Shares by companies, PSA for development of Azeri, Chirag and Guneshli oil fields

Company	%
BP Exploration (Caspian Sea) Ltd	17.1267
Amoco Caspian Sea Petroleum Ltd	17.01
State Oil Company of the Azerbaijani Republic (SOCAR)	10.0
Lukoil Joint Stock Company	10.0
Pennzoil Caspian Corporation	4.8175
Unocal Khazar Ltd	9.52
Den Norske Stats Oljeselskap as (Statoil)	8.5633
Turkiye Petrolleri AO (TPAO)	6.75
Exxon	5.0
Itochu	7.45
Ramco Hazar Energy Ltd	2.0825
Delta Nimir Khazar Ltd	1.68

Note: Amoco was taken over by BP. Pennzoil and Ramco sold their stakes.
Source: Bagirov (1996).

economy. In 1995 Terry Adams, the first president of AIOC, made predictions of total foreign involvement from 750 000 bbl/day to 1 mln bbl/day coming on stream in ten years, with a peak of 1.2 mln bbl/day by 2010 (*Argus FSU*, 24 April 1995).

In order to sustain an increase in oil production, other projects are required to prove their viability alongside the successful AIOC project, but prospects to date are not very good. Some projects proved to be drilling failures (those in the Lenkoran–Talysh, Oguz, Apsheron and Ateshgah blocks) and were abandoned. In addition, there are some potential projects located in waters disputed by Azerbaijan, Iran and Turkmenistan (e.g. Araz–Alov–Sharg). If the ownership of these fields were legally identified, the size of the investment into these projects could be significant, but so far no evident progress has been made.[38] However, as David Woodward highlighted, 'BP is still reasonably optimistic about Inam' (interview, 22 March 2007).

In terms of gas development (see Map 3.2), a major deal for Azerbaijan, the Shahk Deniz PSA, was signed in 1996. The contract parties to its development include BP (25.5 per cent) – PSA operator; Statoil (25.5 per cent); Lukoil (10 per cent); Elf (10 per cent); National Oil Company of Iran (10 per cent); Turkish Petroleum (10 per cent) and SOCAR (10 per cent). The Shakh Deniz gas field discovery in 1999 (approximately 62 miles south of Baku in water depths ranging from 164 to 1640 feet) was the largest discovery for BP since the Prudhoe Bay oil field in the early 1970s. The reserves are estimated at 1.8–3.6 bln bbl (250–500 mln tonnes) of oil and 2–4 tcf of gas.

Turkmenistan

In the Soviet era, the Turkmen Socialist Republic had been a medium-sized gas producer (second after the Russian Federation), although estimated oil reserves appeared to be smaller than in Kazakhstan and Azerbaijan. Therefore it was logical to expect an independent Turkmenistan becoming a serious gas supplier for Europe.

However, the Turkmen gas industry went into a deep recession once the provision of know-how from other parts of the FSU had stopped, equipment was ageing without replacement and the infrastructure of

---

[38] The Azeri government has recommended that SOCAR develop Caspian fields that have been dropped by international oil firms. The intention is that SOCAR uses Karabakh and Ashrafi fields for oil production, and Umid and Babek for exploration work with higher oil and gas prices. Some foreign companies, including BP and Total, have expressed interest in further exploration in Azerbaijan.

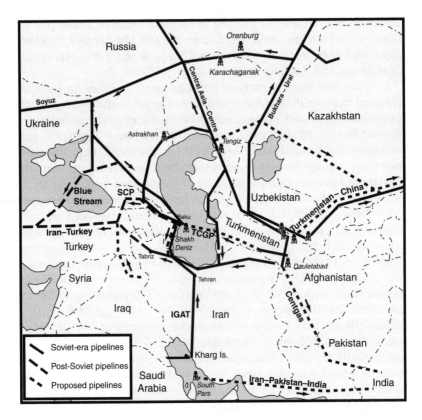

Map 3.2   Major gas fields and pipelines in the Caspian Sea region
Source: Courtesy of Julian Lee, CGES.

the gas pipelines fell apart (e.g. no maintenance work has been carried out since 1992).[39] In exploration, all work has been stopped. Russia was rising as a new strong competitor in gas supply to Turkmenistan. The only successful project of that time was the gas pipeline to northern Iran, bringing around 70.6–141.2 bcf to a power plant.[40] Poor and indirect access to gas export markets influenced Turkmenistan's earnings between US$1.25 and US$1.6 per mmbtu (million British thermal

---

[39] In recent years there has been some maintenance work done, reported by the official press.

[40] There are plans for laying an oil pipeline from the western oil fields of Turkmenistan (Nebit Dag, Korpedzhe) to the Tehran Refinery and on to the Persian Gulf.

units) from its exports to Russia and Ukraine, while other producers have higher earnings from direct access (e.g. India earns US$3.0 to US$3.5; Egyptian producers, US$4.0 to US$4.25; and US$6.0 to US$6.50 per mmbtu earned by producers in the USA).

Therefore the Turkmen oil and gas industry desperately needed foreign capital as well as know-how. However, the country did not attract a significant number of international energy companies. This reflected the 'difficult' geographical position of Turkmenistan (a land-locked country, with Russia as a strong neighbour–competitor for gas routes, as well as a supplier to customers at the end of these routes); an uneasy foreign investment climate under the rule of the late President Niyazov; and limited oil resources in comparison to other Caspian neighbours.

The jewels in Turkmenistan's oil and gas crown are five projects with foreign participation under PSA terms. These comprise two onshore projects: Khazar and Nebitdag, and three offshore projects: Cheleken, Block –1 and Block 11–12.

The Khazar PSA was signed in 2000 with a consortium comprising Turkmenneft (52 per cent), the operator, and Mitro International (48 per cent), which is handling the financial side of the project. Under the terms of the PSA the consortium obtained a licence for oil production in the Gyundogar (eastern) Cheleken field for 25 years, with a right of further extension for five years. The project envisages the workover of idle wells and putting them back into operation, as well as the drilling of 30 new development wells. In 2004, the consortium produced 2.68 mln bbl of oil.

Oil exploration and production in the Nebit Dag area started in the early 1940s. At the time of signing the PSA in 1996, the Burun field had been producing since the 1970s, though it was still under development. Therefore the first logical step after signing the PSA was for the consortium (Monument, Mobil and Burren) to start a rehabilitation and development phase for Burun. As a result, oil exports began in May 1998. The Nebit Dag PSA area covers 258 719 acres in Western Turkmenistan, approximately 31 miles from the Caspian Sea. The PSA area is subdivided into an 'exploration area' and five 'production areas', which comprise three oil-producing fields (Burun, Nebit Dag and Gum Dag) as well as two gas fields (Gyzyl Gum and Gara Depe). Since 2000, Burren Energy (UK) has been the project operator. Production in 2006 averaged over 7.2 mln bbl (980 000 t) and over 21 500 bbl/day in the first half of 2007.[41]

---

[41] See detailed description of Burren Energy's activities in Turkmenistan in Chapter 4.

The Cheleken block consists of the Chelekenyangummez (Pricheleken dome), Dzheitun and Dzhygalibeg oil fields (more commonly known as LAM and Xdanov), whose cumulative reserves amount to 513.1 mln bbl of oil and 2.19 tcf of gas. A PSA between Dragon Oil (69.4 per cent) – as operator – and the government was signed in 1999 (with effect from 2000). This has a duration of 25 years, with the possibility of extension for a further ten years. At the time of writing, commercial oil is produced at two fields: Zheitun and Dzygalibeg. In 2006 oil production was around 20 514 bbl/day and in the first half of 2007 it was 28 300 bbl/day.

Block 1 includes the fields of Garagol–Deniz, Diyarbekir, Magtymguly, Ovez and Mashrykov. A PSA for 25 years was signed in 1996 between Petronas Carigali and the government. From the beginning of the project, several cycles of exploratory drilling have been carried out. Initially it was gas and gas condensate only; then commercial oil flows were obtained from all drilled wells. In the short term, plans are for the drilling of further oil wells. Production of the first oil began in 2006.

The Integrated Offshore Block 11–12 project is being carried out by Maersk Oil under a PSA which started to be implemented in December 2002. During preliminary estimates of Block 11–12 a structural feature, classic pinch-outs, and a carbonaceous superstructure scenario were developed. These engineering methods reflect the structure that had formed at the Garashsyzlyk prospect, which is a target of the first exploratory well. However, this well turned out to be dry. Further estimates will be made after the first drillings.

The PSAs described above were viewed as political-economic 'blessings' for Turkmenistan, allowing the creation of jobs for Turkmen nationals (around 85 per cent of staff working under PSAs are local) and preserving a skilled labour force for the country's oil and gas industry. In the conditions prevailing in Turkmenistan, PSAs are the only possibility to keep ageing equipment at modern operating standards, as well as to equip the industry with modern technology.

3.3   Commercial challenges and transport issues

It is important not to underestimate the role of potential market power, and influence over resources, in decisions concerning the Caspian oil and gas business: the oil and gas fields of the region have incomparable values. Against the strategic value of access to these reserves, however, oil operators have had to weigh the major challenges that are typical of the region. In particular, Caspian oil has high costs of production and transportation. Average production costs in the Caspian Sea are around three times those in the Persian Gulf. There are some exceptions such as the Tengiz field, which ChevronTexaco is aiming to produce at around US$2/bbl at peak production, and the Burun field in Turkmenistan, which Burren is developing with US$3–4/bbl costs, but the majority of the Caspian fields are expected to cost around US$5/bbl, and in some cases more.

Other commercial challenges in the region include additional costs for the construction of new export pipelines; the high cost of importing different types of resources (including human, technological, capital, etc.); and high price discounts to Brent on oil exports from the Caspian. For instance, according to Brian Lavers, in recent years discounts to Brent on oil exports from Turkmenistan have been as high as US$8 per barrel. These discounts mainly reflect transport costs, which include trans-Caspian shipping, pipeline tariffs and shipping to market within the eastern Mediterranean area; but quality issues also play a role.[42] (Brian Lavers, presentation at the conference 'Hydrocarbon Wealth and Development in Resource Rich Economies', June 2005, University of Reading).

A key constraint affecting costs throughout the region, and constraining export capacity in Kazakhstan and Turkmenistan, is the inadequacy of pipelines and port facilities. Oil transportation has been a perennial problem in the Caspian region, with a limited pipeline network (most of which went north into Russia), seasonal shipping through the Volga–Don canal system and rail transport. Since the early 1990s there have been many delays in obtaining political approval and finance for cross-border oil pipelines to the West.

As major Caspian oil fields have been brought into full production, it has become increasingly obvious that oil output from the region has the clear potential to grow rapidly over the next decade. There are projections that, by 2010, output could approach levels higher those enjoyed by the Soviet oil industry in the late 1980s. However, despite a number of pipeline projects, the region's export infrastructure is not fully prepared for the size of the increase. 'Together, future oil production from already discovered fields in Kazakhstan, Azerbaijan, the Russian sector of the Caspian Sea and Turkmenistan is expected to reach a peak level

---

[42] Quality issues arise when high-quality crude is blended with low-quality (usually heavier) crude and sold at a price which reflects the quality of the blend. Unless there is a mechanism, such as a quality bank, to pursue the relative values of different grades of crude put into the pipeline, the high-quality producer will be penalized and the low-quality producer rewarded. Quality banks exist for both the CPC and BTC pipelines, but not for the Russian pipeline system.

of around 5 mb/d shortly after the middle of the coming decade' (Lee, 2007a: 36).

In 2001 the Caspian Pipeline Consortium (CPC) opened its pipeline from Tengiz to Novorossiysk on the Black Sea – Baku–Supsa. The new line provides around 600 000 bbl/day of export capacity to the region. This was a major breakthrough for oil development in the Caspian region. The next major step was the then controversial Baku–Tbilisi–Ceyhan pipeline (BTC), which connects the Azeri–Chirag–Guneshli fields to the Mediterranean on the south coast of Turkey. This pipeline was officially declared open in 2005, although first exports were not made from Ceyhan until mid-2006. (For discussions on BTC, see Soligo and Jaffe, 2001; Olcott, 2005.)

The transport challenge concerns gas as well as oil. In order to realize the full potential of its gas fields (as well as a more efficient utilization of associated gas reserves), the Caspian region needs additional gas pipelines and infrastructure. The political and financing challenges that were finally overcome in constructing the CPC and BTC oil lines remain to be solved for gas. For the moment the most promising development is a planned upgrade of the existing gas lines from Western Turkmenistan, through Kazakhstan into Russia.

3.4   Economic impact

After this description and discussion of oil and gas projects in the Caspian region, it is clear that their impact on the host countries (including governments and economies) is expected to be quite significant. The logical consequence of the implementation of such projects (and in fact the final goal for the host country) is the collection of oil and gas revenue in the form of taxes, royalties, bonuses, etc., which are potentially very important for the national economy.

Moreover, the scale and preconditions of such projects differ importantly from those of other projects undertaken in the economy. This is due to the different profile of this type of project as compared with, say, manufacturing or agricultural projects. Oil and gas projects operate with large economies of scale, and sizeable costs and investments during a defined period of time (the time of the contract) with a highly specialized group of workers who are facilitating the project. All this will only take place if sufficient oil and gas reserves are found in the country and if their extraction proves to be commercially viable.

The fundamental criterion here is the commercial value of the project. However, there are other variables which should be taken into account when we assess the success of the oil and gas projects, namely local factor determinants (as in the employment pattern, in purchases of input composition, and use of the local technologies, if the last are available in the country).

In an ideal world a project should be both commercial (when internal rate of return (IRR) exceeds the cost of capital) and competitive (where IRR and other criteria that maximize shareholder wealth exceed those available from other projects worldwide). This will be assessed on a comparative basis between states and countries, and between competitor companies. However, it is important to bear in mind that companies differ in IRR hurdle rates (financial performance, capital structure, segment of business and its available returns for projects). As a result, a project's IRR may be commercial but not be competitive (Seba, 2003). Overall, a project should be socially beneficial, i.e. with positive cost–benefit ratio when costs and benefits include environmental and other externalities.

All these activities are taking place against the background of crude oil prices that vary in a pattern that does not match the global economic cycle in a predictable manner. Variations in corporate financial performance from one calendar quarter to the next, which are such a mainstay of security analysis in most industries, have little, if any, meaning in the oil and gas industry. Income from new capital expenditures in the upstream sector of the business will take many years to achieve, if at all. Cash flow per share replaces earnings per share as the best gauge of current financial performance of an oil company. Thus the short-run performance of a project is an important indicator; but only once a project is complete can one assess its full impact on the local economies in the Caspian Sea region.

However, one fact can (even now) be stated with a high degree of certainty: the oil and gas sector has an important impact on the host economies and makes it an ideal taxpayer for the government. At the same time, the capital return goes to the shareholders and banks of the companies who are conducting these projects. The domestic economic impact of oil and gas projects depends very much not only on how much revenue the government has collected and on how much local content was developed, but also on how well the government succeeded in utilizing this revenue in the host economy and in its international investments.

Overall, the direct economic impact to date of oil and gas projects on the Caspian economies must be characterized as mixed (Table 3.5), and the local content factor has varied greatly. One of the positive impacts has been the creation of employment: a major plus of the oil and gas

Table 3.5   Impact of the major oil and gas projects on the Caspian economies*

Positive		Negative
Direct	Creation of work places	Environment pollution
	Education, training of local staff	Higher living expenses
	Investment to local budgets	Capital outflow from the region due
	Purchase of local equipment & services	to preference of foreign contractors/ suppliers over local
	Innovations	
	Globalization	
	Access to world market	
	Implementation of safety principles	
	Experienced local staff	
Indirect	Population inflow	
	Improvement of public services sector	Depletion of natural resources
	Mix of cultures	
	Expansion & development of private business	
	Development of financial sector	
	Development of infrastructures	
	Additional funds to the budgets from contract & subcontract	Demoralization

Note: *The table is a very rough attempt to capture the impact of the major oil and gas projects. The entries are far from equally important and some may be positive or negative (e.g. 'mix of cultures' has led to ethnic riots at Tengiz).

projects is that they are 'reinjecting' life into the resource-rich regions, which are as a rule deprived and obsolete from Soviet times. This offers the possibility of developing more experienced local staff, assuming that education and training are involved; but it also results in rising living costs in the area. A second direct impact is that of investment in local budgets and, in principle, some purchase of local equipment and services. At the same time there is the risk of capital outflow from the region due to a preference for foreign contractors/suppliers over local firms.

In terms of externalities, better access to world markets has the potential to give a positive spin to local content development, the expansion and development of private business, and the improvement of public services. But there is a real challenge of depletion of resources and environmental pollution.

More broadly, oil and gas projects can lead to a loss or gain of host-country sovereignty. History demonstrates that companies could have certain reactions to host–government interventions and related investment risks (Yergin, 1992). However, the perceived bargaining strength of any operator of a major oil or gas project might be overshadowed by the high degree of risk involved in the long run. Obviously, an initial 'honeymoon' between host government and foreign investors will end and be replaced by a period when, due to high oil prices, high taxes or other benefits of the projects, the government may to attempt to change, or at least have regrets about the conditions that were agreed with the investors at the beginning. That could create a nervous and risky situation, making the investors quite vulnerable to further government action.

4
Companies and Governments

4.1 The learning curve

Since the region gained independence in the early 1990s, policy-makers in the Caspian states have given top priority to developing strategies for national hydrocarbon development, as many documents of that time confirm. The first generation of foreign investment in the region went overwhelmingly to the hydrocarbon sector (see Figure 4.1). The experience during this period can be viewed in terms of a learning curve in relations between the newly independent states and international companies, as they sought to develop cooperative relations.

Before their engagement in the Caspian region, major oil and gas companies such as BP, Shell and Chevron already had significant operating experience in resource-rich developing countries. It has long been apparent, indeed, that a sizeable proportion of some companies' future production and profits would come from activities in developing or transition economies. Nonetheless, in the early and mid-1990s companies had not developed a clear understanding of how to operate in the specific conditions of the transition from central planning. The economic decline during the 'transition recession' was very steep. Corporate governance as a concept was non-existent, and governments had little or no experience of structuring economic relations with private companies. 'The host government should realise that respect for foreign investors will encourage more investments' (interview with Clare Bebbington, communications and external affairs director, BP Azerbaijan, 27 April 2007, Baku).

At the same time, it was clear that the Caspian oil and gas industry required massive capital investment up front, often running into billions of dollars. It was obvious that the expected returns would accrue over a long period of 20 years or more, following the initial investment.

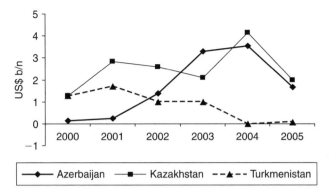

Figure 4.1   Foreign direct investment, net flows (BoP, current US$bln) (data shown in units)

Note: BoP – balance of payments.

Source: International Monetary Fund, International Financial Statistics and Balance of Payments databases, and World Bank, Global Development Finance.

Therefore, the first signs of reassurance of their right decisions that foreign investors were looking for were those typical in such circumstances: a climate of stability, the rule of law, long-term stakeholder partnerships, and wealth creation that benefits all. This setting would be essential to ensure recovery of initial investments.

During the first phase of oil and gas development, governments in the region lacked both financial resources and expertise, while the need for investment capital was very high. For a period, this imbalance between private resources and public needs served to simplify commercial relations. In the course of the late 1990s, and around the turn of the century, however, these relations gradually began to evolve. Governments became more insistent on their claims to participate in the industry and to ensure gains for the local economy that would go beyond tax revenues and public expenditure.

The commercial climate of the second generation of investment in the region is characterized by a greater diversity of interests among the Caspian states, but a common theme is more assertive market regulation. Moreover, a key issue recurs in all cases: the concern of host governments to improve the capabilities of local companies involved in supply and services.

The change in government–company relations potentially holds the seeds of fruitful cooperation on a more equal footing, but it can also give rise to many possible tensions. The recent history of the region is full of evidence of the efforts of governments and companies to channel such tensions in a productive manner and reach frameworks that could address the legitimate concerns of each side on a cooperative basis. This is true at the over-arching level of production agreements, but also in the more concrete and sensitive field of local content (which merits specific discussion in Chapter 5).

By and large, the years since 2000 have seen further development in political-economic relationships between governments and companies, with parallels to earlier experience in regions such as the Gulf. But uncertainty about future political trends in the region means that it is, as of now, an unfinished story. To understand the dynamics at work it is helpful to consider the varying strategies of companies as they entered the region, including the special case of national oil companies; and then to turn to the somewhat more uniform concerns of governments as they gained experience in dealing with commercial interests.

4.2   Commercial strategies

The fundamental purpose of an oil company is to provide oil and gas to customers and, in so doing, to build shareholder value (see Figure 4.2). Risky investments need to be assured of commensurately high returns to ensure a successful company strategy. This said, any oil company would acknowledge its duty to act responsibly, foster sustainability and safeguard its reputation. However, the question arises of how to give specific meaning to the term 'responsible' – and, moreover, a meaning that is intelligible on both sides of the company–government

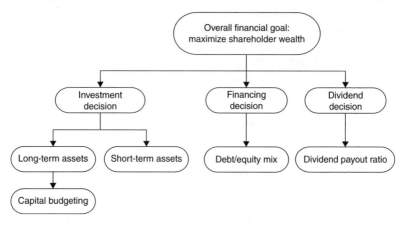

Figure 4.2   Composition of maximization of shareholder wealth by company

interface. Achieving some clarity in this area, as it specifically affects host governments, is essential if companies are to build a sustainable role in resource-rich nations.

First, there are those issues directly within the company's sphere of *control*: legal compliance; and being a progressive operator with high and consistent standards of safety, the environment, recruitment, procurement and financial transparency. Second, the company can use its sphere of *influence* to work with governments (and vice versa), business partners and civil society by using its skills and resources to deliver better outcomes for society in areas such as the environment, investment in education, encouraging enterprise and enabling communities to gain access to energy. The company can also work with host governments to help them manage the impact of the company's investments and the wealth that is created, often simply by transferring knowledge of best practice from around the world and by investing in further research to create global centres of excellence in resource management. Exxon is a market leader in such activity, but BP adopted an alternative strategy through outsourcing many of the conventional R&D functions.

In analysing the behaviour of any oil and gas company one should not look at a particular project or country in isolation. Analysis needs to be based on a broader framework for capital budgeting. The first step would be to identify company strategy overall, and then to assess how the strategy works to maximize shareholder wealth. To be effective, such concepts must be capable of translation into concrete principles and practice. They may lead to different types of solution across the countries and projects of the region, which is characterized by uneven endowments, widely differing types and scales of project, and varying types of company. The starting point must be the decision-making process of oil and gas companies, against the background of basic investment principles. This is the channel through which the philosophy of any oil and gas company operating in the Caspian region has to find expression.

Capital budgeting and allocation in a company to decide what projects to approve is of a paramount importance (see Figure 4.2). Major project investments are the most significant financial activities of a firm. From a company's point of view, it is very important to define core long-term activities correctly. The budgeting process will then include the evaluation of existing and potential activities, and confirmation of which projects receive capital for immediate implementation. As illustrated in Figure 4.2, capital constraints force an allocation process that selects a project mix that is expected to maximize shareholder wealth. Whatever the scope and timing of activities, decisions must be made carefully and rationally with owners, i.e. shareholders, in mind. History testifies to the problems in cases where projects have been approved that are not commercial or competitive. However, prices have risen so much since investment decisions were made on the major Caspian projects that everyone ought to be earning well from them, exploitation problems notwithstanding.

For the purposes of this academic analysis it is important to set out how systems for evaluating projects are structured, and how capital allocation is dealt with in order to be consistent with overall company strategy. Such a system will include several phases, namely: a concept phase (where the idea about a new project is brought up), a preliminary evaluation phase (where the first feasibility study will be presented), a business evaluation phase (where the business plan together with financial figures will be in place), and then a 'go-ahead or reject' phase.

In this formal sense, business decisions are structured to ensure that a project must pass all these phases in order to be approved, but an accompanying element, beyond these formal structures, could be termed the 'culture within the company': the set of shared values which will influence strategic choices and the judgements made in the capital evaluation system. This culture reflects some identifiable factors such as risk preferences; but it also involves human factors and value judgements that may be much more complex to tie down.

Capital project portfolios for different companies could vary from very diverse one (BP, Shell, etc.) to more focused (BG Group, Burren Energy). This is generally a function of the size of the company, with larger companies usually having a more diverse project portfolio.

As Table 4.1 shows, in order to undertake any expansion, it is important to allow a certain percentage of capital for each component of the

Table 4.1 Expansion in existing businesses, % of capital

Expansion in existing businesses	Major oil co. capital, %
Upstream: exploration	10
Upstream: development and production	50–60
Midstream: pipelines, natural gas processing	10
Downstream: oil refining and retail marketing	20
Chemical manufacturing	10

Source: Author's companies analysis.

activities. For instance, in upstream sectors activities such as exploration require around 10 per cent of capital, while development and production account for perhaps 50–60 per cent of capital. And of course the decision criteria for a capital project, to be even considered, will include a system of indicators such as internal rate of return (IRR) – which should be commercial (i.e. exceed 'cost of capital' plus premium) and competitive (create the best mix of future cash flows when multiple projects can be selected from). There are complementary financial indicators such as net present value (NPV), payback period and profitability index, which provide additional reference points in evaluating projects.

An overlay on this process is the ultimate risk assessment of the project, which must factor in many types of political, economic and market uncertainty, and the possible occurrence of compound risks. In other words, companies will need to assess a wide range of factors that include forecasting risks (including production, costs, taxes, etc.), exploration geological risks, political risks, permit risks and capital cost prediction risks. A positive conclusion about the investment decision will only be reached when there is evidence that the proposed project is sufficiently resilient to risks.

The notion of risk is itself quite debatable. Some authors equate or relate risk with uncertainty: 'we will consider the words "risk" and "uncertainty" to be synonymous'. (Newendorp, 1975: 59). Others distinguish between the concepts: 'risk is a measurable possibility of losing or not gaining value. Risk is differentiated from uncertainty, which is not measurable' (Barron's *Dictionary of Finance and Investment Terms*, 1998: 521).

The crucial challenge for companies, of course, is not to avoid all risks but to mitigate them – and diversify them – sufficiently. 'For any long term in any mega project the longevity of contracts is required. This must be underpinned by the contract enforceability under the law, internal commercial stability with undisputed rights to the international arbitration' (interview with Terry Adams, founding president, AIOC, 26 August 2007, Reading). In the hydrocarbon industry this involves, first of all, sufficient front-end engineering and assessment, as well as selection of the right technologies (including the development of new technologies). A tight control of capital and operating costs is crucial, especially with complex projects in difficult geographical and geological situations, which abound in the Caspian region. Then there is the scope and credibility of government assurances or incentives such as permits or loan guarantees to lower project costs in terms of interest rates, availability of tax credits, and

low-side price risk protection. Vertical integration mitigates price volatility. Downstream production prices are less volatile than upstream
production prices.

The key question, always, is why and how to enter specific projects
overseas. The answer lies in the strategic fit between, on the one hand,
business opportunities offered by each country, and, on the other, the
overall risk–return features of a company's portfolio of activities.

Companies vary in their strategies, and risk assessments inevitably
differ. An example of diverse company strategies in one country,
Kazakhstan, will illustrate this. In Kazakhstan, BG Group faced an
excessive concentration of risk, accompanied by insufficient leverage,
a potentially very demanding long-term investment, and an energy sector (oil) which was not fully in line with its commercial strategy. These
considerations led it to disengage from a key project. In Kazakhstan, to
diversify its holdings in the region and global production areas, BG
Group 'completed the disposal of its share in the North Caspian Sea
(PSA) (BG Group 16.67%) in April 2005' (BG Group, 2006: 14). By that
time the company had decided to concentrate more on gas rather
than oil (Kashagan is a large oil discovery). BG Group itself is a result-
oriented company; it is more focused on a rapid rate of return. The last
reason is related to the fact that BG Group has grown into a major company and wanted to be involved in projects where it could use significant
leverage rather than being a small shareholder (interview with Mehmet
Ogutcu, global manager, international government & corporate affairs,
BG Group, 8 August 2006). The company's internal calculations show
that Kashagan is a long-term investment. For instance, in Kazakhstan,
Kashagan is claimed to be the largest and most challenging oil field
development project. 'Caspian drilling requires equipment tailored for
deep, high-pressure reservoirs, with sour gas and other contaminants'
(Rach, 2004: 44).

By contrast, ConocoPhillips decided to remain as a minority investor
in the Kashagan project, although their share is only 9.26 per cent and
they do not operate the development. 'We like Kashagan; it has its technical challenge and certainly has its cost challenges. But the Caspian is
an area for ConocoPhillips that we are really interested in and we are
pretty aggressive trying to get more acreage, in particularly, well in the
Caspian' (from ConocoPhillips Q4 2006 Earnings Call Transcript, John
Carrig, EVP of Finance and CFO).

The Bridas story in Turkmenistan (see Box 4.1) demonstrates that the
relations between companies and governments could be strained and do
not always lead to a successful partnership.

Box 4.1   The experience of Bridas in Turkmenistan

Not every company working in the Caspian Sea region has a story of success. One such example concerns Bridas, an Argentinean corporation in Turkmenistan that is closely related to the initial privatization programme conducted by the Turkmen government in the mid-1990s.[43]

In February 1993, Bridas entered into a joint venture agreement (JVA) to conduct hydrocarbon operations in the Keimir area of Turkmenistan together with an entity[44] designated by the government of Turkmenistan. 'The Turkmen Party to the agreement was an entity wholly owned by the Government, whose identity was designed and re-designed at will by the President of Turkmenistan and has changed a number of times during the life of the joint venture' (United States Court of Appeals, Fifth Circuit, 2006: 2–3).

According to the initial agreement, the Turkmen government was entitled to oil and gas production up to the November 1992 levels, while both sides would split any further increase in production. The joint venture managed to secure an unrestricted export licence for oil and gas. 'Within three years of its inception, the Keimir joint venture (and Bridas' JVA rights) had been fatally compromised by a series of unilateral actions by the State of Turkmenistan, including a decree forcing the joint venture to cease work, as well as a 1995 governmental suspension of exports or imports by Bridas' (Nelson, 2006: 592).

The International Chamber of Commerce (ICC) Tribunal was presented with arbitration proceedings against Turkmenistan by Bridas, resulting in awards in 2000 and 2001 holding Turkmenistan liable for Turkmenneft's violation of the JVA.[45] The ICC Tribunal,

---

[43] Here are the facts of just this particular case. It is interesting to note that Bridas was successful in other regions of Turkmenistan.

[44] Originally it was PA Turkmenneft.

[45] On 1 July 1996 Turkmenistan reorganized its state-owned enterprises by decree, ordering that all rights and obligations of CB be transferred to another entity, the State Concern Turkmenneft ('Turkmenneft'). In 1997, Turkmenneft was added as a respondent to the ICC arbitration.

in its final award, granted a total of US$495 000 000 in damages to Bridas (The American Society of International Law, 2003).

In its response, the government of Turkmenistan and Turkmenneft rejected the ICC Awards on numerous grounds, including that Turkmenistan was not a signatory to the JVA and as a consequence was not bound either by the JVA arbitration clause or the ensuing ICC Awards.

However, the Texas District Court dismissed all these objections and confirmed the ICC Awards in all respects. They found that 'Turkmenneft acted as the "agent" of the state and that the state could not deny its obligation to arbitrate'. Turkmenistan and Turkmenneft appealed.

In 2003, the United States Court of Appeals for the Fifth Circuit reversed the Texas District Court's 2001 order confirming the ICC Awards, and remanded the case for further reconsideration by the district court.

The Fifth Circuit found that Turkmenistan had misused Turkmenneft's corporate structure to commit fraud. It was provided with plenty of evidence that 'after the 1995 export ban the Government misused Turkmenneft to harm Bridas by destroying the value of the JVA' (Nelson, 2006: 595). As in 1996, Turkmenneft was dissolved and replaced by the Turkmen government. Turkmenneft was initially capitalized with the equivalent of US$17 000, and was funded by a State Oil and Gas Development Fund. However, Turkmenneft became a full partner of the JVA (in fact representing the Turkmen government). At the same time the Turkmen government attempted to distance itself from the JVA (in order not to assume any liabilities) by issuing several decrees. 'The Government's manipulation of Turkmenneft to prevent any substantial damage award satisfied the "fraud or injustice" prong [of alter ego liability]' (Nelson, 2006: 595).

The overall conclusion of the Fifth Circuit was that an investor in the Caspian Sea region is stuck with the risks it takes when investing in that turbulent region. From our point of view all the international oil companies should envisage and calculate the degree of such risk that they are prepared to meet if they decide to invest in the Caspian. No doubt in 1993, before entering Turkmenistan, Bridas was aware of such risks, and thought through the possibility that its investment could be affected by the political decisions of the Turkmen state, which is what happened in the end. To conclude the story, Bridas still is awaiting the compensation from the Turkmen government.

4.3 Company case studies

The experience of BG Group and ConocoPhillips in Kazakhstan underscores that it is worth probing in more depth the varying strategies that different types of companies may pursue. It helps, here, to think generically in terms of three stylized groups of corporate players in the Caspian region: oil majors, independent international companies,[46] and the national oil companies of the producing countries. All of them will pursue different strategies. Well-defined examples of each type of company can be found in the Caspian region, and here the discussion will focus on the activities of BP (a major) in Azerbaijan, Burren Energy (an independent) in Turkmenistan, and KazMunaiGaz (a producer-side national oil company) in Kazakhstan.

Case study 1: BP in Azerbaijan

At the time of writing, BP is the operator of major projects in Azerbaijan and is 'responsible for managing and carrying out development and production activities on behalf of the various project partnerships within agreed management frameworks' (BP Azerbaijan Sustainability Report 2004: 9). The history of BP in Azerbaijan is briefly presented at Table 4.2.

As an oil major, BP has an overall group strategy which is the fundamental basis for its Azerbaijan exploration and production activities, which are substantial long-term assets. In all cases, BP's strategy is based on the company's overall responsibility, and the Azerbaijan operations are no exception in this respect. As Terry Admas pointed out, 'the test for any major oil company is the materiality of expenditures on reputation management under their contract within the context of their total investment' (interview with Terry Adams, founding president, AIOC, 26 August 2007, Reading).

The company follows applicable Azerbaijani laws, and it also operates according to a BP code of conduct covering the areas of health, safety,

[46] This term is used to describe any oil company that is not one of the largest integrated oil companies.

Table 4.2   History of BP in Azerbaijan

Date	Event
Sep. 94	ACG PSA signed by BP, its partners and the Azerbaijan government to develop offshore resources
Feb. 95	Formation of AIOC comprising 10 companies, including BP as the largest single shareholder
Oct. 95	ACG 'Early Oil Project' (EOP) sanctioned to allow exports from Chirag
Jun. 96	Shakh Deniz PSA signed
Sep. 97	Planning begins for Baku–Tbilisi–Ceyhan (BTC) pipeline project
Nov. 97	First oil produced from Chirag
Jul. 98	Inam and Araz–Alov–Sharg PSAs signed
Dec. 98	Western Route Export Pipeline (WREP) starts operations
Aug. 01	ACG Phase 1 sanctioned
Sep. 02	ACG Phase 2 sanctioned
Feb. 03	Shakh Deniz Stage 1 sanctioned
Apr. 03	Construction of BTC pipeline begins
Feb. 04	Financing of BTC project agreed
Sep. 04	ACG Phase 3 sanctioned
Oct. 04	Construction of South Caucasus Pipeline (SCP) begins
Oct. 04	BTC pipeline on Azerbaijan/Georgia border welded together
Feb. 05	Production at Central Azeri in Caspian Sea begins
Mar. 05	Azeri crude oil exports starts
May. 05	BTC linefill starts; delivery of associated gas to Azerbaijan section of BTC inaugurated
Oct. 05	Georgian section of BTC inaugurated
Dec. 05	Deepwater Guneshli pre-drilling programme commences. West Azeri production begins
May. 06	First gas flows into the SCP
Jun. 06	First tanker filled with Caspian oil at Ceyhan terminal; record ACG daily production rate of over 500 000 bbl/day
Jul. 06	Inauguration of the Turkish section of the BTC pipeline, the Ceyhan terminal and the BTC pipeline export system
Nov. 06	East Azeri produces first revenue oil
Dec. 06	Gas production begins from Shakh Deniz; South Caucasus Pipeline operations commence

Source: BP Azerbaijan Sustainability Report 2004, 2005.

security and the environment; employees; business partners, governments and communities as well as company assets and financial integrity (see BP Code of Conduct, 2005). In its long-term business strategy, BP has identified three main areas to which it is committed. These are supporting targeted learning activities in Azerbaijan; helping to create jobs in the areas of operations; and enabling the Azerbaijani community to gain access to modern energy services.

In 2005 the BP-led AIOC group began to be interested in developing the Karabakh and Dan Ulduzu–Ashrafi blocks in the Azeri sector of the Caspian.[47] These blocks were abandoned as commercially unattractive by other investors in the late 1990s but remain a high-risk investment for possible additional reserves that could give BP and its partners more oil for the 1 mln bbl/day Baku–Tbilisi–Ceyhan (BTC) pipeline – which incidentally confirms the fact that, at the current rate of production, Azerbaijan would hardly satisfy the supply capacity for BTC. In addition it would enhance the consortium's position in talks with Kazakh crude suppliers wanting access to BTC, and also boost the chances of expanding the route's capacity to 1.4 mln bbl/day.

BP is keen to find reserves to maintain an export production rate of around 1 mln bbl/day once production from the Azeri–Chirag–Guneshli fields (ACG) begins to decline.

In addition, BP became interested in possible development of prospective offshore structures north of the Apsheron peninsula. The company has confirmed its interest in expanding its activities but declines to identify specific projects, saying 'nothing will materialise quickly' (*Argus FSU*, 24 June 2005).

Also in 2005 the BP began filling one of the new major pipelines, the BTC pipeline. BTC started to operate in 2006 and reached its design capacity of 1 mln bbl/day in the second quarter of 2007.

In 2006, the investment into development phases of BP's main projects in the country were coming to an end and expenditures started to decrease as a result. Investment in Shakh Deniz, the ACG field and the BTC pipeline amounted to just over US$4 bln in 2006.

The total project cost of the ACG offshore block is expected to be US$20 bln, according to BP. This forecast covers the whole period of the contract and includes construction of new infrastructure, drilling of wells etc. It compares with earlier projections on the order of US$13 bln–16 bln. Observers have attributed the rise in costs to US dollar inflation and higher contractor and material costs. The AIOC group boosted output of Azeri light crude from the ACG fields to 439 000 bbl/day in 2006, from 262 000 bbl/day in 2005 and plans an average production

---

[47] 'SOCAR signed a PSA for Karabakh in 1995 with Lukoil, Italy's Eni and Pennzoil, a US firm later acquired by Devon. But this was annulled in February 1999 after the partners found only 58.64 mln–73.3 mln bbl of crude and 811.9 bcf of gas. A PSA for the Dan Ulduzu–Ashrafi block was signed in 1997 with Amoco, Unocal of the US, Japan's Itochu and US–Saudi venture Delta Hess. The partners carried out exploration drilling revealing up to 293.2 mln bbl of crude and 811.9 bcf of gas, but the PSA expired in March 2000' (*Argus FSU*, 24 June 2005).

rate of more than 700 000 bbl/day in 2007. As the result of a third development phase, output from this field will reach a peak of some 1 mln bbl/day in 2008–2009. Production from phase three would begin in the second quarter of 2008.

At the Shakh Deniz field, some 19 000 bbl/day of condensate should be produced (see Table 4.1). The first delivery of gas from Shakh Deniz to Georgia was made early in 2007, with deliveries to Turkey following in June. Problems with construction of the Baku–Tbilisi–Erzurum gas export line to Turkey delayed shipments that had been expected to start in October 2006.

As a result of the exceptional geo-hazard, there are lessons to be learned from the Shakh Deniz project, including in particular the need to better tolerate risks undertaken when there are multiple applications of 'serial number one' equipment – new designs to meet specific challenges posed by a project. Notably, the Shakh Deniz team faced difficult circumstances when designing high-pressure gas wells on the specific type of platform used here (*Compass*, 12 March 2007).

As Table 4.3 shows, the volume of annual investment made by BP as operator for these major projects demonstrates a challenge faced in spending in excess of US$216 mln per day.

Why is BP so successful in Azerbaijan? In his interview with me, Terry Adams explained:

> BP is the most successful oil investor in Azerbaijan because it had a well defined geological model that reflected reality. It enabled us to identify where the best performing oil fields would be. We also took an early lead in commercial negotiation of a PSA in which some 3.5 bln bbl of proven oil had been found. This led to future operatorship. 'Be first–be Operator' has always been a successful maxim for the global oil industry. This has been very clearly proven for BP in Baku. (Interview with Terry Adams, founding president of AIOC, 26 August 2007, Reading)

Table 4.3 Investment plans

US$ mln	2006	2005
ACG	2552	2711
BTC	641	1287
Shakh Deniz (inc. gas line)	865	1299
Total	**4058**	**5297**

SOCAR and BP

To characterize relations between SOCAR and BP, one needs to start from the ultimate goals and aims of the two parties.

Obviously the classic dilemma for SOCAR as a national oil company is to reconcile political and business interests. Like other national oil companies, SOCAR was created to correct a perceived defect in the energy market: a distribution of benefits that the host government considered to be unjust and politically inappropriate. There is a clear set of objectives which SOCAR is pursuing. For BP it is important to understand SOCAR's objectives and to adopt the appropriate policy responses from micro and macro points of view, taking into account not only the company's maximization of stakeholder wealth, but also a broader political and economic perspective. From SOCAR's point of view the commercial question could also be asked: how to make better returns to its shareholders?

What would be a win–win partnership? On one hand it is clear that the energy sector is facing a serious shift in host-government requirements, where the state is using the national oil company as an arm and instrument in its governmental policies (domestic and foreign) in order to reach the desired result in its non-energy policy objectives.

As David Woodward recalls from his time in Azerbaijan,

> SOCAR had people who were very knowledgeable about the geology of the region but limited in their understanding of modern technology and management practices. Whereas BP has a world-class technological capability and ability to manage major, complex projects, and so, in effect, a win-win partnership formed. The ACG, BTC and Shakh Deniz projects are a testimony to the success of that partnership. (Interview with David Woodward, former president, BP Azerbaijan, 22 March 2007).

However, there can be conflict over division of the winnings when only two actors are involved (as in the ultimatum game).

What could BP offer to SOCAR? At least five points could be highlighted here: leading modern technology; capacity to manage such big projects as the Azeri–Chirag–Guneshli or Shakh Deniz; additional risk capital; experience of cutting costs in order to have more efficient operations; access to diversified markets such as through participation in BTC. However, the obstacle here is that SOCAR is under pressure from the state to pay less attention to commercial interests, in favour of its broader mandate.

It is interesting to note when ACG contract was first signed the key elements required from the government were the shareholders' ability to self-finance the project, with a proven ability to deliver an offshore project, and who would bring a high level political access to their respective governments. (Interview with Terry Adams, founding president AIOC, 26 August 2007, Reading)

Case study 2: Burren Energy in Turkmenistan

Burren Energy plc[48] was created in 1994 by Finian O'Sullivan, the current president, under the name of Volga Sumo Transportation and Trading Company. O'Sullivan's concept and strategy with regard to the Caspian Sea region was to create a Western-managed oil transportation company, and through this to look at upstream opportunities in the region. After establishing a Caspian tanker-based export route in partnership with Volgatanker, Russia's biggest shipping company, Burren then set about acquiring upstream assets (see Map 4.1).

In Turkmenistan Burren commenced operations in 1995, expanded rapidly and in partnership with Monument Oil & Gas and Mobil, the Nebit Dag PSA was signed in August 1996, covering an onshore site in Western Turkmenistan.

As discussed earlier, oil exploration and production in the Nebit Dag area had started in the early 1940s, and the Burun field was already producing (see Figure 4.3); a rehabilitation and development project there in 1996–1998 led to the start of oil exports in May 1998. The Nebit Dag PSA area is approximately 31 miles from the Caspian Sea. Following relinquishments over the years, it is now only 49 421 acres.

Following the takeover of Monument by Lasmo plc in 1999, they decided to exit the FSU and Monument's interest was sold to Burren.

Similarly, with the merger of Mobil with Exxon in December 1999, the new integrated company lost interest in Nebit Dag, so Burren acquired the rest of the package from the partners and took a 100 per cent working interest from August 2000. Since that point Burren has reconsidered its managerial strategy. 'From the second half of 2000, we cut onsite overheads and administrative and head office costs. In addition we terminated a significant number of sub-contracting agreements, by bringing the services in house' (interview with Finian O'Sullivan, president of

---

[48] Burren Energy plc is a UK independent oil and gas exploration, production and shipping company, which operates in the Caspian region, West Africa, India and the Middle East.

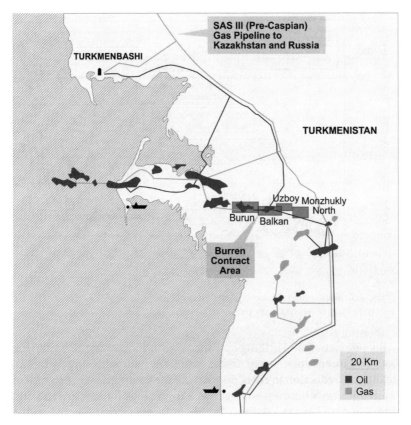

Map 4.1   Burren Energy in Turkmenistan
Source: Courtesy of Burren Energy plc.

Burren Energy, 5 November 2004). The oil price environment has changed dramatically from the time when the oil price was below US$12/bbl to a period when it is now consistently above US$100/bbl.

Operational efficiency has been streamlined through the review of all service companies' contracts, and as a consequence Burren manages most of the services. Burren Energy reorganized its operations into cross-functional teams comprising geologists, reservoir engineers, production engineers, geophysicists and drilling engineers.

This management organization was designed to improve coordination and communication problems inherited from Burren's partners. These changes cut operating costs and led to field operations becoming cash-flow positive. The field camp accommodates 70 people in support of

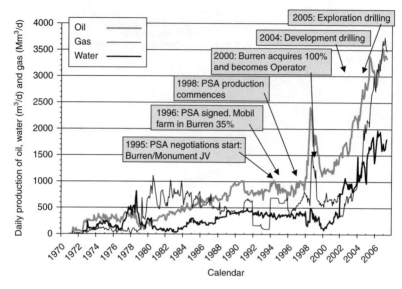

Figure 4.3   Burun field: historic production profile
Source: Courtesy of Burren Energy plc.

daily production and drilling operations, with the remaining staff living locally. Burren replaced expatriates with local staff, achieving by this an additional reduction in costs. So what are the determinants of success of Burren Energy's business strategy? 'We always look for new licences and ideas, and we have the skills to do this. Most of our staff is native to the region where they work and, wherever possible, we cut out any middle-men' (interview with Atul Gupta, chief operating officer, 12 September 2005).

From 2000, Burren Energy has been the project operator of five Turkmen fields: Burun, Nebit Dag, Garadepe, Gumdag and Gyzylkum. At the time of writing, it has sole production rights to and operates the Burun field under the PSA, while production rights for other fields remain with Turkmenneft. The main elements of the PSA include Burren meeting 100 per cent of field expenditure. Since the award of the PSA, cumulative expenditure from 1997 up to 30 June 2007 amounted to US$500 mln. Cumulative production over this period was 29 mln bbl, of which 22 mln bbl were delivered to Turkmenneft in satisfaction of its entitlement to Initial Oil under the PSA.

Burren takes a share of oil and gas over and above a declining annual volume specified in the PSA (known as initial oil and gas) due to

Turkmenneft. The term of the PSA under the terms and agreements is for 25 years, with the option of further 10 years' extension by mutual agreement. The balance of net production, after deducting cost recovery petroleum, is called 'profit petroleum'. The profit petroleum is shared between Burren and the Turkmenistan government, based on the R-Factor.[49]

Assessing the first years of operations, the chairman of Burren, Brian Lavers, remarked: 'after a slow start, oil field developments in the Caspian region are moving ahead steadily with a changing of transportation logistics (completion of major export pipelines). Independent Western companies, after establishing mutual trust, play an important role, particularly in the countries like Turkmenistan' (interview with Brian Lavers, chairman of Burren Energy, 12 September 2005).

There are a number of specific risks for Burren's activities in Turkmenistan, namely the operational, staff and political situation in Turkmenistan. As discussed in Chapter 3, transportation challenges are far from absent in Turkmenistan. Logistics problems are typical of the region. In the case of Nebit Dag there is a limited number of transportation options, and this presents an operational risk factor. The company relies heavily on a group of very talented individuals who are the key players and in the event of their departure the staff substitution problem might be crucial. Although from my interviews with chairman, chief executive and operational officers it came clear that Burren believe that the present Turkmen government is stable, the danger of changing governmental policies and regulations exists, which might negatively impact Burren's operations and profit.[50]

Burren's president, Finian O'Sullivan, in an interview with *Argus FSU Energy*, says that the country's internal politics have 'no impact on our commercial reality', adding that in the ten years since the Nebit Dag PSA was signed Burren has experienced 'no disruption or interference' from the authorities. 'The only change they have made to the whole PSA is that they have reduced the tax from 25pc to 20pc' (Finian

---

[49] The R-Factor is the ratio of total cumulative contractor receipts to the total cumulative costs, both calculated from the beginning of PSA operations to the end of the most recent calendar year. The R-Factor is set at the beginning of each calendar year.

[50] Since the collapse of the Soviet Union, Turkmenistan has created an investor regulatory framework enshrined within a petroleum law and regulated by a single entity called the 'competent body'. The competent body is empowered to act as a 'one-sstop shop' and is responsible for dealing with all other ministries. Petroleum law takes precedence over any other conflicting laws or regulations.

O'Sullivan, *Argus FSU Energy*, 10 March 2006). Nonetheless, there is no guarantee that Burren's contractual relationship to with the Turkmen government will always provide for unfettered export rights – a factor that is crucial for realization of revenues.

In an interview with me, Atul Gupta insisted: 'Our challenge in the Caspian is commercial – getting the oil and gas to market. Elsewhere, there could be perceived political threats but I don't feel this is the case where we have chosen to work' (interview with Atul Gupta, chief operating officer, 12 September 2005). Chairman Brian Lavers emphasized

> Burren is operating in a frontier area, more a politically sensitive area, working with developing and transition countries, countries with high political risk, we believe that we can minimise this risk by good economic returns. Some other independent companies look for the countries with low political risk, they feel that they should not work in the back of beyond. (Interview with Brian Lavers, chairman, 12 September 2005)

The external risk for Burren (as for any other oil-producing company) lay in oil market trends. Historical data show that the market price of oil fluctuated widely, and was of course affected by factors wholly beyond Burren's control. With oil prices expected to remain firm in the medium term, the company's strategy was straightforward: to increase output. Production averaged over 21 500 bbl/day in January–June 2007 and in the last quarter reached a peak of over 24 000 bbl/day.

Summing up the reasons for Burren's successful operations in Turkmenistan, it is important to emphasize the following factors: good oil field management, introduction of improved artificial lift (gaslift and water injection); bringing operations in house, eliminating turnkey contractors; tight cost control; and insisting on Western standards of health, safety and environment (HSE). In his interview with me, O'Sullivan emphasized Burren's impact on the Turkmen economy: 'Turkmenistan is not only making money on taxes, it is also making money on its daily oil production – this is a 100 per cent success for it' (interview with Finian O'Sullivan, chief executive officer, 5 November 2004). Relations with the Turkmen authorities were made easier by twice-yearly meetings with the country's vice president, and by the fact that nearly all contact was carried through the so-called 'competent body', which acts as a 'one-stop' link with the government.[51] The company also

---

[51] The competent body was closed down in August 2005, but introduced again in 2007 as the state agency.

considered that the PSA structure was better than a joint venture in terms of reducing possible conflicts or tensions. Nevertheless, both government and investor also benefited from the dramatic rise of the oil price.

As can be seen from the Burren example, an independent oil company's overseas strategy is built on the exploration and development of resources that are unattractive (and in the case of ExxonMobil, unprofitable) to majors. The Turkmen part of the Caspian Sea represents a mature basin with low-cost production, which is appealing for a smaller-scale company. In general it is characterized by modest entry cost; small field size, and possibilities to commercialize 'smaller resources' for local markets. As a result Burren became an attractive company with a simple structure, significant volumes of oil and healthy cash flows to a number of international oil companies in 2007, including ENI of Italy and the Korea National Oil Corporation. On 30 November 2007 Burren agreed to a £1.74 bln ($3.59 bln) takeover from ENI.

The 'acquire and exploit' strategy has been a major method and phenomenon of Burren's growth. As it was illustrated above, major oil companies have been attracted to new mega projects in the Caspian (e.g. Kazakhstan) that diverted funds away from more mature areas, and as we saw from the Burren story assets that no longer fit the portfolios of major oil companies were a great fit for Burren (as an example of an oil independent) because these assets had a large inventory of projects and a large land position. Assets divested by majors provided Burren with production and room to grow. Commenting on the ENI takeover, Finian O'Sullivan said: 'Takeover is a logical conclusion of the life-cycle of any independent company. Burren has been very successful and now reached this point. I think it should be good for the country [Turkmenistan], for the company, for the people' (interview with O'Sullivan, 30 November 2007, London).

There are different opinions with regard to whether or not the ENI deal makes sense for the Italian oil major. As a result of buying Burren, ENI expands its stake in the M'Boundi field in the Republic of Congo and gains access to deposits in Turkmenistan. FitchRatings, for instance, believes that

> Burren Energy's assets, principally located in the Republic of Congo and Turkmenistan, represent an important addition to ENI's reserve base and are a good fit for its geographical diversification. While Turkmenistan is considered to be the perfect entry point to the

rich central Asian market, the assets in the Republic of Congo comple-
ment ENI's latest E&P asset acquisition in the country early this year.'
(Reuters, 4 December 2007)

However, some analysts think that the deal does little 'to vault ENI into
the ranks of the super-majors, as it adds less than 2 per cent to the
group's total annual production' (*Financial Times*, 'ENI and Burren',
December 2007). Whatever the outcome is for ENI, it is clear that the
situation will not be the same for the Burun field. Whether ENI will be
able to continue to maintain this small field size, and create possibilities
to commercialize 'smaller resources' for local markets, time will show. In
any case, the story of Burren, its rise and its end, is a success story in the
history of the creation of independent oil companies as well as in the
history of the oil development in the Caspian Sea region.

Case study 3: KazMunaiGaz (KMG) in Kazakhstan

JSC NC KazMunaiGaz (KMG), the Kazakh national oil company, was
formed in accordance with Presidential Decree N811 of 20.02.2002 by
merging Kazakhoil CJSC and Oil & Gas Transport CJSC with a large network of diverse operations (see Table 4.4). This company is solely owned
by the Kazakhstani government and is a closed joint stock company with
a vertically integrated structure of assets. These assets cover six sectors
and 39 organizations.

JSC NC KMG includes exploration and production, transportation,
oil refining and petrochemical activities, marketing and sales of oil,
gas and oil products, servicing of oil and gas projects as well as performing the role of competent authority in PSA. While KMG exploration
and production (E&P) key assets are mature, and KMG's holdings
in growth projects are limited to minority stakes, KMG E&P has
several subsidiaries (Figure 4.4). In 2005 KMG contributed 7.6 per
cent to Kazakhstani GDP.

The creation of a national oil company is a natural route for producing
governments to follow, even if some industry specialists are very much
against this. It helps 'the producing states to nationalize oil by giving
them the technical and organizational means to take over operations
from the private companies when the time is right' (Marcel, 2005: 29).
Any national oil company, and KMG is no exception, generally espouses
three principal objectives on behalf of their respective governments: to
reduce dependence on multinationals for oil supplies; to provide the
government with an 'inside window' on the industry to enable its
bureaucracy to judge the performance of multinationals within the

Table 4.4 Structure of assets of KMG (six sectors, 39 organizations)

Development and production (9 business structures)	Transportation of oil and gas (5 companies)	Auxiliary profile sector (6 business structures)	Non-profile sector (15 business structures)
Razvedka Dobycha		Kazakh Oil and Gas Institute CJSC (100%)	Atyrau International Airport OJSC (100%)
KazMunaiGaz	KazTransOilJSC (100%)	Kazakhstancaspiishelf OJSC (90%)	KazMunaiGaz-Service LLC (51%)
Zhambai LLC (100%)	KazTransGas JSC (100%)		KSB group OJSC (50%)
Kazakhturkmunai LLC (51%)	cPc-K cJSC (19%)	Kazakhoilkurylys LLC (100%)	Astanaenergoservice OJSC (0.1 1%)
Kazakhoil Aktobe LLC (50%)	cPc-R CJSC (19%)	Tengiz Service LLC (50%)	KazMunaiGaz-Consulting JSC (100%)
Damunai-Daoil JSC (50%)	Kazmorrtransflot JSC (50%)	Kazakhstan Pipeline Ventures LLC (50.1%)	Komakinvest CJSC (10%)
Tenge LLC JV (69%)		Kylysh TP (50%)	KazTransCom JSC (47.2%)
Embavedoil tLC (52.7%)			Euro-Asia Air OJSC (100%)
KazMunaiTengiz JSC (100%)	Marketing and sale (4 business structures)		Kazakhoil-Ukraine CJSC (33.34%)
TengizChevroil LLC JV (20%)			KazMunaiGaz Finance BV (100%)
	KazMunaiGaz Trade House JSC (100%)		Rauan Media Group JSC (73.98%)
	KazRosGas CJSC (50%)		KBTU JSC (100%)
	Kazakhoil-Petrol LLC (100%)		Kazakh Contract Agency JSC (50%)
	Kazakhoil Products LLC (100%)		Unified Centre for Personnel Development (49%)
			AstanaGasService JSC (8.56%)

Source: Petroleum Encyclopedia of Kazakhstan, 2005, Vol. I: 362.

114

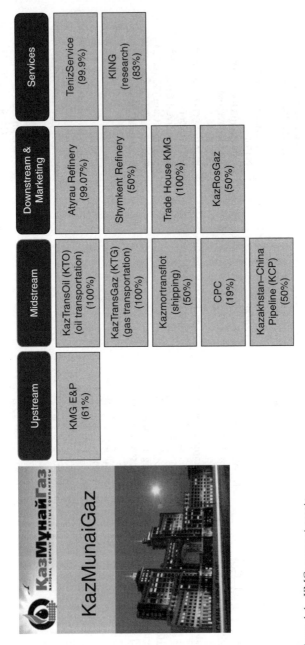

Figure 4.4   KMG: current assets
Source: Courtesy of Julia Nanay, PFC Energy.

country; and to ensure continuity of supply at the crude oil producing, refining and marketing stages at home.

In an interview with me Zhaksybek Kulikeyev, first vice president of KMG, stated that the KMG strategy is based on the priorities of achieving a high level of competitiveness in the Kazakhstani economy and hence development in the energy sector that maximizes the value of national resources, controls or influences local energy sector development, and secures oil and gas supply through domestic development and ownership of international reserves. The company sees its mission as providing maximum benefits for the Republic of Kazakhstan from development of the oil and gas sector (interview with Zhaksybek Kulikeyev, first vice president, KMG, 24 May 2006).

Describing the mission, Uzakbai Karabalin, president, stated that JSC NC KMG, it was the 'provision of maximum benefits for the Republic of Kazakhstan from development of oil-and-gas industry' (Karabalin, 2007: 1).

In February 2002, the government gave authority to KMG to act on its behalf in the PSAs for the Karachaganak and North Caspian projects. This was the first step in increasing state control over the oil and gas sector. Since 2004 it is clear that one of the key objectives of the government has been to increase the participation of KMG. The evidence speaks for itself: at the time of writing, there is a required minimum 50 per cent equity participation in all new contracts (provided in the draft PSA Law and Decree 708). In addition, there is the regulatory oversight by the new authorized state agency (provided in the draft PSA Law and Decree 708). And finally, there is the concept of a 'strategic partner' which was added to the petroleum law. The strategic partner is a foreign or Kazakhstan company selected by KMG to be its partner in a contract which it obtained by direct negotiation. The company selected to be the strategic partner will be responsible for paying the signing bonus and exploration costs unless otherwise provided in the terms of a joint operating agreement.[52]

All this has allowed KMG to become the largest producer in Kazakhstan (240 000 bbl/day), leaving behind such major players as Chevron, PetroKazakhstan, CNPC, etc. Some experts predict that the production could triple by 2015 (see Nanay, 2005).

It is evident that KMG is trying to become, in the long run, a major offshore player. Logically, its production growth substantially relies on offshore fields. The main obstacle, as perceived by industry experts, is a lack

---

[52] The legal aspect of the petroleum regime changes in Kazakhstan was kindly provided by the legal firm Denton Wilde Sapte.

of technology, funds and offshore experience. These should be resolved through partnerships with international oil, gas and service companies. However, across the resource-rich countries there is a concern that independent oil companies (IOCs) do not care about the long-term prosperity of their countries of operation, but more about short-run profits. This creates an obstacle to NOC–IOC partnerships (Marcel, 2005). There is always an interface of conflicts where government and investor accountabilities overlap.

Among industry experts there is a certain apprehension as to whether KMG will in fact become a fully commercial company, or whether it will remain a state monopoly and an arm of the government in the oil and gas sector, with a risk of becoming the only serious cash source for the government. There are grounds for such worries. Taking into account a long history of state firm behaviour before transition, reliance of on government subsidies and management is understandable. Even in the transition period the desire to enjoy a soft budget constraint regime might still be high. However, 'in transition economies there is a close causal relationship between healthy development of the private sector, hardening of the budget constraint' (Kornai, 2003: 19). Such an environment will, it is hoped, boost a competitive environment in the oil and gas sector, and make a positive impact on KMG's development. The presence in Kazakhstan of oil majors and other international oil companies, possible diversification of its asset base outside of Kazakhstan and implementation of ISO international standards[53] should help KMG to establish itself as a competitive and commercial identity.

Discussing possible routes to diversification, the president of the company, Uzakbai Karabalin, remarked that the company sees at least three dimensions to this challenge: the development of a resource base and acquisition of new assets; output of products with high added value; and development of the infrastructure and directions of oil and gas transportation, (Karabalin, 2006).

The first dimension concerns the development of a resource base and acquisition of new assets. In terms of offshore projects, to date KMG owns 8.33 per cent of the North Caspian project.[54] As mentioned earlier, in any future development of new Kazakhstani fields KMG will own not less than 50 per cent in PSA. Current onshore projects of KMG include:

---

[53] To date KMG has already received certificates of conformance of JSC NC KMG with the requirements of international standards ISO 9001, ISO 14001 and specification OHSAS 18001.

[54] Recoverable reserves of the North Caspian project are appraised as 16.13 bln bbl.

Tengiz–KMG possesses 20% in TCO, Karachaganak–KMG is the competent authority. In 2005 KMG had acquired 33 per cent of the shares of PetroKazakhstan Inc.[55] In July 2006 RWE Dea AG, the German gas and oil exploration and production company, had sold its 25 per cent stake in the KazGerMunai joint venture (KGM) in Kazakhstan to KMG. In late 2006, China's CITIC agreed to sell half of Nation's Energy to KMG in order to secure the government's approval for its takeover of the Canadian company. KGM has been producing crude from the Kazakh oilfield Akshabulak[56] in central Kazakhstan since the end of 1998. Other partners in the joint venture most recently were Petro-Kazakhstan (a subsidiary of the China National Petroleum Corporation) with a 50 per cent stake, EEG Erdgas-Erdöl GmbH (a subsidiary of Gaz de France) with 17.5 per cent, as well as the World Bank Group (7.5 per cent). EEG Erdgas-Erdöl GmbH and the World Bank Group have also sold their shares.

At the time of writing, KMG is trying to expand its geography of acquisition as well as including in its expansion strategy a retail component. In 2006 KMG acquired the assets of Tbilgazi JSC (Georgia),[57] which includes low- and middle-pressure gas pipelines with a total length of 1940 km. On the retail front the company is pursuing an expansion of a network of petrol stations. In 2006 KMG had 52 petrol stations with a capacity of 0.7 mln tonnes;[58] however by 2010 the company plans to expand the petrol station network by 500 with capacity of 1.9 mln tonnes, which will represents 27 per cent of overall petrol stations' capacities in the country.

Thus, with regard to the resources dimension, KMG has a significant advantage in the offshore area. Potential reserves in the Caspian offshore region are providing KMG with an opportunity to become a world-class firm. However, current lack of technology and management capacity could prevent the company from achieving its strategic goal of becoming an independent offshore player or operator. Other than Tengiz and Karachaganak, onshore producing fields have limited benefits.

The second dimension concerns the output of products with high added value. Here, KMG is conducting an upgrade of Atyrau Refinery (see Table 4.5). The company has 86.49 per cent of assets of this refinery. In addition, KMG is involved in the following petrochemical projects:

---

[55] The reserves are 521.16 mln bbl. Annual production volume is 1.06 mln bbl.
[56] The reserves of the fields are estimated as 178.12 mln bbl. Annual production may reach 16.13 mln bbl of oil.
[57] Supplier of gas for the consumers of Tbilisi city.
[58] This is 11.9 per cent of total petrol station capacity in the country.

Table 4.5 Main indicators of Atyrau Refinery functioning

Indicators	Before reconstruction	After reconstruction
Oil refining depth, %	57.00	82.00
Increase in production of gasoline, thousand tons per year	326.00	699.00
Production of diesel fuel, thousand tons	1005.90	1024.00
Production of aviation fuel, thousand tons	43.01	87.00
Reduction of residual fuel production, thousand tons per year	1426.00	399.00
Production of vacuum gas oil, thousand tons	0.00	657.50
Production of liquified gas, thousand tons	48.00	86.00
Production of electrode coke, thousand tons	43.95	70.20

Source: Karabalin (2006).

development of petrochemical complex in the Atyrau region (US$4 bln), benzol production project at the Atyrau Refinery (US$250 mln) and, finally, manufacture of road bitumen at the Aktau Plastics Factory (US$50 mln).

The third dimension concerns infrastructure, and directions of oil and gas transportation. Here, there are number of projects where KMG is attempting to find its own niche: (1) supporting the base of oil offshore operations in Bautino: CAPEX is US$22.8 mln, including the first stage of US$14.5 mln; (2) disposal site for toxic industrial wastes with a plant for recovery of oil effluents: CAPEX is US$1.9 mln, including the startup of US$1.2 mln; (3) sea-craft fuelling station: CAPEX is US$30 mln. KMG was also involved in the construction of a new runway at the Atyrau International Airport,[59] which has a guaranteed life without restoration and routine maintenance of 20 years due to the use of the state-of-the-art composite and synthetic materials. The company is engaged in the developing of pipeline networks (see Table 4.6); KMG's transportation monopoly helps with route diversification.

As can be seen from Table 4.6, the oil pipeline connection from Caspian to China and the Aktau–Baku–Tbilisi–Ceyhan pipeline give KMG strengths in the market. In addition, KMG has developed an investment programme for modernization of the Central Asia–Centre (CAC) gas system; this is an attempt by the company to become regional gas

---

[59] This is the highest-specification runway in the Republic with a length of 3000 m, width of 45 m, and area of artificial pavements 285 820 m^2.

Table 4.6 KMG oil transportation, present and future

Present	Future
1 Atyrau–Samara	3a Kenkiyak–Kumkol
1a Baltic pipeline system	4 Aktau–Baku–Tbilisi–Ceyhan
1b Druzhba	4a Iskene–Kuryk
1c To Odessa	5 Odessa–Brody–Plock
2 CPC	*Projected oil pipelines bypassing the Turkish Straits:*
3 Atasu–Alashankou (Kazakhstan–China)	6.1 Burgas–Alexandropolis
Also by sea from Aktau	6.2 Constansa–Triest
To Baku and further to Batumi (railroad)	6.3 Samsun–Ceyhan
– to Neka (Iran)-swaps	6.4 Kiikoy–Ibrikbaba
– to Makhachkala and further by Makhachkala–Novorossiysk oil pipeline	6.5 Burgas–Vlore

Source: KMG.

hub. This reconstruction programme provides a gradual increase in the gas pipeline capacity from 1.94 to 3.53 tcf.

As illustrated above, the company is trying several options to develop and diversify its business activities. Moreover, its role and goals could be said to be still evolving. In some ways it is very much a Kazakh company with a Soviet legacy and mentality. While interviewing one of the heads of KMG's subsidiaries I was challenged by the question: 'Who gave you the responsibility to write such a book'. When I answered that it was simply research and not a 'state order', the interview became very shallow with no information given away. In other respects the management team of KMG in Astana is quite dynamic and competent, giving hope for further positive changes in the years ahead.

Because KMG's talent pool is still limited, a logical suggestion would be involvement of international oil companies in order to help this young company to develop managerial skills. However, IOCs are in direct competition with KMG, and therefore in practice such a suggestion might not be workable. Meetings with different levels of KMG's employees yield the impression that KMG's desire to be treated on an equal basis among IOCs is very high (interviews conducted in November 2005 and May 2006). The only way to achieve this will be through joint projects and developing the ability to absorb the expertise of other partners in such projects.

Taking into account the fact that the future of Kazakhstani oil is offshore, the biggest challenge for KMG is to develop engineering expertise, financing and management skills needed in this sector. KMG's experience offshore is non-existent, and managing offshore projects is not an easy task. Petroleum industry history could name many lessons to this effect, including Statoil (Norway), Petrobras (Brazil) and Petronas (Malaysia).

Is KMG's profile similar to that of other NOCs? There are several factors that suggest exploring such a parallel. Starting from relatively large oil reserves and growing production, we could compare KMG with Aramco (Saudi Arabia). As was already mentioned, offshore potential leads to a comparison with such 'super-titans' as Petronas, Petrobras and Statoil. There are lessons to be learnt from all these benchmark companies (see Box 4.2).

Box 4.2   Lessons from the Petrobras experience

Petróleo Brasileiro S.A. (Petrobras) is one of the most powerful examples of a national oil company that has managed to develop expertise and become a competitor to the likes of BP, Royal Dutch Shell, ExxonMobil and Chevron around the world. Today Petrobras is a world-recognized industry leader in the development of deepwater technology.[60] What are the ingredients of the company's success that could be taken into consideration by new arrivals SOCAR and KazMunaiGaz? To start with, Petrobras has substantial proved hydrocarbon reserves and increasing upstream output. In addition, the company has a unique recognized leadership in offshore exploration and production.

Right from the beginning Petrobras based its strategy on investing in the development of the company's personnel (today Petrobras even has its own university – Petrobras University with campuses in São Paulo, Rio de Janeiro, and Salvador, Bahia – a teaching institution established by the Brazilian oil company to train its employees) as well as in relations with the subcontractors. José Sergio Gabrielli, CEO of Petrobras, thinks that the strength of the company is in its very integrated structure. 'My advice to the Caspian national oil companies would be to build as much as they can vertically integrated company. That helps a lot, and Petrobras' experience proved it' (interview with the author, 19 June 2007, London).

---

[60] Brazil has 92 per cent of its oil proven reserves offshore as well as 78 per cent its production.

KazMunaiGaz and SOCAR should take into account the main principles of building a company's strategies from Petrobras's experience. In the initial period (1953–1995) Petrobras had a monopoly over the exploration, production, refining and transportation of crude oil and oil products in Brazil. This has clear analogies with the pattern currently emerging with regard to the positions of KazMunaiGaz and SOCAR in the Caspian. However, since 1995 the Brazilian government has introduced market reforms and a constitutional amendment changed Petrobras's monopolistic status.

Should we blame Caspian governments who are attempting to do almost the opposite, giving to their NOCs almost exclusive rights with regard to all aspects of the domestic oil and gas industry? As we can see from Brazil's experience, it took almost 43 years for the government to realize that a regulatory framework which would enable competition in the hydrocarbon sector would be more beneficial to the country, or perhaps it was an inevitable period of economic nationalism in the infant national oil and gas industry. 'Political feelings regarding the development of the nation's oil resources are deeply entrenched in the societies of developing countries' (Marcel, 2005: 43). This is not just a rhetorical statement; it reflects the reality that the Caspian governments are facing at this point in time, and it would be counterproductive just to put economic arguments that monopoly is bad for overall development. However, one argument could be highlighted: both KazMunaiGaz and SOCAR desire to become internationally important players.

Petrobras is continuing to pursue market-oriented reforms, which are reflected in the company's mid-term objectives, namely expansion of the company's production and reserves, upgrading downstream facilities, and growing further internationally. The core of the company's corporate strategy is based on three main principles: growth, profitability, and social and environmental responsibility. The company is focused on consolidating and increasing its competitive advantages in the Brazilian and South American oil and oil products markets; developing and leading the Brazilian natural gas market and performing in an integrated manner in the gas and power market in South America; selectively expanding interest in the petrochemical market; etc.

In 2006, Petrobras announced its 2007–2011 business plan, which reflects new projects (five new projects for 2007 with total additional capacity of 590 000 bbl/day and seven new projects in 2008–2011 with total capacity of 1 120 000 bbl/day) to increase production and refining both domestically (in Brazil) and internationally. The plans are to invest US$87.7 bln through 2011, an increase of US$34.7 bln (66 per cent) over the comparable period under the previous plan. Approximately US$49 bln (56 per cent of the total), up from US$31 bln (59 per cent), has been allocated to exploration and production (E&P) activities, representing a slight shift in allocation percentage toward downstream activities (US$23.1 bln). All this could be positively viewed for the long-term credit quality of the company.

In recent years the company has been blessed with a favourable international product price environment, as well as with successful implementation of corporate and industry restructuring. Today we can see the positive effects of the reforms and corporate governance. 'At the present time we have much more transparent financial standards and dominant domestic market shares' (interview with José Sergio Gabrielli, 19 June 2007, London). Gabrielli thinks that the free float of shares was a guarantee of the company's high degree of freedom from the government. 'We have never been a cash cow of the government. The government realised that the commercial success of Petrobras will be a success of the whole Brazil.' Without doubt, the company has a dominant domestic market position, however; Petrobras also benefited from material international operations (the company operates in 26 countries of the world) and since 2005 has a net export position. All this strongly supports the generation of foreign currency cash flow.

Obviously there are some unavoidable weaknesses which Petrobras has recognized and is trying to alleviate. Like any oil company, Petrobras is affected by fluctuations in international commodity prices; this vulnerability is unavoidable and could only be managed by the reduction of operational costs to a certain extent. The company is also exposed to local political interference and currency risk. The current increase in costs of related services and equipment in the productive chain, and a stronger local currency, have also had an impact on capital spending.

Assessing the initial impact of the market-orientated reforms, it is already possible to see the positive credit effect which was given by FitchRatings in 2006: the company moved from a BB rating to BB+, as well as improvements in corporate governance, the desire of the management of the company to increase financial transparency, and corporate reorganization.

The overall lesson for the NOCs in the Caspian region from Petrobras would be to seek to establish themselves as recognized international companies, participating in all facets of the value-added chain, by broadening their international portfolio and by thus reducing the their operational risk, providing more opportunity for generation of hard currency and, through this, being in the position to reduce the cost of capital.

One lesson, in particular, deserves to be remembered: the degree of companies' autonomy from the state. The path followed by all these companies could be considered as a potential model for KMG. As Figure 4.5 suggests, all of them have a greater autonomy from their respective states. Although, for example, Statoil was originally created on the assumption that it would pursue the political agenda of the Norwegian government in its early stages of developing state oil industry, nevertheless over the years Statoil gained its freedom and became a fully commercialized

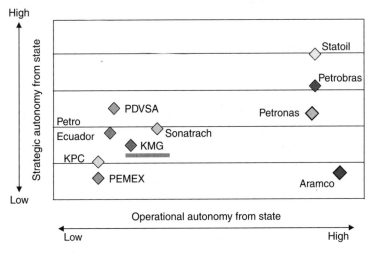

Figure 4.5   Comparison of NOCs' degrees of autonomy from the state
Source: Courtesy of Julia Nanay, PFC Energy.

company in which the BP–Statoil alliance played a significant role.[61] That gives reason to hope that one day KMG will become a strong international player. Yet KMG remains in its infant period: its potential is emerging more strongly every year, but it still has a very long way to go in redefining itself and finding that 'golden middle' place – a suitable balance in its relationship with the Kazakhstani state.

In his interview with me, CEO of Petrobras José Sergio Gabrielli said,

> There is no country in the world where the hydrocarbon policies are free to the market. Every government is trying to keep control on strategic energy issues. However, the fact that the NOCs are the main providers for the countries' energy market pushes both parties (governments and companies) to have a convergence of the interests. (Interview with José Sergio Gabrielli, 19 June 2007, London)

These considerations make clear why we must now turn to explore the other side of this partnership: the role of the state as it seeks to develop its relationship with the hydrocarbon sector across a multiplicity of linkages that now include ownership as well as regulation.

At the time of writing, KMG is making steady progress in terms of increasing its liquids production. 'KazMunaigaz, seeking a bigger role in the giant Kashagan oil development in the Caspian Sea, reported a surge in profits and its production division . . ., underscoring its determination to emerge as champion on the central Asian republic's oil industry' (Gorst, 2007a). For KMG, one constraint on its growth is the ability to create efficient management structures within the company in order to keep pace with the demands of producing and handling large volumes of oil. In order for KMG to reach the efficiency of Statoil, Petronas or Petrobras national oil companies, it must compete and cooperate domestically with IOCs.

KMG is clearly emerging with a good prospects of developing a bargaining position to aim for upstream and gas activities in Russia, Turkmenistan, Iran and Iraq.

Strategic alliances with Russian oil companies may be used by KMG for joint activities in Kazakhstan as well as for partnering in Russian projects. KMG expects that a joint venture with Russian Gazprom based on the

---

[61] BP–Statoil alliance: in the early 1990s the senior management of BP and Statoil entered into a formal arrangement whereby they would jointly develop new global investments in which both parties would benefit from their mutual but different strengths.

Orenburg gas-processing plant will start to operate shortly. In October 2006 the agreement was signed between the government of the Republic of Kazakhstan and the government of the Russian Federation in order to create a joint venture between JSC NC 'KMG' and OJSC 'Gazprom'. Clearly this venture could be a very interesting development in the future.

There is no doubt that the NOCs, in both Kazakhstan and Azerbaijan, can facilitate achieving benefits for their societies, which will include technology transfer, together with the development of human resources (human capital). They also could result in a redistribution of income from other players to the state. There is a danger that political interventions in the energy market through the NOCs could leave everyone worse off than they could be otherwise. Whether or not that is unavoidable is an open question.

Experience shows that there is a need to design effective frameworks and institutions that will help channel productively the interaction the 'power of international capital', on the one hand, and the 'power of the state', on the other. NOCs have a role to play in this. However, in my view, there is a strong tendency in the Caspian region for such companies to be – rather than commercial entities – a bureaucratic arm of the government that manages the state hydrocarbon monopoly and possibly performs, in addition, a regulatory role.

4.4   New directions in governance

In order for hydrocarbon activities to flourish in the Caspian region, the challenge for governance is very specific. Governments need to find modalities that secure their legitimate national interests but offer a sufficiently predictable and supportive operating environment for companies to engage in the major risks of exploration and development. But there is a corollary: companies, on their side, need to engage actively in a dialogue to help arrive at such a governance framework, which balances legitimate interests. They also need to work in ways that help deliver the common goals. In this sense, effective governance is a two-way street.

Overall, it is clear that there is a long way still to go for the companies establishing business in the Caspian region and for the host governments. An equilibrium should be found between the interests of both sides to take into account both parties. When the gap is very wide, as it has become with current oil prices, it is difficult to agree where the equilibrium should be – especially when both sides believe that they have right on their side (the territory is national and the company has a contract). The successful project must be based on proven reserves

and partners' agreement. This includes agreement on competitive financing and a sufficient level of local content (which we shall tackle in more
detail in Chapter 5). That should ultimately bring high economic yields,
and improvement of local infrastructure construction.

In order to ensure continuing investment, government attitudes
towards NOCs, IOCs and foreign direct investors in other sectors has
been evolving in the direction of improved corporate governance. As we
can see from the case study of KMG discussed above, the migration
towards internationally accepted financial reporting and management
standards is gradually forcing the Caspian NOCs to adopt better managerial and production practices. With regard to IOCs, governmental perceptions are gradually changing, because the approach and role of companies
have been transforming throughout the last decade in the Caspian region.
This has implied a pragmatic rebalancing of the attention paid to IOC
interests which belies the simplistic views that they have either an over-
whelming influence or no influence at all in the formation of government
policies throughout the region.[62] And corporate governance approaches
towards other direct investors may also have begun to shift.

The most prominent example of a shift in the way investor interests are
channelled and perceived is in Kazakhstan. A key development was the
creation in June 1998 of the Foreign Investors' Council (FIC) chaired by
the president of the republic. The main aim of FIC is 'to provide direct dialogue between the Republic of Kazakhstan and investors in order to efficiently address the key issues related to investment activities' (http://
www.fic.kz). The list of representatives from the government side is very
impressive: the prime minister, the chairman of the National Bank, the
Minister of Foreign Affairs, the chairman of the Investment Committee
and the chairman of the Inter-departmental Commission on Consideration of Foreign Investors' Appeals. In addition, FIC includes CEOs and
senior executives from leading foreign companies operating in Kazakhstan.

The FIC has four working groups, whose activities are directed to fulfil
the major objectives of the FIC.[63] These are

> to submit to the President of the Republic of Kazakhstan for his
> consideration proposals to improve the laws regulating investment
> activities, proposals on issues related to the implementation of invest-
> ment programs and projects; to draft recommendations for the

---

[62] My interviews with various industry specialists and some governmental
officials.

[63] Legislation, taxation, operation and image enhancement.

improvement of the investment climate as well as strategy to attract foreign investments and to develop proposals on the integration of the country's economy into global economic processes. (http://www.fic.kz)

The idea of bringing together representatives of the Kazakhstani government and the international business community with the aim to discuss and solve critical issues affecting the investment and business climate in Kazakhstan is very prominent and unique in the Caspian region. Although the aims and objectives of the Council are praiseworthy, it has yet to live up fully to these goals. One criticism that I encountered during interviews with industry specialists (including present members of the FIC) is that very often this forum is 'just a place to see the President and a platform for public relations for the companies rather than a functional establishment'. Nevertheless it is important that such a forum does exist, and over the past decade it has signalled and symbolized a certain commitment to work with investors. To date none of the other states has a similar forum, although they are showing attention and support in different ways.

In addition to the FIC, there is the Kazakhstan Petroleum Association (KPA), which was registered in the Amsterdam Chamber of Commerce and Industry on 9 December 1997. To date it unites 62 companies from 20 countries that are engaged in the development of Kazakhstani hydrocarbons as well as in its service sector. The KPA pursues the following objectives:

- To facilitate exploration and production activity in the petroleum industry in Kazakhstan.
- To share non-proprietary information between member companies and the Government with the view to advance investment and the operating climate for the industry in Kazakhstan.
- To monitor legislative developments affecting oil and gas industry, and coordinate industry efforts to comment on draft laws.
- To communicate industry viewpoints on issues important for KPA. (KPA, 2006: 10)

KPA holds regular meetings of the general membership in Almaty. I had the privilege of participating in one of them and observing its work.[64] The agenda was clearly defined. The chairman (Sagandyk Nuraliev) opened the meeting with a briefing, giving an overview of the important energy

[64] The meeting took place on 19 May 2006.

issues, and posing some routine administrative questions. Then the meeting followed the agenda. A first impression was the high percentage of representatives of the companies who are Kazakhstani citizens. This could be viewed as a very positive step, because such forums represent a platform for mastering inter-company communication. Developing such skills among Kazakh nationals has paramount importance in the longer term.

However, the main criticism of the current situation is related to the fact that the Kazakhstani participants are very quiet, and it is possible to see a clear contrast between expatriates representing companies and their Kazakh counterparts. It would be wrong to blame any participating side of the meeting in this situation. One contributing factor may be related to the level of participation on the Kazakhstani side and specifically the extent to which representatives feel authorized to express official positions or indicate flexibility in changing them. From various interviews which I conducted with both foreign and local nationals in the Caspian region one conclusion could be drawn. Sometimes the dominance of foreign expertise, and the way of conducting business, is putting the locals off initiatives and constraining their ability to articulate (possibly alternative) points of view. Still, the managers of the companies (especially foreign and JSV), should pay attention and attempt to prepare their Kazakhstani colleagues to act as real voices for their respective companies. The management of companies very often does not pay attention to these weaknesses. This explains why a large majority of the interviewees (expatriate managers) firmly answered in the negative questions about the possibility of substituting the foreign part of company's top management by the locals in 10–12 years' time. Commenting on this, Terry Adams stated that 'its practice against the interest of both government and foreign investor should be excised and should be replaced by effective succession planning.' (interview with Terry Adams, founding president, AIOC, 26 August 2007, Reading)

In Azerbaijan, the situation in government–company relations in the hydrocarbon sector is currently characterized by a high degree of legal and fiscal stability. Acreage has been abandoned or transferred to second-division players. However, less progress has been made so far in the non-oil sector and on institutional issues. For example, in Azerbaijan foreign investment plays major role in financing the development of much of the country's industrial sector, in particular the oil- and gas-related industries. A number of laws have helped to create a sound framework, e.g. 'the 1992 Law on Foreign Investment provided many basic guarantees to foreign investors, including non discriminatory treatment, the repatriation of profits, guarantees against expropriation, and dispute settlement. The Privatization Law passed in 1995 allowed foreign investors to acquire shares in state companies and purchase real estate jointly' (*Encyclopedia of the Nations: Asia and Oceania* – www.nationsency-clopedia.com/Asia- and Oceania/Azerbaijan.html).

Turkmenistan, meanwhile, is currently characterized by a tolerable investment climate, but this is eclipsed by political governance issues. Some progress has been made by independents and regional players. Nonetheless, the government is continuing 'to play a highly interventionist role in the economy' (Gleason, 2002: 9), and the competent body for use of hydrocarbon resources is directly coordinating governmental relations with the companies.[65] There are no similar establishments to FIC or KPA.

4.5   The business environment

The issue of corporate governance in the hydrocarbon industry cannot be viewed in isolation. Governments' concern to achieve linkages between foreign-owned industry and local suppliers, and to see hydrocarbon development as one part of a broader development strategy, inevitably directs attention to the case for enhancing the overall setting for business. Moreover, as this re-evaluation takes place, the experience that governments have gained in the hydrocarbon sector in dealing with foreign investors, and in fostering the post-transition domestic private sector, can be seen as a learning process that should shape policies towards the general business environment.

First, the business environment will be an important influence on the willingness of foreign companies to set up or expand operations – including but not limited to the specific contractual framework surrounding the hydrocarbon industry. Second, the business environment will be crucial for the broader objective of the state, which is to see, over time, some 'trickle-down' and multiplied effects from the oil industry to the rest of the economy through market-driven routes – including to some degree the 'local-content' issues that are the specific focus of Chapter 5.

The difference between first- and second-generation waves of post-Soviet investment into the region, in the hydrocarbon sector and beyond, will thus increasingly reflect the ability of the host countries to accommodate investors' requirements in a way that balances these with legitimate state interests. In this respect, as Caspian economies develop and tap

[65] For more information, see details in the discussion of the Burren Energy Case (case study 2 in this chapter).

international expertise and capital, the global investment market is becoming more sophisticated. Far greater attention is focused today on business climate and competitiveness indicators, and on investment ratings by agencies such as Fitch, Moody's, and Standard & Poors.

Such ratings allow potential foreign investors to assess opportunities and risks via qualitative and quantitative analysis, indicating the hospitality of the climate to business; governments' ability to service debt in a timely manner; and the risk factors that could limit the ability to freely transfer profits and interest abroad. They also provide ample scope to make comparisons across countries and industry sectors. The decision by the Kazakhstani government to focus on enhancing its 'Davos' gradings in terms of international competitiveness is a litmus test of this trend.

Among the key factors that could affect the decision of the foreign investors with regard to the new opportunities for their investors are: economic stability (contractual and non-contractual income streams, fixed and variable costs, market, relative position in market, past, present and future); risk allocation (basic principle 'risks should either be insured or allocated fairly to those parties in a transaction best able to manage them', risk–reward balance, back-to-back contractual structures – ideal, vertical integration – control of the value chain, clear and stable independent regulatory framework); legal environment (stable and predictable, non-arbitrary decision record, clear and due process, independent judiciary (not state-influenced), enforceability, arbitration); strategic importance of assets (to state; to locale; to business expansion plans); synergies and stable favourable fiscal regime.

Clearly, perceptions of the Caspian Sea region by the foreign companies have been changing since the first decade of transition. New accents characterizing the second investment generation have emerged, related to investment promotion through stability of macroeconomic policy, identification of the national players versus foreign companies, and introduction of local content. Even in the oil and gas sector the emphasis has been a shift towards technology and services development. From the various interviews with investors I concluded that although the perceived risk level in the Caspian region at the time of writing remains high, there is a real sign of improvement overall compared with the beginning of the 1990s.

To evaluate where countries stand now in terms of investment conditions, it is useful to consider first the traditional investment ratings by agencies concerned with sovereign and corporate risk, and then broader indicators of the business environment.

In terms of international investment ratings, assessments are available for most Caspian region countries (Table 4.7). All the countries started from the BB level, and most have advanced significantly. However, as can be seen from the table, the picture is not uniform, with Turkmenistan withdrawing rating by the agencies due to the lack of interest in cooperation from the government side.

Transparency International, Heritage Fund and WB Cost of Doing Business also provide rough guides on the situation in the countries, and are commonly used.

In terms of more broadly based assessments of competitiveness and the business setting, the Caspian economies have a strong potential but a fragile business environment. Host governments should realize new high legal and technical demands from the international business community. In addition, the question of local content is becoming highly debatable in the light of the desire by some of the Caspian states to become members of the WTO. The non-discrimination principle of the WTO could be an obstacle in pursuing the local content programme. That brings our discussion to the questions of a 'level playing field' and governance standards. This is a very sensitive and delicate area between local content and international standards. 'This concept was a major issue in Baku at the beginning of joint operations where it was seen as criticism of local practices. Issue was resolved once it was understood by the SOCAR that this meant insurable standards based on either API or GOST'[66] (interview with Terry Adams, founding president, AIOC, 26 August 2007, Reading).

The host governments should balance their approach, viewing local content versus international skills, employing criteria of track record, equipment, and quality and safety standards. The area of public and private governance issues is still rudimentary in the Caspian region.

According to the World Bank investment surveys, which were conducted in Kazakhstan (2002) and Azerbaijan (2002), such impediments as economic and regulatory policy uncertainty, and macroeconomic instability and corruption were not major obstacles for the business environment in these countries (see Table 4.8), which no doubt gave a positive spin to further development of businesses (second generation of investments) in these regions.

As was discussed in Chapter 1, the prime aim of the second transition decade for the countries of the Caspian region should be not just the

---

[66] API and GOST are regulatorary standards by official government institutes in the USA and the USSR.

Table 4.7 Sovereign rating history

| Country | Date | Foreign currency rating | | Outlook/watch | Last updated: 23 February 2007; local currency rating |
		long-term	short-term		long-term
Fitchratings sovereign rating history					
Azerbaijan	5 Feb 2007	BB+	B	stable	BB+
Azerbaijan	22 Nov 2004	BB	B	stable	BB
Azerbaijan	25 Jul 2002	BB-	B	positive	BB-
Azerbaijan	20 Jul 2001	BB-	B	stable	BB-
Azerbaijan	21 Sep 2000	B+	B	positive	BB-
Azerbaijan	3 Jul 2000	B+	B	-	BB-
Kazakhstan	20 Dec 2005	BBB	F3	positive	BBB+
Kazakhstan	27 Oct 2004	BBB-	F3	stable	BBB
Kazakhstan	19 Nov 2003	BB+	B	positive	BBB-
Kazakhstan	11 Oct 2002	BB+	B	stable	BBB-
Kazakhstan	12 Jul 2001	BB	B	stable	BB+
Kazakhstan	21 Sep 2000	BB-	B	stable	BB
Kazakhstan	5 May 2000	BB-	B	stable	BB
Kazakhstan	15 Feb 1999	BB-	B	-	BBB-
Kazakhstan	27 Jan 1998	BB	B	-	BBB-
Kazakhstan	5 Nov 1996	BB-	B	-	-
Turkmenistan	25 Feb 2005	Withdrawn	Withdrawn	-	-
Turkmenistan	18 May 2001	CCC-	C	Withdrawn	-
Turkmenistan	21 Sep 2000	B-	B	stable	-
Turkmenistan	29 Jan 1999	B-	B	-	-
Turkmenistan	7 Jan 1998	B	B	-	-

S&P Sovereign Rating History

Country	Date				
Kazakhstan	2 Nov 2006	BBB	A2	stable	BBB+
Kazakhstan	13 Jun 2006	BBB−	A3	positive	BBB
Kazakhstan	20 May 2004	BBB−	A3	stable	BBB
Kazakhstan	28 May 2003	BB+	B	stable	BBB−
Kazakhstan	18 May 2001	BB	B	stable	BB+
Kazakhstan	28 Jul 2000	BB−	B	stable	BB
Kazakhstan	22 Dec 1999	B+	B	stable	BB−
Kazakhstan	16 Sep 1998	B+	B	negative	BB−
Kazakhstan	5 Nov 1996	BB−	B	stable	BB+
Kazakhstan	5 Nov 1996	BB−	B	stable	BB+

Moody's Sovereign Rating History

Country	Date				
Azerbaijan	14 Sep 2006	Baa1	P2	stable	Ba1
Kazakhstan	9 Jun 2006	Baa2	P1	stable	Baa1
Kazakhstan	3 May 2006	Baa3	P2	Review of upgrade	Baa1
Kazakhstan	13 Jul 2004	Baa3	P3	positive	Baa1
Kazakhstan	19 Sep 2002	Baa3	P3	stable	Baa1
Kazakhstan	18 Jun 2001	Ba2	NP	positive	Ba1
Kazakhstan	7 Mar 2001	B1	NP	Review for upgrade	B1
Kazakhstan	4 May 2000	B1	NP	positive	B1
Kazakhstan	25 Jun 1999	B1	NP	stable	B1
Kazakhstan	18 Feb 1999	B1	NP	stable	–
Kazakhstan	1 Oct 1998	Ba3	NP	Review for downgrade	–
Kazakhstan	11 Nov 1996	Ba3	NP	stable	–
Turkmenistan	20 Jul 1999	B2	NP	stable	B2
Turkmenistan	4 Dec 1997	B2	NP	stable	–

Source: Courtesy FitchRatings.

Table 4.8 Business constraints in Kazakhstan and Azerbaijan (2002)

Value	Business constraints (in %)							
	Economic & regulatory policy uncertainty		Legal system/ conflict resolution		Macroeconomic instability (inflation exchange rate)		Corruption	
	Kazakhstan	Azerbaijan	Kazakhstan	Azerbaijan	Kazakhstan	Azerbaijan	Kazakhstan	Azerbaijan
No obstacle	28.81	62	55.36	86.13	35.1	59.73	48.71	50.34
Minor obstacle	34.98	19.33	26.34	7.3	23.67	21.48	17.67	12.08
Moderate obstacle	17.7	12	14.29	4.38	24.08	14.09	19.4	18.12
Major obstacle	18.52	6.67	4.02	2.19	17.14	4.7	14.22	19.46

Source: World Bank Database: http://iresearch.worldbank.org/ics/frontcontroller/registration; http://iresearch.worldbank.org/ics/frontcontroller/mainFrame.htm.

expansion of the energy sector, but its integration in an effective development strategy. But sustainable development of the local economy can be achieved only with the full support of the government. The business environment needs to foster local energy and non-energy-based companies, which participate in projects through the complete supply chain, and whose operations ultimately go beyond the local market to become global in scale and scope. The ideal goal would include a technology hub that creates a setting for innovation and entrepreneurship. Among other factors, strong educational institutions will be key to developing the highly skilled and competent local personnel needed for this. The Caspian economies could thus become a regional energy and finance centre, with an adequate capital market. To achieve such goals, the energy sector will remain key – its influence radiating by enhancing competitiveness of sub-sectors, including supplies and services. In setting such a strategy in motion, the issue of local content deserves specific consideration.

5
Developing Local Content

5.1 Strategic goals and constraints

The broad shift in the region towards more assertive market regulation was discussed in Chapter 4, which highlighted the common concern of host governments to improve the capabilities of local companies involved in supply and services. This concept of local content is not a new one. It emerged in the USA in the 1900s, and in the 1920s it spread to UK industry.

In general, by 'local content' in the oil and gas industry, policy-makers understand value-added activities in which local businesses compete for subcontracts or service contracts in the industry, as well as broader 'social' participation by the foreign investors. In other words, 'local content' could be defined as the amount of local or indigenous inputs employed or utilized in carrying out all the operations of exploration, development and production of oil and gas.[67] Here, one could include expertise, in terms of human resources, technology, equipment and materials; finance, in terms of the availability of capital and investment funds; and facilities and infrastructure. Overall, local content builds up the locally owned and adapted knowledge of a community. It is thus an expression of a community's capacity to appropriate knowledge, and technical and managerial skills, from external sources, and to transmit this to others in the locality and the broader economy.

A legitimate question is why governments should be concerned to develop local content in the host country. There are several strong arguments which could be presented in favour of this. For companies, local content potentially provides a lower-cost engineering resource, and

---

[67] 'Value creation in the country' is the definition used in Norway and the UK.

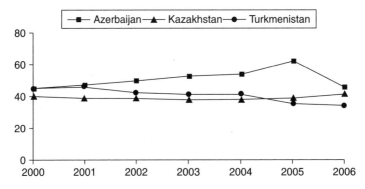

Figure 5.1   Industry, value-added, % of GDP
Source: World Bank national accounts data, and OECD National Accounts data files.

also facilitates relationship-building with host governments and national oil companies. For host countries, it broadens the knowledge base of local capabilities, customs and regulations. In the Caspian region, it has become a fact of life for operators, and engineering and construction (E&C) contractors.

This priority is certainly understandable. The first and foremost feature of all Caspian economies is a high level of dependence on the energy sector (see Chapter 1 and Kalyuzhnova, 2001). Figure 5.1 shows that industry as a share of GDP has remained at almost the same level in all Caspian economies throughout the years of oil price recovery.

The data for Azerbaijan could be misleading because they also include figures for oil-related industries. More accurate data would be desirable, such as for manufacturing, but available sources do not allow such a distinction.

Based on the experience of the other resource-rich countries, it is evident that governments can seek to maximize value from the hydrocarbon sector through two main routes. The first lies in fiscal instruments: government royalties, taxation policies and expenditures. The second embraces all other, non-fiscal, instruments, which include local content and local participation. The latter may, of course, develop fairly naturally, without a mandatory policy. For example, in 'the UK content of orders place by the petroleum industry has increased dramatically since the early 1970s (when it was under 40%) to over 80% in the later 1980s' (Kemp, 1990: 600). But many host governments in emerging market economies are concerned that this process may not occur in the circumstances of their economies, or may occur only very slowly.

The immediate priority of host countries, in terms of development, is to foster stronger local output and employment related to the energy industry itself, and the ultimate challenge is to reduce natural resource dependence. Developing local content related to the foreign-owned energy industry is thus one step in a longer-term strategy. It can increase the share of final manufacturing production in overall economic output, thus broadening the impact of energy beyond the mere receipt of tax revenues. It can also be seen as a step towards building the skills and business networks of the local economy in areas outside the hydrocarbon industry. Ultimately, economic diversification means the development of competitive industries outside the hydrocarbon and related sectors.

Thus, from Sakhalin, in the far east of Russia, to the North Sea, the Middle East, Africa and Latin America the underlying message is the same, even if degrees of emphasis differ: 'we want to maximize value creation and build competence in our country'.

This concern is a summary of the broader issues concerning the role of the state and its interaction with corporate strategies, which were discussed in Chapter 4. It is high among the current preoccupations of governments and companies.

In the Caspian region specifically, there is an understandable desire by authorities to create an environment that involves local business wherever possible, and to train the indigenous population. The experience of the early 1990s was characterized by the dominance of foreign over local companies in industrial and service sectors of the hydrocarbon industry. For almost a decade these supply/service companies were operating on an 'expatriate' basis – in terms of human resources but also without establishing factories, plants, research centres and so on locally.

This experience led host governments to seek legally based ways of boosting local content to develop the industrial capacities of the local economy, which in principle is open to interaction with the international companies. Governments intend to maximize the involvement of local ownership within the entire value supply chain, maximizing the usage of the local labour force, businesses, goods and services, etc.

The fundamental question underlying such strategies concerns the level of local capability development and absorption capacity. How rapidly can the technology, know-how and professional skills be transferred to deepen and broaden capability and international competitiveness of local business and labour forces? And how can government policies help foster a spillover to other sectors of the economy?

So far, Kazakhstan is the only case in which serious attempts have been made to ensure competitive cost levels in the non-hydrocarbon sector, to reduce the share of the hydrocarbon sector in the total national income, and to develop a broad non-oil economy. It has introduced policy measures in this direction, including the Programme on Industrial Development (2004), which is at present just another document on the shelf of history.

In all cases in the region, however, one finds the narrower aim of pressing international companies to use their expertise to build local capabilities related to the energy industry through subcontractors and services. The concern about local content has found its expression in a range of approaches:

- In Kazakhstan, since 2001, the government has been pressing local content requirements (through laws, degrees, labour quotas), as well as obliging companies to invest in social projects in the area of operations.
- In Azerbaijan the issue is not as high on the government's agenda as it is in Kazakhstan. However, the government is employing a soft approach mainly related to the impact of the major operating companies on 'sustainable growth in Azerbaijan'.
- Turkmenistan clearly lacks local (Turkmen) staff, although there is a governmental local content requirement for employing local staff (regardless of in what capacity). As a result, oil and gas companies have to employ expatriates. During interviews I conducted with them, Turkmen officials tended to emphasize 'the importance of the local staff in the hydrocarbon sector' and the government's wish to support a significant role for local content (interviews with Turkmen officials, April and November 2006).

Initial approaches to local content in major producing regions have included legal frameworks that did not prove satisfactory. It is worth considering a few examples before turning to the question of how to develop realistic goals in light of industry conditions, and how to evolve viable modalities to pursue these goals.

5.2 Experience with legal frameworks

Local content regulations are designed to foster a more favourable environment for a 'trickle down' of skills and output to host-country economies. If not well designed, however, they can lead to significant economic and commercial problems. Experience in recent years clearly illustrates the pitfalls. These include the fact that the increase in local content is not costless; that a badly designed policy may create a less predictable environment for investors as well as increasing their costs; and that there are risks of creating a climate of permanent protection, inferior industry development and infrastructure, coupled with a prolif-eration of red tape and corruption. In other words, a badly designed pol-icy may damage growth by consuming the wealth rather than creating value, and it may have knock-on effects to other sectors of the economy.

Thus, while it is logical on the side of resource-rich governments to seek to capture and extend local value from the hydrocarbon sector by building local capabilities that support the sector's growth, this is in practice becoming a debatable area between the local governments and operating companies.

In one country in which we operate we were asked by the local gov-ernment to achieve 100% local content, whereas on similar projects in the past, levels of only 15–20% had been achieved. While the intention was clear, this was obviously an impossible target which lead us to look very closely at the liabilities associated with not achieving the target in a situation where we were certain we would not do so. We think very seriously about our contractual risks in such a situation. (Interview with Malcolm Harrison, director of Oil and Gas Division, Foster Wheeler Ltd, 10 October 2006, Reading)

As discussed in Chapter 4, Kazakhstan is an example in the Caspian region of a country experiencing a change in the legal regime applicable to its petroleum industry since the beginning of 2004. This has had major implications for the industry in terms of increased participation of the national oil company, increased attention to the use and develop-ment of local content and 'high technologies', a change in government take, and increased regulation and oversight.

Here, the issue concerns key changes to increase the focus on local content and technology, to further Kazakhstan's policy for the economic development of the country. The Petroleum and Subsurface Laws have for many years required parties carrying out petroleum operations to use goods and equipment manufactured in Kazakhstan and to hire Kazakhstan enterprises for the performance of services provided that they meet the requisite standards. Preference must be given to hiring Kazakhstan personnel and the contractor is obligated to conduct train-ing and to transfer technology.

In order to ensure that Kazakhstan suppliers of goods and services are given priority, the amendments provide for discounting their bid price by 20% when comparing bids to determine the winner of a tender for provision of goods, work and services. The new amendments to the Sub-surface Law further strengthen the domestic requirements by providing that subsurface contracts may be suspended for violations of the obligations with respect to Kazakhstan content. Finally, it should be noted that the Tax Code provides no recovery for costs incurred in violation of the local content requirements.[68]

An obvious conclusion from experience in the region is that companies cannot expect to ignore the local content concerns of governments. Companies, however, tend to adopt a cautious approach. The information in Table 5.1, later in this chapter, explains why companies are often reluctant to invest time and resources in training their local staff for semi-professional and professional jobs, and preferred entry-level jobs, skilled jobs, apprenticeship jobs, technical and office jobs. In some cases the scale and the time of the projects/contracts might not be sufficient to make the training viable. Thus governments need to monitor company training programmes and make sure that the local content element will be sufficient there.

Legal frameworks may be most effective in areas where they reinforce the economic opportunities and incentives facing companies. At the time of writing, there is a saturation of the expatriate employment market. Several international recruitment agencies are in the region (particularly in Kazakhstan). A majority of expatriates, who were interviewed with regard to their location of work, characterized the Caspian region as one of their favourites (interviews conducted in Atyrau, 18–19 May 2006).

According to Jason Goodall,[69] clients' development manager of KIS/Orion LLP,[70] the Caspian (and notably Kazakhstan) is considered as one of the most interesting and attractive places in a world where at

---

[68] The legal aspect of these changes was provided by the legal firm Denton-WildeSapte.

[69] Interview at KIS/Orion LLP, Atyrau, 19 May 2006.

[70] KIS Orion is the Orion Group's joint venture in Kazakhstan. The venture is a local Kazakh company formed in November 2001 between Tengizneftestroy (TNS), a major construction company originating from Kulsary in the Atyrau region of West Kazakhstan, and Orion Engineering Ltd. KIS/Orion LLP now has an annual turnover of US$120 mln and a core staff of 60 that manage an even split of over 950 local and expatriate contractors from the headquarters based in Atyrau. The continued expansion has resulted in the venture now having regional offices in Tengiz, Aktau, Aksai and Almaty. They have an extensive client list in Kazakhstan which requires the supply of contract hire personnel, executive search, permanent placement of local and expatriate staff, visa and work permit support, meet and greet, local and rotational transportation, accommodation and catering. The supply of equipment, drivers and vehicle hire can all be facilitated from one of the five locations in Kazakhstan where they have offices. (*Source*: http://www.orioneng.com/Offices/Atyrau/index.htm)

present the majority of oil and gas production comes from unstable environments. In terms of a challenging engineering environment, opportunities for young engineers, and development of new technologies, it could not be better placed for expatriates' and nationals career progression.

On the other hand, there are limits to the scope and speed of training local staff. As Victor Temnikov, the manager of Pump Equipment Plant, stated,

> apparently it is not easy to become a worker. People from auls [rural areas] cannot become accustomed to the regime of work from 8 a.m. to 5 p.m. They could leave work earlier. They cannot tolerate the noise or achieve a quick speed of work. ... To people who are accustomed to livestock-life activities, such 'science' is very difficult. However, some people are adapting to the new conditions, starting to earn good money and became more accustomed to the good life. (Vologodskii, 2006: 26)

In addition, the capacity of local subcontractors can be an obstacle to local content. In particular, it is quite difficult to develop local content with the ageing technical base of some Caspian enterprises, unless investors put in resources for upgrading.

On the government side, a form of local content which is sometimes considered is the involvement of companies in contributing to social projects in the region. That is a debatable area, which is very germane to the issue of defining realistic boundaries for local content and corporate and social responsibility. As we can see from Figure 5.2, such boundaries are not easily identified. Very often there is a cross-reference between core business, social investment and policy dialogue.

From the analysis of Figure 5.2 it is evident that IOCs in the Caspian region legitimately expect to gain rents from their direct investments, expressed in location-specific benefits, such as access to the Caspian resource-rich countries; and to gain also from the internalization process (working with local and other international partners in the region), which is connected to vertical and horizontal integration (Dunning, 1981).

It is clear that supporting local content can only be achieved realistically through an overall integration with corporate and social responsibility. This includes elements such as community development, human rights, environmental stewardship, education and training, rule of law, transparency, capacity-building and stakeholder engagement. It is also

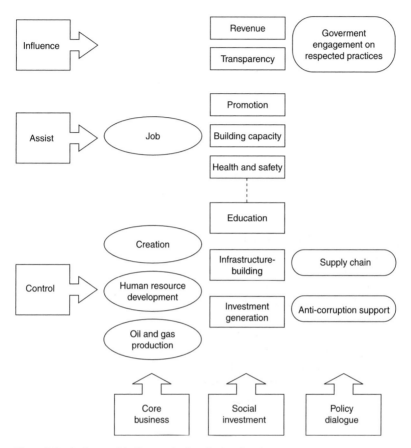

Figure 5.2 Action and influence in developing local content
Source: International Alert – Conflict Sensitive Business Practice.

important to ensure adequate budgetary provision for the running (maintenance) costs for the social projects.

In Kazakhstan one of the big contributors to the social projects (considered by the local government as part of local content operations) programme launched by the Kazakhstani government is KPO. To date the total volume of KPO mandatory investments into social projects has exceeded US$126.4 mln and will reach US$400 mln during the 40-year life of the PSA. Beside the requirements of the PSA, BG Kazakhstan contributed total voluntary investments into social projects in excess of US$2.6 mln (US$500 000 in 2006) (courtesy of BG Group). For an illustration of BG involvement in social projects, see Box 5.1.

Box 5.1   Some examples of social projects

Case study: Kazakh British Technical University (KBTU) Graduate School

In Kazkhstan, BG Group has been exploring approaches to local involvement that make sense in terms of commercial interest as well as the country's concerns to achieve favourable social outcomes. In addition to investing in personal development programmes to build technical competencies and behavioural skills, the company considered that supporting formal education programmes is key to attracting and retaining the best local talent. To this end, BG Kazakhstan, together with its joint sponsor, Shell, launched a new graduate school at the Kazakh British Technical University (KBTU) in Almaty in 2004. KBTU was established in June 2001 and is one of the few universities in Kazakhstan providing specialist training for professionals in the oil and gas sector.

KBTU has partnered with three British universities to deliver a number of postgraduate master's programmes, including Human Resource Management and Petroleum Engineering. In little over two and a half years, BG Kazakhstan has committed some US$340 000 in support of this initiative. More recently BG opened a state-of-the-art video conference hall and lecture theatre. Such facilities have been important not only in generating cost savings, but also in enhancing the quality of the teaching year. The 2006 was the first graduate year for the master's programmes, and a number of the graduates are working in the Karachaganak venture. In the view of the company, such initiatives support the transfer of skills and demonstrate a commitment to broader corporate responsibilities, while also helping to build a pool of skilled labour from which it can attract future employees.

Community projects in Uralsk, West Kazakhstan Oblast

Zhas Dauren Orphanage programmes

For the past three years, BG Kazakhstan has worked in cooperation with the IBC Group Ltd to deliver a range of development programmes for students at the Zhan Dauren Orphanage in Uralsk, a neighbouring community to the Karachaganak facility in the West Kazakhstan Oblast (WKO). During this time, BG Kazakhstan has contributed some US$100 000 to educational and career development programmes.

In 2005–06 BG Kazakhstan, together with the Eurasia Institute, awarded two scholarships to graduates for further study at WKO universities. Under a job placement programme, a number of graduates have also completed internships with the IBC Group. This work experience has enabled them to apply their skills in a real working environment and has helped them to secure employment.

Mini-MBA Training for small and medium-sized entrepreneurs

To date over 70 students have benefited from programmes that cover information technology and language skills training. More recently, BG has incorporated additional business skills such as book-keeping, as well as motivational training and business. Building on the existing training programmes, a series of business training courses for small and medium-sized entrepreneurs within the West Kazakhstan Oblast (WKO) is now being conducted in order to develop and enhance their business skills. During the past two years, four mini-MBA training courses have been held and more than 150 students have enrolled.

In sum, the demand and supply of skills provides some economic reinforcement to the development priorities set by governments in terms of training programmes and recruitment, although there are some limitations in this field. On the other hand, the condition of subcontractors is in some cases discouraging. And participation in social projects is something of a grey area. So the picture is complex, offering both opportunities and risks. As with other risks and challenges affecting the industry, the issue here is not the avoidance of local content; it is careful management on the company side, and the design of a realistic framework on the side of governments.

5.3   Defining realistic goals

To arrive at a framework within which to set realistic goals for local content programmes, it is important to clarify several issues: the operational meaning of the term 'local content'; the opportunities and constraints faced by foreign companies, notably in their management of subcontractors and

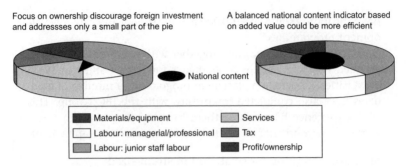

Figure 5.3 National content pie

the supply chain; the perception of the market by foreign companies; the types of professional positions and other jobs in the supply chain; and the way local content decisions can be integrated in the project management strategy. These issues are discussed in turn below.

First, in line with the general definition at the beginning of this chapter, 'local content' can be defined as 'composite value added to, or created in the country's economy'. This categorization, it should be noted, is much broader than one based only on ownership of firms in the supply chain. A comprehensive Local Content Indicator (LCI) includes ownership, local content of materials, percentage of local labour, percentage of locals in professional and management positions, services (contracts) and local taxes. If governments concentrate on a narrower definition based on ownership alone, that will discourage foreign investment in the country, and will not stimulate substantial growth (see Figure 5.3).

Another expression of measurement of the local content (LC) could be a metrics based on *ad valorem* criterion, checking on values of imported components.

$$LC = \left(1 - \frac{X}{Y}\right) \times 100$$

where X consists of the following:

- values of materials and equipment directly imported by the operator company, including importation tax;
- values of materials and equipment directly imported by the main contractor, including importation tax;
- values of imported materials and equipment purchased by the operator in the local market, excluding internal tax;
- values of foreign services needed for the project;

- values of imported materials and equipment purchased by the main contractor in the local market, excluding internal tax.

Y is total value of the project, excluding internal tax (Brazilian measurement).

Second, the specific opportunities and constraints for developing local content need to be defined within the operating framework of the oil and gas industry. This involves understanding the approach taken by the industry as it operates through contracts between the operating oil companies and their suppliers. These relations are often characterized as hierarchical. Supplier companies call on subcontractors and all activities and information up to the final product comprise the 'supply chain'.

The approach towards subcontractors taken by oil operators in the Caspian region can thus be characterized as typical supply chain management, which mainly involves choosing a number of preferential suppliers from the base of qualified suppliers with whom it is possible to secure long-term contracts. In addition, the operating companies are always in the process of evaluating suppliers for quality, cost performance, delivery, etc. A crucial factor here is the ability of the suppliers themselves to manage subcontractors and to conduct performance improvement strategies when required.

In discussion with Terry Adams (founding president, AIOC), it became clear that the four key elements in provision of local content are quality (fit for purpose and insurable), delivery (capacity to supply), price and procedural transparency. Consequently one should realistically expect a material presence of national staff at all levels within the foreign operating company. But in terms of goods and services both government and foreign investor should be aware where these would best fit in the business cycle. A government would be disadvantaged if a local content were to dilute their revenue stream (when the local content provision undermines the pace of project delivery). Cost–benefit analysis applies equally both to government and investors.

The local enterprise development strategy by BP in Azerbaijan is to maximize spending with local suppliers and JVs to meet the target of doubling local spending by 2010. It also includes development and implementation of a Local Content Delivery Plan in targeted supply sectors. As in Kazakhstan, there is a desire to increase nationalization of the workforce with international suppliers to meet PSA targets as well as to assess demand for specialist financing solutions for SMEs (small and medium-sized, enterprises) i.e. innovative investment projects to provide transparent sources of finance.

One of the tasks that the strategy has highlighted is the creation of enterprise development and training opportunities for local suppliers, and finally to communicate BP's demand and ensure transparency of BP's local spending targets. As a logical continuation of the above-described programme, an enterprise centre in Azerbaijan was set up in May 2002 by BP on behalf of its partners in oil projects. The Centre assists Azeri-owned and Azerbaijan-based companies to develop their business in support of major oil and gas developments in Azerbaijan. It provides training on safety and technical standards, ethics and business practices. One of the aims of the Centre is to make sure that local businesses have access to BP's supply chain. The Centre is aiming not just to develop suppliers for BP but also, over time, to help create a more competitive environment in which SMEs can thrive. This is part of BP's commitment to do all that is possible to (help) ensure that oil and gas wealth generates benefits for all.

A sound enterprise policy for a small open economy should rest on the twin pillars of FDI and domestic SME development. Central to a well-designed policy is the notion that vertical linkages should tie local SMEs into the supply chain of foreign enterprises. In Azerbaijan, oil-based FDI has been strong, but attracting non-oil FDI is very difficult. The crucial advantage of Azerbaijan is that the high level of oil-based FDI offers a solid platform for SME development. Supply chains are a key mechanism through which engineering subcontractors can deliver sustainable social and economic benefits to the host economy. Overall, the engineering subcontractors are well positioned to contribute to their clients' local content requirements. The subcontractors can explore this issue in partnership with government. 'Our aim is to push the supply chain in order that what we do and how we do it makes a real contribution to Azerbaijan economic health'. Interview with Clare Bebbington, communications and external affairs director, BP Azerbaijan, 27 April 2007, Baku).

Within this framework local industries in the Caspian region have to perform adequately in order to earn the right to become subcontractors and be a part of the oil and gas industry's supply chain. The main selection criterion in this supply chain will be a degree of value added by local businesses that compares well with that of other (non-local) subcontractors.

Third, in order to spell out the appropriate strategies with regard to increasing the role of local content in Caspian hydrocarbon development, it is important also to understand the local business context in which the Caspian suppliers are operating. Foreign investors' perception of local companies can be summarized from my various interviews with the foreign players in the Caspian Sea region as follows.

Very often the foreign investors have found that their local partners are not familiar with non-local standards. Over the years this situation is rapidly improving. Nevertheless, quality assurance and quality control issues remain key obstacles in the project implementation process. As a rule, local companies are not known outside their countries (or region), which creates additional hesitations and a cautious approach in the selection of local partners.

In addition, local companies are often able to provide only a limited range of products, which means that reorientation of production is required, and local managers need to include this as a part of their strategies. There are other 'technical' problems which are related to low-volume production and problems of financial stability and control.

In some cases, foreign investors also pointed out a lack of clarity on import duties and on taxation issues, which ultimately puts them off. Another challenge, but at the same time a possible advantage, could be the factor of the mix of cultures, which to date already has both good and bad examples from the region (various interviews I conducted in the Caspian Sea region in 2003–2007).

Fourth, having defined local content, and sketched out the working of the supply chain, we now need to consider the many types of jobs with different requirements in the oil and gas industry and its satellites. One can define at least eight levels of such jobs. As shown in Table 5.1, some types of jobs require no or minimum experience (e.g. entry-level jobs) and some require many years to master the skills (e.g. semi-professional and professional jobs).

Ultimately this brings us to the long-term labour agreements needed to provide the base for development (Figure 5.4).

While there are concerns about the impact on profitability of developing local content, many of the expatriates I interviewed (in 2003–2007) praised the principle of involving locals in their operations.[71] However, the question *'Could the managerial staff be completely replaced by the locals in 10–12 years' time?'* was, amazingly, answered identically: 'Not at all with regard to the top management'. The explanation of such answers can be seen in two ways. First of all it is very comfortable to be an expatriate manger working in the Caspian Sea region at the present time (good working conditions, excellent package from the company, etc.). However, there is another explanation, not expressed officially by the interviewees, which is related to the obstacles and pressure within the

---

[71] The answers were vary: from 'this is much cheaper', 'this is a policy of any international company' to 'locals are very nice people'.

Table 5.1 Levels of jobs in the oil and gas industry

Levels	Description	Examples
Entry-level jobs	Require little or no previous experience	Supply vessel worker, offshore worker, cook's helper, seismic driller's helper, janitor for camps, mechanic's helper, electrician's helper, survey helper, equipment operator
Skilled jobs	Require some previous experience	Derrick hand, power tong operator, motor hand, welder, diver, gas utility operator, compressor operator, control room operator
Apprenticeship jobs	Require that the person will be a certified tradesperson. Apprentice is usually a four-year training programme where a person is taking a short course and usually gets paid to train on the job	Pipe fitter, cook, mechanic, welder, electronics, plumber, carpenter, electrician
Technical jobs	Require a technical college certificate or diploma. Generally they are one or two-year programmes	Seismic recording technician, survey technician, petroleum technician, mechanical technician, geophysical technician, instrument technician
Office jobs	Require at least completed secondary education and some training and experience	Accounts clerk, secretary, purchasing agent, materials clerk
Semi-professional jobs	Require a college diploma, although it is possible to work your way up to these positions through work experience and on-the-job training	Warehouse manager, catering manager, safety officer, environmental monitor, drilling foreman
Professional jobs	Require a university degree	Geologist, engineer, research analyst, IT Systems, land surveyor, accountant, nurse, land agent, general manager, human resources
Goods and services	Ample opportunities to create goods and services for the industry	Expediting, security, equipment rental, cooking/catering, pilot/transportation, fuel supply and haul, trucking, supply of explosives/chemicals, geophysical surveying, camp management and construction, remote communications, supplying materials, retailer

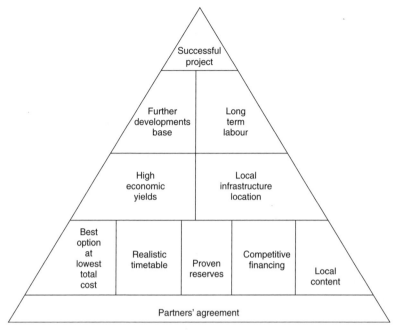

Figure 5.4 Successful project components

Caspian environment for the potential local top-level managers, namely related to the level of autonomy and protection from interference of the government (local, city, etc.) as well as from the general public (some people who might be acquaintances, relatives, etc.).

There is a constant source of contradiction between the reality of and desire for local content. The oil and gas industry operates with huge operational costs, and needs to make commensurate profits, or developments will not make any commercial sense. Meanwhile, the concept of local content is laudable but potentially very expensive if not implemented properly. It should be appreciated that this is not 'a quick fix'; it must be supported by a long-term development plan. It will require a sustainable project workload and clients have to accept that it can increase a contractor's risks in the early days.

One way of formalizing the framework to integrate local engineering and project management capability is to integrate this within the company's project management system. Typically a company will undertake the following five key steps. First, an appropriate market analysis needs to be conducted. Second, the regulatory and fiscal framework of the host country needs to be understood. Third, a business plan must be developed (which would include the crucial decisions about the creation of a joint venture as well as a design for organic growth). Fourth, a technology transfer and training programme (with elements in the country as well as out of the country) needs to be developed. Fifth, it is necessary to identify the expatriate/local resource ratio and, building on this, a programme for expatriate reduction (interview with Steve Spicer, director, Global Business Lines, Foster Wheeler Ltd, 3 February 2006).

In terms of this framework for project management and contracting, the crucial question for the execution stage is: at what stage in the project life-cycle does the centre of gravity shift from the contractor's home office: conceptual, front end engineering design (FEED) or detailed engineering?

Let us take an example from the service industry, where one of the common types of contracting strategy is engineering procurement construction (EPC) and a frequently used type of agreement is the lump sum amount contract. Within the boundaries of such a contract it could be very difficult to fit local content activities without making losses. Table 5.2 presents the various contracting strategies and their 'adaptiveness' to the inclusion of the local content element. As we can see, the most difficult one is a lump sum EPC. More 'relaxed conditions' could be adopted on reimbursable and incentivization types of contracting strategies. In any case, the equilibrium of cost, time and quality remains valid in any of the contracting strategy, and that would be a prerequisite of any local content development.

This discussion has provided us with some key elements for a legislative framework (see Figure 5.5) in which to consider local content, including the operational meaning of the term; the operating approach of companies in their management of subcontractors and the supply chain; the types of professional positions and other jobs in the supply chain; and the way local content decisions can be integrated into the project management strategy.

5.4   Partnership in new modalities

The true substance of local content, as already discussed, is connected to value creation within the host country. It is a full utilization of oil and gas wealth, together with the capacities established in the service sector, to create a local manufacturing sector – with employment opportunities and with other multiplier effects on the local economy. At the time of writing, the dominance of foreign over local oil and gas companies (and their service sector) in the Caspian region is evident. In response,

Table 5.2 Types of contracting strategies and local content factor

Type of contracting strategy	Description	Local content element
Lump sum engineering, procurement, construction (EPC) lump Sum turn key (LSK)	Generally large construction and engineering projects such as process plants, oil rigs, offshore facilities and pipelines with the lump sum amount agreed up front with full responsibility for detailed design, procurement, construction and interfaces between contractors. This type of contract represents minimum risk to the owner, a higher risk to the Contractor.	Inclusion is very limited, highly inflexible, in some cases contract could stipulate minimum requirements for local content by volume (hours) or cost These sums have to be spent in the host country.
Engineering procurement, construction management (EPCm)	Provides for all planning and communications, maintains a close relationship with the client, ensures strict compliance with contractual requirements, monitors quality assurance and control systems, maintains reporting methods to ensure an accurate information flow, directs accounting and project cost management, and responds to any and all execution issues.	Inclusion depends on the client's agreement as well as on the length of the project.
Reimbursable with various forms of incentivization (a) Cost plus fixed fee. (b) Gain or pain share to an agreed percentage of the potential contract price (c) Liquidated damages for late delivery of the programme. (d) Target cost.	The contractor is paid his costs including overheads and preliminaries together with a fee which may be either a percentage fee or fixed. This payment mechanism is appropriate where an early start is required but the project lacks sufficient definition. Cost reimbursement has also been used in projects where the particular physical conditions are considered too variable to allow other methods of payment to be adopted, and the overriding consideration has been to ensure the full and open cooperation of the contractor to allow the construction problems to be overcome. Incentives to the contractor usually tied into performance-based incentives, with appropriate milestones being agreed with subcontractors before contract award.	This is the easiest type of contract for the inclusion of the local content element into the costs. The contracts with incentivization mechanism by which owner and contractor objectives are aligned are the most 'favourable' to build up the concept of local content for the host government, which could be based on additional incentives for the contractors if they develop the local content programme while implementing the project.

(Continued)

Type of contracting strategy	Description	Local content element
Schedule of rates	The contractor is paid for the actual amount of work carried out if any shown in the schedule. If the final quantities differ markedly from those in the approximate bill or the schedule, then the contractor may have an entitlement to a re-evaluation of the rate. A variation of the Schedule of Rates contract is that of a schedule which is issued with the rates already inserted and contractors are then asked to tender on the basis of a plus or minus percentage addition to the actual rates. The use of such Schedule Contracts as with 'Approximate Quantities Contract' is that they allow the preparation of quantities from preliminary drawings at a very early stage. Whilst the quantities will not be accurate they should be sufficient to give the contractor a reasonable idea of the scope of work to be executed. In all cases the schedule should be prepared so that preliminary items are priced and identified separately and not included within the unit rates.	There is 'room' for inclusion of local content aspect in this strategy. However, it is clear that in terms of profitability the companies might prefer not to do it.
Build own operate (BOO)/Build own operate transfer (BOOT)	The contractor under BOO constructs and operates a facility without transferring ownership to the public sector (hosting government). Legal title to the facility remains in the private sector, and there is no obligation for the public sector to purchase the facility or take title. A BOO transaction may qualify for tax-exempt status as a service contract if all Internal Revenue Code requirements are satisfied. Three elements are required for BOO/BOOT types, namely: a feasible and viable project; a willing host government to grant concession agreement which empowers a concessionaire the right to operate and benefit from the constructed project by that concession; and finally, funders who are willing to take the financial risk of undertaking the project. BOOT assumes that on the expiry of the concession period contractor has a requirement to revert the project to the authority that has granted the the concession.	The proliferation of local content procurement regulations would be practically impossible under concession rules after the contract has been agreed with the host government.

Sources: The definitions of the contracts were taken from http://www.atkinson-law.com/cases/CasesArticles/Articles/Contract_Strategies.htm and http://ncppp.org/howpart/ppptypes.shtml; Bunni (2005) and Wright (2002).

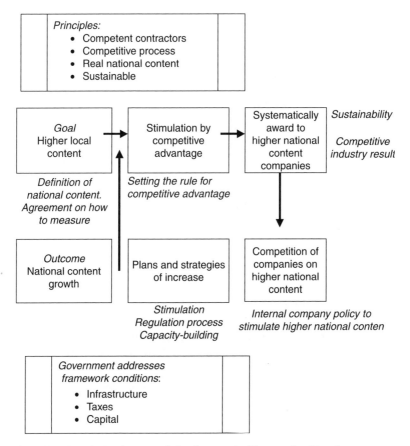

Figure 5.5 Legislative framework for the sustainable growth of local content

host governments have been seeking to establish a framework that would set incentives to develop local content. And indeed it would be strange if, in 10–15 years' time the Caspian countries' supply and service sector were still to rely entirely on the import of finished goods and services, in the absence of local contractors.

But there is a fine balance to be struck. Ultimately, the corporate entities governments are dealing with (similar to the PSAs) are not forever. The history of oil and gas joint ventures proves that joint stock ventures tend to drift apart over time. This means that in changing the costs and benefits facing the industry it will be important not to overplay the local content factor. There is a question of how to define targets and in what contractual framework to embed them.

As noted above, not every Caspian government has set a firm target for local content. In an interview I conducted, the mayor of one of the oil regions in Turkmenistan simply stated, 'we encourage the companies operating in this *oblast* to use more local staff and goods, but we do not put any precise targets' (interview conducted on 7 November 2005). Overall, the Turkmen government has to approve any purchasing over US$50 000.

So the industry is experiencing, and in some cases developing itself, a range of approaches. Some ideas and approaches are emerging on both sides that may contain the seeds of a new partnership between companies and governments in the area of local content. Companies indeed have every interest, as do host governments, in seizing on and fostering realistic frameworks that fit well with business priorities, including cost containment by the industry. Companies need to develop and gain experience with modalities that may subsequently be applied elsewhere, adjusted for different country circumstances. In this respect, two interesting examples of initiatives coming from the industry side deserve attention.

The first example is the promotion of a Code of Conduct by KPO in Karachaganak field in Kazakhstan. The Karachaganak Code of Conduct was first issued September 1999. Following rapid growth in the workplace during the Phase 2 construction project, in 2004 a decision was made by the partners in the Karachaganak venture to appoint an independent guarantor and re-launch the Code. Vital to the success of this re-launch was the highly visible commitment of the senior management and an extensive communications campaign. A company-wide poster campaign together with individual leaflets and booklets reinforced the series of senior management briefings. The trades unions and manpower service providers were also included in the awareness campaign.

The principles embedded in the Code are that company activities must be carried out:

- in a safe and environmentally sound manner
- in compliance with the relevant law
- in fair competition
- with honesty, integrity and good faith
- with due respect for the legitimate interests of customers, employees, shareholders, commercial and financial partners and the communities where it operates.

In support of these principles there are six key values that determine the character of the organization, as do behaviours. Any action, operation and negotiation performed by company employees, or those acting on behalf of the company, must be guided by these values:

- Cultural sensitivity
- KPO has a multinational workforce who must respect the culture of others and of the communities in which we operate.
- Integrity
- Business dealings will be conducted with integrity and consistently high ethical standards.
- Trust
- Effective business relationships inside and outside the Company are possible only with high levels of trust and mutual respect.
- Openness
- The Company will strive to be as open and straightforward as is possible.
- Partnership
- The sharing of information, knowledge, experience and skills helps to develop the partnerships so vital to KPO's business.
- Teamwork
- Working together as a team is more effective than working in isolation.

These principles and values are enshrined in the Code of Conduct, which covers the following key areas:

- Business   Personal Conduct, Business Relationships
- HSE   Karachaganak and Surrounding Environment
- Information   Confidentiality, E-communication
- HR   Behaviour Standards, Staff Development
- External Relations   Community and Media

It is clear that developing this common culture will require time and the commitment of KPO employees and management. This desire for a common culture, and the associated development of human resources, can be considered as a very particular aspect of the development of local content.

The Code is now well established throughout KPO, and in order to maintain the high profile a new communications campaign was conducted in 2007. The Code is fundamental to the way in which KPO wishes to conduct its operations and business, and indeed it is now included in KPO's standard contractual terms.

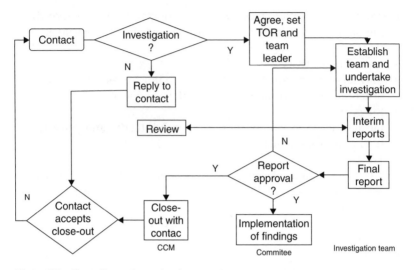

Figure 5.6   Compliance investigation process
Source: Courtesy of Howard Burrows, Compliance Coordination Manger of KPO.

Associated with the Code is the Compliance Assurance Policy. Through this policy, the guarantor provides an independent and confidential assurance role for employees. Questions or concerns about the Code are referred to the compliance coordination manager. For the most serious matters, a formal investigation may be required, in which case an investigating team is appointed by the Code of Conduct Committee. The investigation would then be carried in accordance with the schematic presented in Figure 5.6.

It is important that the employees are able to exercise their rights to express concern, and to identify areas that require attention. Table 5.3 provides a good idea of such possible areas, which include crucial aspects of the day-to-day operations such as government contracts, employment law, international business issues, etc.

There are already some lessons to be learned from this process, which are related, for example, to the process of investigations itself. This process usually takes longer than expected. The team leader/members must not have a conflict of interest. Sometimes allegations may be subjective or vague, and may concern events from some time ago. The process has more similarity with a police investigation than an incident investigation.

For the future it will be important to gain a professional opinion, which is independent, but the crucial question here is: from whom?

Table 5.3   Possible areas of employee concern

Safety	Improper use of company assets
Conflicts of interest	Falsifying reports
Harassment and discrimination	Workplace violence
Gifts and entertainment	Drug or substance abuse
International business issues	Government contracts
Copyright usage	Environment
Unlicensed software	Antitrust
Employment law	Insider trading
Theft	Misuse of confidential information

Sources: Institute of Business Ethics.

Table 5.4   Breaches of Code of Conduct, 2006

Types of breaches	Examples
Substance abuse	Following positive tests for alcohol and drugs, 14 agency employees were dismissed from various sites.
Inappropriate safety behaviour	Two agency employees showed unwillingness to work within BP's safety culture and systems. Their contacts were terminated
Misuse of company assets	An internal investigation confirmed that an agency employee was accepting unauthorized payments and misappropriating company assets. The employee's contract was terminated.
Fraud	An agency employee's contract was terminated after the discovery that confidential data had been manipulated and concealed to avoid the disclosure of underlying records.
Theft	One BP employee and five agancy staff were sacked for theft at sites in Azerbaijan and Georgia.

The practice of KPO has already demonstrated that it can be difficult to close out internally. Competent closure of each sub-part of the investigation is vital – one poor link can invalidate the whole process. In close-out with the contact, what information should be provided? This is a crucial issue to underscore. In addition, formalized terms of reference and a formalized process flow are required (interview with Howard Burrows, compliance coordination manager, KPO, 28 February 2006, Reading).

In comparison with KPO's experience, a complementarity can be found from BP's history in Azerbaijan. Table 5.4 presents recent examples of breaches of the Code of Conduct in 2006 when one BP employee and 23 agency staff were dismissed for non-compliance with laws, regulations and BP's Code of Conduct.

A second example relates to the local content programme for Tengizchevroil, which has several dimensions. These are mainly concerned with education (postgraduate programmes, short courses, etc.), training programmes in house, as well as creation of Caspian Technical Resources LLP – Caspian Training Centre (CTR) in Atyrau. According to Renee Lagorio-French,[72] the main strategy of Tengizchevroil in Kazakhstan is to leave the country as a better place (interview conducted on 19 May 2006, Atyrau). Tengizchevroil's workforce consists of 80% local staff.

The functional organization chart of the supply management department is presented in Figure 5.7, where the local content part is located under strategic management. Overall, local machineries and fabrication processes are lagging in Kazakhstan, being old, and sometimes obsolete. However, if the local goods and technologies are competitive, then preference would be given to Kazakhstani goods and services (interview with Renée Lagorio-French, Atyrau, 19 May 2006). The process of selection is quite linear. The Kazakhstani companies who want to work with TCO send information to the company and then TCO puts them into a pre-qualification process. Working with TCO, local companies benefit from Chevron's culture, which is considered to be open, collaborative, employee-friendly (with a number of educational benefits), less bureaucratic than other companies, and well managed.

Of course, there are some challenges for local staff in this and other programmes. They are facing new techniques and methods of work, which in supply management are complex. Another obstacle picked up by many interviewees is a weak knowledge of English among local staff. According to a number of managers of joint stock ventures, 'if you are an international company which wants to work internationally, you must speak English'. In addition, the local staff needs to gain familiarity with Western business practices, including a proactive approach. The Soviet legacy is not to question a process, and this passivity remains an obstacle today.

In an important development designed to help overcome training barriers, Caspian Technical Resources LLP (CTR), came to an agreement to acquire all the assets and maintain the operations of Tengizchevroil's craft training centre operated by Parsons Flour Daniels (PFD), through a competitive tender in June 2005. PFD implemented a training programme that Flour Daniels utilizes worldwide, developed by the

[72] Manager of supply chain management, Department of Tengizchevroil.

161

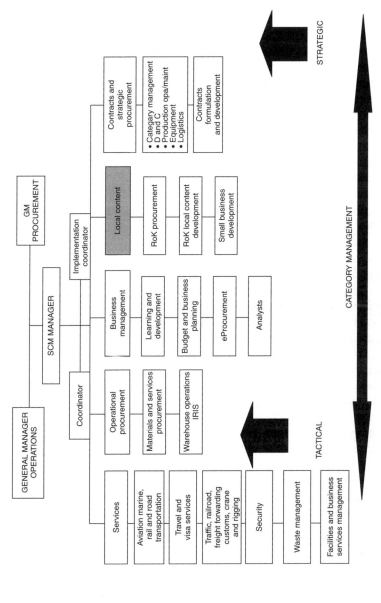

Figure 5.7 TCO: supply chain management – functional organization chart
Source: Courtesy TCO, Supply Management Department.

National Centre for Construction Education and Research (NCCER).[73] NCCER has developed standards for the operation of accredited training programmes to ensure that standardized quality education is provided for all construction and maintenance trainees.

CTR was formed in April 2005 by Aliya Dosmukhambetova (51% Kazakh), QED (43% UK), and Kerry Karvas (6% US), after several years of planning, for the purpose of training Kazakh citizens for the construction and oil and gas industries in the Republic of Kazakhstan (CTR, 2006: 7). The CTR West Kazakhstan Project Curriculum was primarily developed by Tengizchevroil, PFD and their subcontractors to develop the local labour market for TCO's SGI/SGP.

This curriculum is designed to take Kazakh nationals with some experience and bring their skills up to a level to meet project needs and standards. The curriculum works for any project in the region, and can be modified to the requirements of the client. It also allows the contractor to increase productivity with the utilization of the Kazakh labour market at minimal cost and time, at the same time reviewing the competence of the workers for future training and future development of the national labour force. On 30 December 2005 the Department of Education in the RoK issued a licence to CTR specifically for Skills Enhancement and Competency Development (see Appendix).

Currently CTR is developing and maintaining a standardized training process in partnership with the construction, maintenance and pipeline industries operating in Kazakhstan. The training process itself is portable, meaning that the knowledge and skills learned by students and workers are taken from project to project, from company to company.

Here are a few of the benefits as listed in the CTR training information (CTR, 2006: 11):

- As industries compete more fiercely for fewer qualified workers, a professional, accredited training program that offers industry-recognized credentials and a clearly defined career path will attract and retain high-caliber workers.
- Standardized training will create a national pool of construction, maintenance and pipeline workers with documented, portable skills.

---

[73] The NCCER is a not-for-profit education foundation serving a broad spectrum of industry, including construction, maintenance and pipeline. NCCER is supported by the participation of trade associations, contractors, schools, construction and maintenance users, pipeline operators, manufacturers and third-party training providers.

- Training improves productivity, which increases profitability.
- Standardized training will establish construction, maintenance and pipeline industries as industries with credible career opportunities rather than just jobs.
- Career paths defined through standardized training will improve the image of the industry.
- Corporate commitment to improving craft workforce skills and professionalism increases employee loyalty and motivation while reducing absenteeism and turnover.
- Corporate commitment to craft training clearly demonstrates a commitment to quality management, providing a critical competitive edge.
- Well-trained workers are more capable of identifying potential problems and making innovative, cost-reducing solutions.

Overall, the training process should increase productivity, reduced accidents and, in turn, achieve more cost-effective construction, maintenance and pipeline operations. That can be seen as a direct benefit of local content development. Of course, in most cases the benefit of training is not seen initially, only the cost. The operator and/or owner pays this cost, but it is they who ultimately benefit from the training. Therefore it is the operators/owners who should be responsible for ensuring that the workforce is properly trained to standards accepted by the industry.

Another example of an educational establishment is the Caspian Energy Centre (Baku, Azerbaijan) which was set up on 25 May 2005. It is the first science-focused centre in the region for anyone in Azerbaijan who is interested in broadening their knowledge of the Caspian energy sector BP (Azerbaijan, *Sustainability Report*, 2005: 43).

A third promising example of developing local content has been put in place by Burren Energy in Turkmenistan, where at the Burun oil field (within the oil camp) a training centre was created in order to address the limitations of Burren Energy in Turkmenistan in terms of the available local labour pool for both managerial and engineering staff.

Another local initiative of Burren Energy is supporting the local orphanage for 200 children of 3–18 years in Balkanabad city – providing electrical equipment, renovating the orphanage's housing, spending on the children's celebrations, etc.

In 2005 the company also introduced the Burren–University of Reading Postgraduate Scholarship Scheme,[74] providing full scholarships for

[74] A strategic alliance between the University of Reading and Burren Energy.

postgraduate economics studies for Turkmen citizens. It started with three scholarships for the general public in 2005, and then increased to six scholarships per year, with two scholarships specifically designated for Burren employees. The company aims to develop its local employees' managerial skills in preparation for local staff to take more managerial responsibilities in future. 'When I return to the company after my year studying in Reading I will try to apply my knowledge of managerial principles in my day-to-day work. I expect to take on more tasks and to be more involved in human resource management of the company' (interview with Nury Nazarov, Burren employee, 19 August 2006, Reading).

Such a comprehensive programme for local content development by the operating company in a country with quite relaxed governmental local content requirements proves the point that much (although not everything) depends on the willingness and adaptive attitude of the business to be involved in the economic development of the country of their operation in ways that offer an overall synergy with business goals. More generally, these initiatives in Kazakhstan and Turkmenistan are encouraging signs of creativity in trying to craft realistic but substantive approaches. But the situations that encourage such a forward-looking approach are not universal.

5.5 Developing transparent frameworks

The importance of achieving acceptable levels of local content in major hydrocarbon projects is becoming increasingly evident in the Caspian Sea region. Overall, the political agenda of resource-rich countries has expanded, and companies are coming to recognize that local content is a core element in this agenda. It is therefore urgent for both sides to identify approaches and technical modalities that are realistic and investment-friendly. At times countries have defined strategies and set targets that are not realistic or consistent with governments' underlying political-economic goals.

At a broad policy level, governments may seek membership of the WTO, but may not be prepared to envisage the permanent change in policy regimes that this implies. In terms of development strategy, they may want employment and industrial spin-offs from oil and gas production, while failing to take key flanking measures on the business environment. Specifically on local content, they may set aggressive targets, and want to see results delivered promptly – 60–70% local content is often used as a goal – thus pursuing approaches that raise costs and risks, deterring investors. The practical example of Indonesia demonstrates that membership could be quite 'expensive' and will not support the pursuit of local content: 'the WTO Dispute Panel on Indonesia makes it clear that local-content requirements are prohibited in themselves, whether applied to domestic or foreign firms'. (Morrissey, 2001: 69).

'Local content' requirements influence project design and are certain to influence contracting strategy, which in turn may affect project costs and schedules. Thus governments should assess carefully the impact of mechanisms to maximize local value-added in the short term, in order to build capability for increased value capture over the longer run. Modalities must be consistent with overall policy frameworks, and policies should be applied with rigour and time-consistency for current and future projects. Obviously, Caspian region countries are aware of the worldwide importance of their reserves, especially to Western operators and contractors; but they are also conscious of some interdependence with IOCs, which have, to date, affected the development of these reserves with imported staff and technology.

For both governments and companies, it is important to realize that increased local content takes time (sometimes longer than is anticipated), and to be prepared for risk mitigation and cost-sharing incentives. Through my interviews with the various companies working in Kazakhstan, one conclusion has emerged: local content targets must be realistically set. That was particularly evident at the beginning of 2000s when the Kazakhstani authorities tried to force the multinationals to introduce local content elements everywhere, even when it was practically impossible (interviews in Kazakhstan, 2001, 2003, 2005–2006).

In arriving at solutions, both sides need to be proactive – and the evidence cited above is encouraging in that respect. Moreover, they need to move from a conflict situation to a dialogue based on recognition of each side's legitimate goals. To help to develop an understanding between the parties involved in the project development (not only for local content purposes), a mutual awareness of different cultures is required. I have witnessed many cases when the parties have spoken different business languages, making them unable to understand each other.

How, concretely, can governments in resource-rich countries work efficiently with operating companies in promoting a high level of local content in the companies' contracts? It is crucially important that governments are able to set frameworks that enable the growth of national content via a transparent, self-regulating process, which does not deter companies from expanding their operations (Figure 5.2).

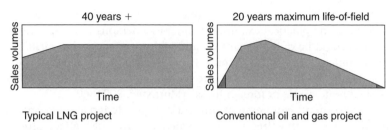

Figure 5.8   Project life-cycles in the oil and gas industry

It is clear that in these bilateral relations (government–company) common initiatives should play a key role.[75] The host country has a reciprocal responsibility to understand the contractor. The contractor is looking for leadership from the host company and the client. Local content development requires a collaborative approach between clients and contractors, managing resources in today's marketplace.

Two questions have been key in this discussion, and remain to be fully answered. How far can the oil and gas industry support the global demand for local content? And how are these demands to be balanced against project requirements of budget, safety, quality and increasingly shorter schedules? Too often, these questions are answered with the rehearsal of sterile statistics. Five elements are needed to help answer these questions on a country-by-country basis.

First, there needs to be a set of criteria to evaluate local content impact, which takes into account the specifics of project life-cycles in the industry. As Figure 5.8 shows, conventional oil and gas projects often last for around 20 years, whereas a typical LNG (liquefied natural gas) project could last more than 40 years. Second, the maximization of local content should be based on identifying opportunities to capture local value-added through the selection of specific (not all) goods and services. Third, a clear definition is needed of ways to deliver maximum local value by increasing participation of local nationals in appropriate functions, backed by specific training programmes. Fourth, approaches to subcontracting are needed that increase the scope, over time, to raise the participation of local firms, on a competitive basis. Fifth, there needs to be a definition of possible additional modalities, including aspects of social responsibility.

---

[75] Obviously this perception varies from country to country but also from company to company. Nevertheless it provides a general set of features familiar to the foreign investors in most of the areas of their operations.

Even at the initial stage a government should establish and agree the definition of 'local content' and present its measurement standards as a basis for agreement on goals. As soon as goals are clearly defined, the next step is to set up the rules for competitive advantage and its stimulation. At the stage of awarding companies with contracts, governments should give preference to companies with higher levels of local content, although that must still result in a competitive industry.

As soon as a contract has been awarded, companies should put in place corresponding internal policies, based on stimulating higher local content. At this stage, the market will consist of companies with higher local content competing with each other, which will ultimately lead to new developments in improving and building new capacities for local content. This will finally bring the country to the goal of maximizing local content.

A clear and mutually understood approach along these lines will help to lay the basis for realistic solutions to 'local content' in technical terms. To be effective, such a framework should be based on the following underlying assumptions, which should be underwritten by both sides: the need for competent contractors, for a competitive process, for real and sustainable national content, and for a conducive local environment ensured by governmental policies in infrastructure, tax and capital.

This last point is important for local content goals to be realistic, but also to ensure ripple effects that benefit the rest of the economy. Resource-rich governments need to set an environment that is favourable to local manufacturing, and the availability of finance, raw materials and provision for local R&D facilities is important. Reopening, or in some cases establishing, fabrication yards is an essential element in promoting local content from the government and company point of view.

In other words, this process needs to take place against a background that is investment-friendly and well disposed towards developing and using competent local suppliers and staff. Here, a proactive role by companies is clearly crucial. More broadly, companies need to work with government to focus on changes that make the development of local content a powerful element in the country's strategy over the long run – underpinned by shared goals, and effected through a genuine dialogue.

Case study of Sangachal (Azerbaijan)

Sangachal is one of the biggest oil and gas terminals in the world. This is the start of the Baku–Tbilisi–Ceyhan (BTC) pipeline. A decade ago Sangachal was just an administrative building with very few staff. At the time of writing, this is BP's largest oil and gas terminal, processing

730 000 bbl of oil daily from the Azeri–Chirag–Gunashli (ACG) oil field and 500 000 m^3 feet of gas from the Shakh Deniz field.

This is the strategic hub for the Caspian, and it is logical that the Caspian Technological Training Centre (CTTC) was established there in 2004 to allow technicians to learn basic skills. This centre is one of the biggest in the world; at the time of writing it is putting around 120 newly recruited technicians through a one-year programme. Approximately 200 technicians recruited and trained by BP are now working on the assets of AIOC, BTC, Shakh Deniz and SCP (South Caucasus Pipeline). In addition to classrooms, the centre also offers a workshop, incorporating instrumentation, electrical, mechanical and production equipment. It is also boasts accreditation to deliver training on complex electrical and instrumentation equipment installed in difficult areas, and potential ignition sources to prevent accidents. 'It is the only place outside the UK accredited for this training', says Andy Buckworth, operations director of the CTTC. The centre has an operations training plant (OTP) which is an impressive core of the whole establishment. It comprises three-phase plant designed to separate oil and gas from water. Overall, there is 90% capacity utilization of the centre, with an equal share of theory and practice.

Following the route of a 'maximization of nationalization' programme, Azeri professionals were promoted in Sangachal to strategically important positions within the terminal's operations team. Some of them went through training in the CTTC. In Sangachal much focus was put on creating a unique programme to cover the development of all core competencies in parallel with management and leadership skills. Regular gap analysis, on-the-job training and, most importantly, people planning to identify the desired route for growth of high-potential individuals were implemented.

Overall, BP, similar to other oil majors in the region, is using a national progression plan. The goals of this are to advance quickly with achieving targets, performing appraisals and arranging mentors. At the same time, in all its activities in Azerbaijan, BP bases its involvement on an assessment of cost-effective performance.

Part III
Models and Policies for the Future

6
Production, Revenues and Transparency

Caspian Sea oil and gas exploitation has made (and will in future make) a significant impact on the Caspian economies. The crucial question in this respect will be the maximization of the potential national benefits. Governmental policy will be of paramount importance. In many ways, the development of Caspian oil and gas production is a remarkable story of the transition era. Since the collapse of the Soviet Union the newly independent countries of the Caspian Sea region found their own place in the international energy arena and have developed their national energy strategies.

6.1 National oil and gas strategies

In Kazakhstan, following the Kashagan field discovery a few years ago, the probable reserves are estimated to be greater than 50 bln bbl in the Kazakh sector of the Caspian. The Development Plan for 2003–2015 for the Caspian prepared by the Kazakhstani government estimates more than US$30 bln to be spent over the next 12 years. An estimated 56 platforms, two new ports, two new export pipelines, among other infrastructure, are planned. At least 23 blocks containing large to medium-sized prospects will be tendered at a rate of not less than three per year.[76] In his address with regard to the strategy of joining the world's 50 most competitive nations, President Nazarbayev clearly stated that 'improving the effectiveness and economic returns from energy' is a crucial element for the country's sustainable economic growth (Nazarbayev, 2006: 6).

---

[76] The above estimates of investment do not include any onshore investment and development.

In Azerbaijan the National Oil Strategy is counted from the date of the signing of the 'Contract of the Century', which

> embarked on a qualitatively new phase in the development of its oil and gas deposits: large investments have been attracted to the country's economy, success has been achieved in ensuring the transportation of hydrocarbon reserves of the Caspian to the world market via Azerbaijan, and since 1999 the country has been continuously receiving foreign currency from the export of profit oil in the framework of the Contract of the Century. (The Long-Term Strategy on the Management of Oil and Gas Revenues.)

The Long-Term Strategy on the Management of Oil and Gas Revenues, which was adopted in 2004, clearly defined the expectations of the Azeri government regarding the profits from the oil and gas resources in the period 2005–2025, with a sharp increase in oil and gas revenues from 2008. However, it was expected that there would be a decline in these revenues after 2010. It would be logical at this stage of development for the Azeri government to set out the state policy on the depletion of the Azeri part of Caspian Sea oil. So far no signs of such a policy have been noticed.

The Turkmen government adopted a programme on mineral resources and hydrocarbon development in 2001, when after a series of high-profile reshuffles the government announced in 2004 an governmental anti-corruption campaign. Patronage networks permeate Turkmen society, which gives rise to a culture of bribery and corruption. Aiming to eliminate corruption, the late President Niyazov enacted legislation giving him direct control over Turkmen hydrocarbon resources.[77] According to Transparency International, the 2006 Corruption Perceptions Index (CPI) captured Turkmenistan's 'significant improvement' in the perception of corruption.

In October 2006 Turkmenistan disclosed plans for the development of its oil and gas resources for the next 23 years. The 'Programme of development of oil and gas industry of Turkmenistan up to 2030' was worked out as the continuation of the plans, stipulated in the National Programme 'Strategy of economic, political and cultural development up to 2020'.[78]

---

[77] One of the consequences of this development is likely to be an even greater siphoning off of export revenues to the presidential special fund.

[78] The Programme defines the scale and direction of work focusing on the output of oil and gas resources, their processing, the means of their delivery to local and external consumers.

The basic exploration works in the period up to 2030 will take place in the western and eastern territories. The intention of the Turkmen government in 2007–2030 is to increase the volume of oil reserves by 26.09 bln bbl and the volume of natural gas by 194.15 tcf.

In accordance with the Programme, the government also plans an ambitious increase in gas production: in 2010, 4.24 tcf; in 2020, 6.18 tcf; and in 2030, 8.83 tcf. In order to fulfil these ambitious targets, the Strategy of the President of Turkmenistan assumes the creation of a multidirectional pipeline system. The infrastructure units for processing and export of gas are planned, along with the development of new fields.

The Turkmen government has realized that not all grandiose oil and gas projects can be implemented relying only on Turkmen capital. As already mentioned in Chapter 4, FDI was attracted on the basis of PSAs. However, only a few of them were able to find their way to Turkmenistan, namely Petronas, Dragon Oil, Burren Energy, Mitro (in consortium with the state concern 'Turkmenneft' [Turkmen oil]).

The governmental strategy also includes the mid- and downstream industries, the development of oil- and gas-processing facilities (upgrading Turkmen and Seydi oil refinery complexes, and the installation of new oil refineries in Balkan, Ahal and Mary).

6.2   Hydrocarbon revenues and taxation

The profound presence of the state in oil and gas production can be clearly seen in the incorporation of the state in the country's licensing regulations and hydrocarbon legislation. As discussed in Chapter 4, there are many ways of justifying the establishment of national oil companies. Kemp (1990) pointed out at least five of them: the national oil company could be a device to ensure national ownership of oil; it could also provide the state with a right to oil; it could be a mechanism of control and regulation by the state of the oil industry; it could be an arm of the government in the process of advising the state; and finally the state oil company could be responsible for security of oil supply.

The concept of resource rent derives from the more general concept of economic rents, which in a broader sense represents the returns accruing to a factor of production in excess of its transfer earnings. It comes from the original Ricardian analysis (Ricardo, 1817; Blaug, 1978: 91–112), where it refers to the difference between what a factor earns and what is necessary to bring it into employment. Following the Paretian interpretation of the concept, the earnings usually refer to those obtainable in the factors' next most valuable alternative use. Applying the concept of general economic rent to oil exploration is quite a difficult task, because oil is not a renewable resource: once it's gone, it's gone. The costs of exploration and development can vary both within and across geographical boundaries. The definition of perfect competition cannot be applied to the oil industry. However, it is obvious that natural resource extraction is an activity that is likely to generate some rents, and therefore the expectations of governments to extract a share of these rents for the benefit of the nation are quite natural. One point should always be checked: that these revenues are raised without distortion in the allocation of resources, e.g. premature abandonment. It is a role of the government to achieve by its fiscal policy a high overall level of tax take consistent with encouragement of exploration and development of fields that are viable on a pre-tax basis. It is the desire and objective of every government to obtain at least part of the fiscal take comparatively early in the life of a field.

From the beginning of independence all the parties were following a learning curve in understanding each other (companies, governments), but also in understanding their role in the hydrocarbon industries. Naturally the rules are changing. As already mentioned in Chapter 5, since the beginning of 2004, Kazakhstan has been experiencing a change in the legal regime applicable to its petroleum industry. Amendments to the Tax Code came into effect on 1 January 2004 and new amendments have been adopted from 1 January 2005. On 8 December 2004 amendments to the Petroleum Law and the Subsurface Law became effective. Finally, a new Production Sharing Agreement Law (applicable to the Caspian and Aral Seas) is soon to be adopted. These will have a substantial impact on the petroleum industry in the future. They reflect the government's policy of increased participation of the national oil company (DentonWildeSapte, 2005).

So let us consider the example of the state's increased participation in the national oil company – KazMunaiGaz. This increased participation takes the following forms. First of all there is a required minimum 50 per cent equity participation in all new contracts (provided in the draft PSA Law and Decree 708). That clearly could provide some disincentives in the exploration or production projects. These can be demonstrated by the calculations of expected monetary value (*EMV*).

$$EMV = P(NPV) - E,$$

where

  P is a probability of success of the project

NPV is net present value of a project
E is exploration costs

If *EMV* > 0, the project will go ahead. If there is full risk-sharing by the state company, participation will never affect the *EMV* in a negative sense.

Another form of increased Kazakhstani government participation is expressed in a provision giving the state a priority right to purchase an interest in a subsurface use contract or in an entity having subsurface use rights that is offered for sale (state pre-emptive right).

This provision states that

> in order to preserve and strengthen the resource and energy base of the country's economy, in new and previously executed contracts for subsurface use, the state shall have a priority right over any other party to the contract, or participants of a legal entity holding the subsurface right, or any other persons, to acquire the subsurface use right (or part thereof) and/or interest (shareholding) in a legal entity holding the subsurface use right being alienated, on conditions which are no worse than those offered by other buyers.

This type of legislatively imposed state pre-emption is rare, and investors have expressed concerns that such a right may reduce the value of their investments. However, this is one type of energy policy that the Kazakhstani government is pursuing.

Another element of the increasing role of the state is the concept of a 'strategic partner', which was added to the Petroleum Law of Kazakhstan. A 'strategic partner' is a foreign or Kazakhstani company selected by KazMunaiGaz to be its partner in a contract which it obtained by direct negotiation. The company selected to be the strategic partner will be responsible for paying the signing bonus and exploration costs unless otherwise provided for in the terms of a joint operating agreement. However, that could damage the *EMV*; if the strategic partner carries the state's share of these costs, which might not be reimbursed, the effect on the investment decision could be a negative *EMV* ≤ 0. In Chapter 5 we discussed the increased focus on local content and technology, which could be summarized as another increase of the government role in their energy strategy, where the promotion of local content and technology is of paramount importance to Kazakhstan's policy for the further economic development of the country.

Before 2004 Kazakhstan's oil and gas tax regime was described as equitable, stable and attractive. However, since the introduction of the Tax

Code in 2004 Kazakhstan has changed its fiscal structure drastically and not in favour of foreign investors. The 'golden' pre-2004 time of the Kazakhstan Tax Code allowed a number of flexibilities 'to customize a tax regime suitable to reflect the feasibility of the field, given particular OPEX, CAPEX, and transportation costs. Under the pre-2004 regime, marginal fields were as attractive as the expensive, offshore prospects, and sometimes more so'. (Fowler, 2005: 4).

The 2004 Tax Code provides no recovery for costs incurred in violation of the domestic content requirements. The 2004 and 2005 amendments to the Tax Code result in an increase in the government take for both tax models: Model 1 (tax royalty) and Model 2 (PSA). Box 6.1 is a summary of the provisions for each model.

Box 6.1   Tax models in Kazakhstan

Model 1 (tax royalty): No stabilization of tax provisions is provided. All taxes are to be paid at the effective rate on the date the tax obligation arises. Signature bonus is paid based on the results of tendering. Commercial discovery bonus is paid for each commercial discovery and is based on the discovered recoverable reserves (as determined by the authorized state agency) and valued at London IPE (International Petroleum Exchange) prices. The rate of the commercial bonus is 0.1 per cent of the calculation base.

Payment of an economic rent tax is applicable. This tax, which was imposed starting in January 2004, is one that the *exporter* of crude oil pays. Rent tax is to be determined on the basis of a sliding scale provided by the Tax Code and depending on the 'market price' of oil. The market price of oil is determined as the value of the exported crude oil based on a basket of published market prices netted back for sales costs and adjusted for the quality of the oil. The sliding scale ranges from 1 per cent if the market price is US$19/bbl to 33 per cent if the market price is US$40/bbl or higher. Royalty is to be paid at fixed rates on a sliding scale based on actual production levels at rates ranging from 2 per cent to 6 per cent. A conversion applicable to gas (to convert to an oil equivalent) is included in the Code as well as how to calculate a royalty for 'free' gas.

Other subsurface taxes apply (e.g. property tax, land tax, etc.). Corporate income tax payable at a maximum of 30 per cent applies. Note that there are changes to depreciation schedules

---

and other deductions that will affect this calculation. Payment of excess profits tax. Note that the basis for the calculation and the rates have changed under the new Tax Code amendments. The basis for this calculation is contractor's net disposable income. The excess profits tax rates vary from 5 per cent to 60 per cent.

Model 2 (PSA): Stability of taxes is provided for Model 2 contracts. The 2005 amendments eliminate royalty obligations for Model 2 (PSA) contracts. The cost of oil will be limited to 75 per cent of production prior to payback and 50 per cent after payback; these ceilings apply after royalty production has been taken into account. Included in the non-recoverable items are signature bonuses, commercial discovery bonus, expenditures in breach of local content rules, etc. Profit production is to be divided between the Republic and the contractor based on the lowest of the following three triggers: R-Factor; IRR-Factor and P-Factor.

R-Factor is the accumulated income divided by the accumulated expenditures. The percentage allocated to the contractor are as follows (this includes the 2005 Tax Code change):

R-Factor $\leq 1.2 = 70\%$

R-Factor between 1.2 and 1.5 = 70% $-2*$(R-factor $- 1.2) * 100\%$

R-Factor $\geq 1.5 = 10$ per cent

IRR-Factor is the annual discount rate at which the net present value of the project is zero. The reporting period is one month, so it is not clear how this will be calculated for the one-month period. The contractor's share is as follows (the following formulae have been modified to include the 2005 Tax Code change):

IRR ≤ 12 per cent = 70%

IRR between 12% and 20% = 70% $-7.50 *$ (IRR $- 12\%$)

IRR $\geq 20\% = 10\%$

P-Factor (price factor) is the sum of the deflated cost production plus the contractor's share of profit production divided by the total volume of oil produced; all for a reporting period. The contractor's share is:

P-Factor $\leq$ US\$12/bbl = 70%

P-Factor between US\$12 and US\$27 = 70% −0.04*(P-factor −12)*100%

P-Factor ≥ US\$27/bbl = 10%

Corporate income tax payable at a maximum of 30 per cent applies. Note that there are changes to depreciation schedules and other deductions that will affect this calculation. The state's total take (including corporate income tax) cannot be less than 10 per cent of the monthly total production value prior to payback and 40 per cent after payback for the reporting period (as provided by the 2005 amendments). This tax is now singled out as a separate tax and called an 'additional payment of a subsurface user operating under a PSA regime'. This tax is excluded from corporate income tax deductions and the R-Factor. It is included in the IRR-Factor calculation.

Model 2 contracts are not subject to the export rent tax, excess profits tax, excise tax, property tax, land tax and, as of 1 January 2005, royalty.

At the end of 2007 Kazakhstan warned international oil companies 'to stop living "in ancient times" as it prepared to tighten the fiscal regime at oilfields and increase state ownership of its flagship Caspian Sea development' (Gorst, 2007a). The draft revisions to the Tax Code are in the agenda of the government. This demonstrates an increase of developing state capacity through the instruments of state governance.

In Turkmenistan the first Tax Code was adopted in November 2004; before this, business operated on the basis of various government instructions relating to different forms and levels of taxation. Oil and gas taxation was based on the conditions of PSAs. The main change which the first Tax Code brought to the contractors was a positive change in the reduction of profit tax in many PSAs from 25 per cent to 20 per cent. However, the downside was related to the position of subcontractors. All subcontractors are obliged to be registered in Turkmenistan and pay their taxes there, even if they are foreign entities and have to pay their taxes in the countries of their origin with which Turkmenistan might not have an agreement with regard to double taxation. As a consequence of this prices for services went up, putting an extra burden on the contractors.

In December 2005 the Tax Code was revised; current tax legislation is based on several tax laws and regulations amended by presidential decrees. Legislation of importance to the foreign investor includes value-added, profit and property taxation, special taxation for small enterprises and reduced taxes in free economic zones. In addition, foreign investors are required to register with the State Chief Tax Inspectorate before beginning operations.

The main current challenge for the oil companies working on the basis of PSAs in Turkmenistan is to negotiate with the Turkmen government the applicability of the Tax Code. At the time of writing, the government position is based on the understanding of the supreme status of the Tax Code with regard to the PSAs, unless in the particular item of the Tax Code there is reference to the Law on Mineral Resources and Hydrocarbon Development; then agreed PSA tax conditions are applied.

The Azeri law is a modified version of the Soviet law, which protects investors from adverse changes in legislation for a period of ten years after their incorporation. Under this law expropriation and/or confiscation is only permitted in exceptional circumstances, and requires prompt and adequate compensation paid in foreign currency.

Azeri law grants the right to foreign enterprises to repatriate profits after payment of taxes and duties, but does not grant the unconditional right to convert profits into hard currency prior to repatriation. Azeri law requires that investment disputes be settled in national courts by arbitration, unless otherwise provided by treaty.

Azerbaijan does not have a law on the subsoil, as does Kazakhstan. The Law on State Property was passed in November 1991, giving the Republic of Azerbaijan control over its natural resources, including those in the Caspian Sea. Foreign investors proceed on the basis of the Foreign Investment Law, which allows the government to grant contracts which are then ratified by parliament. This procedure was adopted by the Western consortium in the contract to develop the ACG fields.

At the time of writing, the profit tax rate is 22 per cent. VAT is payable at 18 per cent on imported goods. VAT paid on the purchase of equipment or intangible assets cannot be offset against the VAT collected from customers. This payment is considered as capital expenditure and is recovered through depreciation. Land tax rates are determined as a percentage of the minimum wage. Export tariffs apply to most goods from Azerbaijan.

Export duty took effect from April 1995. The duty applies to crude oil and the rate is specified as 70 per cent of the difference between the contract price and the wholesale price. Petroleum investments undertaken by foreign investors via PSCs may be exempt from this tax.

Import tariffs are common in Azerbaijan. Exemptions include goods imported as contributions to charter funds of enterprises wholly owned by foreigners, and raw materials, equipment and wares imported for the 'productive needs' of enterprises.

The PSA to develop the ACG fields was signed in 1994. It provides for bonuses, for profit oil sharing based on the investor's rate of return, and profits tax[79] (see Box 6.2).

Cost recovery provisions allow operating costs to be recovered from total production. Capital costs are recovered from a maximum of 50 per cent of oil remaining after the deduction of operating costs.

Box 6.2   PSA to develop the ACG fields

Here we describe the main steps in the creation of the PSA in Azerbaijan. SOCAR, on behalf of the Azeri government, signs a PSA with contractor(s). SOCAR submits the PSA to the parliament for ratification. After the approval of parliament, the presidential degree on PSA will be issued. SOCAR submits the PSA to the contractor with the effective date of the contract.

'PSAs do not divide profit out of market proceeds but instead divide the physical production after allowing a portion of output to be retained by the foreign oil company for the recovery of pre-production and production costs' (Bindemann, 2000: 29). Profit from petroleum is shared between the contractor and SOCAR according to the cumulative after-tax real rate of return achieved by the contractor. This means that the costs will be recovered only when the oil is produced. The precise sharing depends on (1) when early production is achieved and (2) whether transportation costs are determined.

If total transport costs are less than or equal to US$3/bbl and the contractor achieves early oil, Table 6.1(a) applies.

If total transport costs are greater than US$4/bbl and the contractor achieves early oil, Table 6.1(b) applies.

Profit oil is to be split between SOCAR and the contractor on the basis of:

- when the contractor achieves early oil production.
- the cumulative after-tax real rate of return achieved at the end of the preceding calendar quarter.

---

[79] The agreement is complicated by the terms being dependent on whether or not early production is achieved and the transportation costs.

Table 6.1 The shares between SOCAR and the contractor

(a)

Contractor's RROR, %	SOCAR share, %	Contractor share, %
Less than 16.75	30	70
16.7–22.76	55	45
22.75 or more	80	20

Source: Based on PSA to develop Azeri, Chirag and Deep Water Gunashli Fields, http://www.bp.com/genericarticle.do?categoryId=9006654&contentId=7013493

(b)

Contractor's RROR, %	SOCAR share, %	Contractor share, %
Less than 16.75	25	75
16.7–22.76	50	50
22.75 or more	75	25

• total transport costs calculated on a per barrel basis restated in real terms at the effective date.

The contractor is liable for profits tax. This is taken into account in determining the contractor's rate of return. The rate of profits tax is fixed at 25 per cent.

Amortization deductions are:

1. 25% declining balance for equipment and fixed assets.
2. 10%/year straight line for bonus payments.
3. 2.5%/year straight line for permanent office buildings.
4. 5%/year straight line for temporary office buildings.

Losses can be carried forward indefinitely. Interest on loans is a deductible expense.

Abandonment

An abandonment fund in the form of an escrow account is to be jointly opened by the contractor and SOCAR. Contributions to the fund begin when 70 per cent of the reserves identified in the development plan have been recovered. Contributions will not exceed 10 per cent of all capital costs. Contributions are recoverable as operating costs.

Foreign exchange

The PSC allows the contractor to operate foreign exchange accounts inside and outside Azerbaijan. It also allows the contractor to export or dispose of any proceeds from petroleum sales. Exemption from import duties on equipment are provided for in the agreement.

Changes to the contract

The stabilization provision insures the contractor against adverse changes in Azeri law.

Total bonus payments are US$300 mln.

- 50% (minus any payments made) is payable within 30 days of the effective date.
- 25% is payable within 30 days of production reaching 40 000 bbl/day.
- 25% is payable within 30 days from the date at which crude oil has been exported from the main export pipeline for a period of 60 days.

6.3   Companies and governments interests

When discussing oil and gas production strategy it is important to distinguish several players whose interests would be reflected in every governmental strategy/policy.

Any investor seeks to obtain (maximum or satisfactory) profits from oil and gas exploitation. The objective here is to gain from the host government as much freedom as possible to determine the size, characteristics and phasing of plans in exploration, appraisal, development and production. It is an understandable desire for there to be as little governmental interference as possible over pricing of oil and gas as well as equipment purchases.[80] The investor's overall objective is preferential

---

[80] Other types of freedom are in the 'wish list' of every investor, such as freedom to choose investment partners, to source supplies of equipment and labour as well as freedom to import currency and convert local currency to foreign currencies at market rates.

stable and modest levels of regulation applied to oil and gas activities over the contract term. A special item in the list of objectives is taxation, where investors prefer low levels especially in the early years of field life (pre-payback). In general the investor's preferential tax structure is related to profit with tax and regulatory arrangements that share the investment risks. Finally, investors would prefer no residual liability (after the termination of the contract).

On the other hand, the host government has quite different objectives with regard to oil and gas production. In particular, the government's objective is to obtain a large share of economic rents from oil exploitation with the ability to regulate exploration and development, as well as the pace of production.[81] In addition, host governments attempt to enhance local participation in employment, and provision of supplies and equipment. Usually, host governments prefer investors to take a high share of investment risk and cost. Early revenue and predictable tax revenues are a high priority in a governmental strategy. Oil and gas extraction is an activity that is likely to generate economic rents. In this respect it is legitimate for a government to extract a share of these rents for the benefit of the population of the host country. The economic condition here applying here is that those revenues should be raised without causing any distortion to the allocation of resources. There are several points that should be taken into account regarding the application of the concept of economic rents in petroleum exploitation. In particular, oil is a non-renewable resource. Exploration and development costs can differ markedly both within and across geographical boundaries. Petroleum does not conform to the textbook definition of perfect competition; few enterprises have the resources and capacities to perform certain operations, and thus agency problems related to some costs, quasi-extractable rent and low transaction frequencies affect the contractual relationships and ex post renegotiation possibilities between companies and governments. The government might have different expectations than it did in 1994–1995; it is not simply a matter of rent, but more importantly of overall power.

6.4 Transparency and governance

There is scholarly debate whether or not oil wealth is a blessing or a curse for a resource-rich nation (Auty and Mikesell, 1998; Esanov et al., 2006;

[81] The full list of the governmental objectives includes provision of security of supplies for the domestic market; influencing the domestic price of oil and gas as well as obtaining some local ownership of the resource.

Gylfason, 2001, 2007; Sachs and Warner, 1995, etc.). One element of these debates is related to the corruption which the oil wealth brings to the country. The logic is very simple: high mineral (oil) revenues allow a government to maintain power and provide rewards for political supporters, while doing very little for the ordinary people. So what could be a solution in this situation? How is it possible to make resource-rich governments more accountable for their spending? Why it is so important?

Let us start from the last point. Transparency in the management of oil revenues should provide governments with a greater chance of political stability. Historical experience has shown that the lack of institutional development and uncontrolled corruption are the downside of the windfall profits from oil production (Gylfason, 2004). Examples abound, from Nigeria to Iran to Venezuela. In these countries political control over those natural resources makes political power vital and, of course, politics becomes a competition for a near-total control of wealth. The consequences could be very dramatic for the civil society or the establishment of democracy.

It is clear that a great deal is required from resource-rich governments, and strengthening their governance of revenues and spending is of paramount importance. In 2005 the IMF published its *Guide on Resource Revenue Transparency*, which provides a template for assessing fiscal transparency in resource-rich countries. However, the main international vehicle for revenue transparency is the Extractive Industries Transparency Initiative (EITI), which was announced by former UK Prime Minister Tony Blair at the World Summit on Sustainable Development in Johannesburg, September 2002.[82] It aims to provide for greater transparency of the extractive industries. The EITI advocates as the first and most important principle of transparency the availability of information for the general public, including the disclosure of payments related to resources. Transparency and accountability are fundamental to the EITI. The main principles of the EITI are: 'Publish what you pay' for the foreign and national extractive companies; and 'Publish what you receive' for the host governments of the extractive industries. The independent third party is to reconcile information from these reports and then to produce the consolidated EITI report.

The problem and the challenge here is that the EITI is a voluntary scheme, which could potentially be very powerful; however, not every country recognizes it and not every resource-rich country is rushing to

[82] See http://www.dfid.gov.uk.

join it. In a way the EITI seems toothless. A corrupt country probably would not join and follow all the stages of the EITI. At the EITI international conference in Oslo in October 2006 much was said about the need to make the EITI a prestigious club of resource-rich countries, so that joining this club would be self-motivating. In addition, large investors, such as F&C Assets Management, claimed at the conference that endorsement of the EITI and compliance with all EITI criteria by host countries and extractive companies could soon become one of the important factors considered by investors when assessing investment risks. The mechanism of independent validation of compliance by countries with EITI criteria, introduced at the same conference, is well suited to serve this purpose, as only fully compliant countries will be allowed to use the EITI brand. To date there are some 'surprising' countries on the list that have already joined the EITI: Nigeria, Democratic Republic of Congo, Sierra Leone. However, citizens of the resource-rich countries could pressure the governments to support the EITI. Industry would bring further pressures to join it. Thus the main idea of the EITI is to draw together governments, the private sector, civil society and international organizations.

Azerbaijan and Kazakhstan have both expressed their interest in the EITI. However, while Azerbaijan has volunteered to become a pilot case of the Initiative, Kazakhstan was initially hesitant.

In November 2003 President Aliyev of Azerbaijan issued an instruction to the Cabinet of Ministers, which on 13 November established a National Committee on the EITI. Then, after a year, the Memorandum of Understanding was signed between stakeholders: the Committee of the EITI, foreign and local extractive sector companies, and the NGO Coalition (see Box 6.3). Deloitte & Touche was nominated as an independent auditing company. So far Azerbaijan has disclosed five EITI reports.[83]

Box 6.3 Azerbaijan: Coalition to Improve Transparency in the Extractive Industry (ITEI)

In Azerbaijan the Coalition to Improve Transparency in the Extractive Industry was established in May 2004 with 32 members in order to conduct public monitoring and raise the awareness of the citizens of Azerbaijan with regard to transparency and accountability.

---

[83] On the basis of the agreement in the memorandum both the extractive companies and Azeri government should submit their reports twice a year.

Members of the Coalition include representatives from civil society organizations and private individuals. At the time of writing, the Coalition has 107 (94 public associations and 13 private individuals) members. The Coalition is actively involved in the implementation of the EITI in Azerbaijan. From the beginning it participated in preparations for EITI introduction in Azerbaijan, then in improving the Azerbaijan version of the EITI. The Coalition had an active role in the selection of an auditor, and participated in public debate of the auditor's opinion and preparation of feedback on EITI reports (see the main text).

The Coalition views the EITI as an initiative that covers most revenues (profit oil, associated gas, bonuses, per acre payments, taxes paid by contractors, traffic rates); however, there are some types of revenue (taxes paid by subcontractors, rent, social payments, income taxes of employees) that are outside its scope, and therefore the EITI can answer only some of the questions of the public with regard to oil revenues. So from the point of view of the Coalition a step to correct the situation is an improvement of EITI reporting. Another step is the introduction of the surveys among state bodies and companies. However, the latter is doubtful in the current situation in Azerbaijan. As Ingilab Ahmadov, director of the Public Finance Monitoring Centre, told me, 'Azerbaijan as a post-Soviet country has a lack of democracy, and lacks a civil society that plays an active role in the decision-making process in the country. Some of the companies following the government do not consider the NGO as a strong society voice and are sympathetic mainly to government' (interview conducted on 15 August 2007 via e-mail). Nevertheless, it is hoped that further steps to develop the EITI will be taken in Azerbaijan soon.

Based on the last report, the Azerbaijani Coalition of civil society institutions expressed its concern about the degree of increase in the amount of capital expenditures and the extension of the period of recoupment of the ACG project. Concern was also expressed with regard to the total costs of the ACG project, which were initially projected at US$8 bln, and have since risen to US$14 bln. The Coalition refers to the experts' explanation as 'mismatches in the calculations of the equipment and machinery as well as the expected capital expenditures in certain areas of operation, and a significant delay in the commencement of the phase of production in general' (from Conclusion of the ITEI Coalition of civil society institutions on the (5th) report by the Government Commission on the results of the first six months of 2006 in the framework of the EITI[84]).

Another interesting fact that the Coalition highlighted and questioned in its conclusion is that since the implementation of the Contract of the Century, the amount of operating expenditures has worked out at less than expected.[85] The Coalition pleads for stricter control in this matter, but doubts that SOCAR, which is responsible for this, will be able to achieve it, because of the company's dual status. On one side the company represents the government of Azerbaijan (customer in this project), while on the other side, it is among the shareholders who are in charge of the implementation of the project. It is clearly seen as a conflict of interests.

Other pitfalls are highlighted in the auditor's conclusion related to the reporting system at SOCAR and the amount of payments by the company to the government of Azerbaijan, which give rise to contradictions. But fundamentally the effectiveness of the EITI is heavily dependent on a transparent treasury function in government. Clearly this remains to be seen.

Box 6.4   SOCAR financial relations with the Azeri government

It was indicated in the report that over the first six months of 2006, the total amount of contributions from local companies – remittances by SOCAR and joint ventures, in which the company has an interest and who are signatories to the Memorandum of Understanding and operate in the country – to the government of Azerbaijan in the framework of production activities amounted to 403.6 mln manats, down by 119 mln manats from the corresponding figure in 2005 (595.4 mln manats).

Meanwhile, since the beginning of 2006, the amount of payments from local companies to the government of Azerbaijan has more than tripled. Throughout 2005 the companies were not subject to profit tax in the framework of the ACG agreement, while the year 2006 started with the imposition of this levy on

---

[84] http://www.eiti-az.org/ts_gen/eng/feal/5thReport_CoalitionOpinion.pdf.
[85] The operating expenditures are mainly generated in Azerbaijan, while the origin of capital expenses is linked to overseas activities.

project shareholders, including SOCAR. Notwithstanding this fact, the amount of the paid profit tax included in the report is called into question. Over the first half of 2006, local companies have reportedly paid 11.6 mln manats in profit tax, up just 3.1 mln manats as compared to the corresponding figure for 2005 (8.5 mln manats).

A point of concern is that SOCAR, as a company with a 10 per cent interest in the ACG project, should have paid about 23.6 mln manats in profit tax, given that foreign partners who retain the remaining 90 per cent of shares in the same project have met their corresponding levy obligations to the amount of 213 mln manats. The question as to how the difference of 15 mln manats can be explained remains open. As to other taxes to be paid, certain points can be called in question as well; therefore, the Coalition hopes that SOCAR will clarify all the points that have been raised. In the interview I conducted with Anvar Gasimov, he stated first that extra expenses (such as travel) reduced the profit tax of the major companies, while in the case of SOCAR it paid a total of US$41.7 mln but the transfer was made after the end of the second calendar quarter (interview with A. Gasimov, head of Economic and Accounting Department, Joint Projects Division, SOCAR, 29 October 2007, Reading).

Maturity is required from all parties involved: the government, the extractive companies, and the NGOs. As Ingilab Ahmadov has pointed out, 'NGOs and media do not have any strong capacity and skills to demonstrate a competent alternative opinion from the Society' (interview conducted on 15 August 2007 via e-mail). Overall, there is no doubt that Azerbaijan has made significant progress in implementation of the EITI. However, there is an opportunity, scope and a need for improvement.

One of the transparency challenges for Kazakhstan is to follow up this Initiative proactively, moving towards practical implementation. In June 2004 Kazakhstani NGOs formed a coalition 'Oil revenues under public oversight'. The Coalition of NGOs worked in close cooperation with the international campaign 'Publish what you pay', the UK's Department for International Development, the EU governments, the World Bank, the European Bank for Reconstruction and Development and other international institutions in order to initiate the process of Kazakhstan joining the EITI. That was the first step of the Kazakhstan's path to the EITI. In 2005 the decision on Kazakhstan's participation in the EITI was welcomed by the government of Kazakhstan, following consultation with oil companies operating in Kazakhstan on their willingness to participate.

There is a direct benefit to Kazakhstan from joining the EITI. First of all, there is a unilateral commitment to disclose the oil revenues received by the treasury from over 100 legal entities[86] operating in the oil and gas industry; second, it motivates every legal entity operating in the sector to produce reports on the amounts of tax and non-tax payments to the government to be included into a consolidated EITI report, which is to be made publicly available;[87] and third, it ensures that the information base is available to the general public on the National Fund of the Republic of Kazakhstan.

On 5 October 2005, a Memorandum of Understanding (MoU) on EITI implementation in Kazakhstan was signed by the Ministry of Energy and Mineral Resources (representing the government), companies possessing rights to develop natural resources in extractive industries (including petrochemicals), and a group of MPs of the Republic of Kazakhstan. The NGO Coalition refused to sign the MoU because they disagreed with the proposed scheme of publishing aggregated information on companies' payments only (in contrast, the NGO Coalition insisted that the EITI report should contain details on each company's payments and the government's receipts from each extractive company).

The Coalition insisted on further negotiations between the stakeholders aimed at developing the more progressive model. Being forced by the need to bring civil society on board, the government and companies finally agreed on the compromise proposal, the 'Oil revenues under public oversight' coalition to establish the National Stakeholders' Council[88] which would oversee implementation of the EITI and would become a forum for further debates of stakeholders on furthering the EITI in Kazakhstan. The National Council includes three permanent representatives from each of the following establishments: the government, the group of parliamentarians, the group of extractive companies and NGOs.

---

[86] There are conflicting data on the number of extractive companies registered in Kazakhstan.

[87] It should be noted that only aggregated reports will be published; i.e. the public will not see the amount of payments from each company. According to the MoU on EITI implementation in Kazakhstan, information on social investment projects of extractive companies is not to be included in EITI report, however.

[88] On 20 February 2006 the first official meeting of the National Council of stakeholders took place in Astana.

There are some critical points with regard to the MoU that should be highlighted here, namely: so far the MoU has been signed largely by the oil companies (however, some small local oil and gas companies still have not done this) and by only very few mining companies, which are not inclined to do so. This has repercussions on the ability of civil society to take part in the political process of controlling mineral revenue.

Another problem is associated with the fact that the signing parties were the oil companies, but not necessarily their affiliates working in Kazakhstan (e.g. ChevronTexaco, but not TCO; or BG Karachaganak Ltd and not KPO). Through interviews with the companies I received the following explanation for this: the consortia usually consist of more than one operating company; therefore it would be difficult to come to a consensus and the matter would be very complicated if all members were involved. In any case all members of the consortia signed the EITI (interviews conducted throughout 2006–2007). In my view, the issue of the affiliates' accountabilities remains a legitimate concern. In 2007 Kazakhstan became the first participating country *de facto* to require compulsory participation in the EITI by applicants for new sub-soil use rights.[89] However, it is very important to ensure that all companies that already have contracts with the government will be subject to reporting in the framework of the EITI.

Many things remain to be done with regard to joining the EITI in Kazakhstan. At this stage, the first and most important one is to involve all extractive companies that have declined to sign the MoU. So far Kazakhstan is unable to meet the requirements of EITI Criterion 4: participation of 'all companies including state-owned enterprises'. Support and persistence from the government side is crucial, because at the time of writing the EITI in Kazakhstan resembles more a populist campaign: until July 2007, when the costed work plan was finally agreed with all the stakeholders and published on the website, the government did not have a clear strategy of implementation.

In accordance with the MoU between the government of Kazakhstan and the World Bank (dated 1 December 2006), the government made a commitment to establish an EITI Secretariat and a special budget line to fund the reconciliation and validation of EITI reports. In July 2007, these commitments were reinforced at the government's meeting of Prime Minister Masimov with the participation of representatives of the Coalition 'Oil revenues – under public oversight'; however, it is still unclear when the Secretariat will actually start working.

[89] *Macleod Dixon Kazakhstan Legal Bulletin*, 30 January 2007.

According to the government press office, Kazakh Prime Minister Masimov said at the July meeting that 'dragging out the implementation of the Extractive Industries Transparency Initiative (EITI) in Kazakhstan any further is absolutely unacceptable'. He is pressing his Cabinet to implement the EITI in Kazakhstan.

Nevertheless, the government still has not selected the auditor to carry out the collection and reconciliation of the government's and the companies' reports. Previous attempts to contract PricewaterhouseCoopers and KPMG failed for procedural reasons. The problem is exacerbated by the provision in the MoU that limits the pool of possible auditors to the Big Four only.

> I think that this provision is totally wrong as it makes selection of the auditor highly uncompetitive. There are a lot of local audit companies which could be considered as credible for doing this work. And we should remember that this is not audit but merely reconciliation of data so it definitely does not require exceptional competencies from the company. Our Coalition has suggested that stakeholders revise the corresponding clause of the MoU. (Anton Artemyev, director of Kazakhstan Revenue Watch programme at the Soros Foundation Kazakhstan, member of the 'Oil revenues under public oversight' Coalition.)

Coalition 'The NGO is in general dissatisfied with the progress of the EITI in Kazakhstan so far' (Malik Isabekov, a representative of the Coalition, press conference in Almaty, 12 July 2007).

In addition to the above-mentioned problems,

> the population's awareness is very low and EITI still remains the topic of interest for a very limited group of people in Kazakhstan. Ask people in the streets, and you will see that almost no one knows about this initiative. However, without citizens being aware and without broader public involvement, EITI is rather senseless. All stakeholders, and the government foremost, should aim their efforts raising public awareness. People should await EITI reports, scrutinize and discuss them after publication, and raise concerns if anything goes wrong with the companies' payments. This is what EITI is for! (Anton Artemyev, ibid.)

Overall, no doubt, revenue audits in both countries are limiting politicians' ability to use oil revenues for their personal use or to take bribes to give foreign companies a desirable deal. As it stands now, citizens of both Kazakhstan and Azerbaijan usually have no idea how much natural resource wealth is being generated or where that money is going; however, as indicated above, significant progress has been made in Azerbaijan as a pilot country for the EITI.

So far the figures for governmental spending in Turkmenistan available through various sources have been rather patchy. According to Global Witness, 'At the end of 2005, the Turkmen Parliament approved total spending for 2006 of 81.3 trillion manat, US$15.6 billion at the official exchange rate, or US$3.3 billion at the unofficial rate' (Global Witness, 2006: 15). There was a lot of speculation that Deutsche Bank keeps several Turkmen government accounts in Frankfurt, but Deutsche Bank kept its silence until the death of President Niyazov. Only after his death did it confirm for the first time that for 'more than a decade it has been managing funds in the central bank of Turkmenistan' (Williamson, 2007). There is a lot of criticism of Deutsche Bank for breaking their own guidelines governing international operations. The weak explanation offered by Deutsche Bank that the Central Bank funds did not belong to the late President Niyazov cannot be taken at face value, bearing in mind that everything in Turkmenistan related to money was under direct control of the deceased president and of course the governors were appointed and dismissed by him.

According to Global Witness, one of the main accounts held in Frankfurt was an account in which money from Ukraine's gas purchase from Turkmenistan was deposited.[90] According to that contract, from 2002 to 2006, 50 per cent was paid in cash to the value of US$840 mln, and 50 per cent of the contract was supplied in barter goods equivalent to the same amount. Accountability is the major issue in Turkmenistan. How is all the money being spent? During the Niyazov era expensive construction projects were undertaken; many of them glorified the late president. In September 2002, US$41 mln went mysteriously missing from the Turkmen Central Bank. Niyazov initiated a special investigation and criminal procedures were brought against those responsible for the theft. In the end Deutsche Bank was blamed for everything that happened.

According to the Russian public prosecutor, the crime was performed by means of illegal electronic payments[91] to the Russian and Latvian

---

[90] The contract was signed in 2002 between the Turkmen and Ukrainian sides (represented by the national oil companies) with regard to Ukraine's gas purchases from Turkmenistan (Contract No. 14/404, signed 14 May 2001 between NAK Naftohaz Ukrainy and GTK Turkmenneftegas).

[91] From a group of people from the Turkmen and Russian banks.

banks from Turkmen Central Bank.[92] The Turkmen authorities were not cooperative at all and failed to provide any information to the Court in relation to US$41 mln. It could not even be confirmed with regard to a sum of US$20 mln that it belonged to Turkmenistan. As a result US$20 mln was never recovered.

The incident demonstrated that the Turkmen authorities would rather abandon the prosecution than allow the scrutiny of Turkmen accounting practices, which leads us to conclude that the authorities are highly incompetent and possibly corrupted.

Under the regime of the late President Niyazov nobody would have imagined that Turkmenistan would decide to join the EITI, and this remains still a big question at the time of writing. However, taking into account that time for more transparency in the Turkmen–Ukraine gas trade has come, at least from the Ukrainian side, there is hope that this could be a step forward in the Turkmen way of governance and the clarity of its management of hydrocarbon wealth, which could be facilitated by potential pressure from Russia (another strong partner of Turkmenistan in the gas business). As Russia is one of the G8 members supporting EITI globally, no doubt the Russian government should press Turkmenistan to accept better accountability and promote transparency in the energy sector.

The overall conclusion is that transparency can improve governance. Throughout the world, experience confirms this principle. For example, many African countries improved the management of public spending in the 1990s. Through openness it is possible to break the links among corruption, secrecy and lack of accountability (Kostopoulos, 1999). It is hoped that the three Caspian economies will follow this path. Greater accountability for natural resource revenues will help these governments to plan for the future.

[92] Turkmenistan.ru/index.php?page...id=en&elern...id=5230&type=event&sort=date...desc.

7
Policies for Sustainable Development

7.1 Optimal energy policy: market failures and the impact of externalities

Any resource-rich country should adopt an integrated approach to energy policy. This should include components such as the principle of a cleaner environment, the sustainable development of the local economy to underpin stable energy suppliers for the future and to ensure a diverse economy that does not rely purely on energy exports. This set of elements is achievable by introducing advanced technologies as well as by improving the processes of energy production and spending of the resultant wealth, which we discussed in Chapter 6. In any case, policy-makers should ensure, through continual strategic review, that these interventions dovetail efficiently and steer private sector activity along routes consistent with the country's long-run development policy.

In order to facilitate the formulation of an optimal energy policy as an integral part of sustainable development, three major priorities should be put forward. These are the energy transport challenge; the nature of instruments to foster oil and gas production development together with the diversification of the national economy; and the need to underpin environmental stability by enhancing sustainable growth in the region. The governments of the Caspian Sea region should conduct their energy policies taking into account externalities in energy sectors where the public sector role is essential in addressing a coordination problem with regard to energy exploration and transport among the interested parties.

A common theme in these three areas is the need to address major externalities. Thus the governments of the Caspian Sea region should conduct their energy policies taking into account possible market failures in energy sectors: in this respect, the role of the public sector (rather than being a question of political choice) may be essential to address the coordination problem with regard to energy exploration and transport among the interested parties.

Moreover, unlike issues discussed in earlier chapters (such as oil funds, local content and risk mitigation), these remain challenges where one cannot yet see clear signs of a way forward in developments across the region. Hence they deserve consideration together in this chapter.

Very recent history underscores the pressing need to achieve a sound approach on these issues, and to develop some measure of agreement between companies and governments on legitimate and consistent official strategies. The recent past illustrates, by contrast, that governments are not necessarily pursuing such interests in a consistent or transparent manner over time. A genuine need to address externalities may become intertwined with narrower political or economic goals; and governments may use some factors such as the environment, taxes, customs, etc. to justify a significant (and opaque) reversal of the policies. Two recent cases clearly demonstrate this concern.

First, in July 2005 Royal Dutch Shell announced delays of at least eight months and a cost of US$20 bln (£11.4 bln), twice the original estimate of the Sakhalin-2 project (the LNG project off the east coast of Russia). After long debates, negotiations and pressure on Royal Dutch Shell, and accusations from a Russian environmental regulator, Gazprom, the Russian energy monopoly took majority control of the project when the foreign developers, led by Royal Dutch Shell, agreed to sell 50 per cent plus one share to Gazprom. As a result Shell cut its stake in Sakhalin-2 in half, to 27.5 per cent, and the two Japanese trading houses partnered with it also cut their holdings to the same extent. Gazprom agreed to pay US$7.45 bln, a price that analysts said was below market value (Kramer, 2006). This story was one of the first cases of governmental attempts to change the conditions of hydrocarbon contracts in the FSU.

Second, the Kazakhstani government learned this lesson very quickly in the summer of 2007. Something similar to Sakhalin-2 occurred with the Kashagan oil field in February 2007 the operator of the KCO consortium, Italian ENI Spa, announced a second delay in the start of production at Kashagan until the second half of 2010 and said that costs for the first phase would almost double to US$19 bln. The company explained the delay and higher cost in part on the basis of the need to meet environmental standards.

In response, Kazakhstan revoked the ENI-led group's environmental permit for at least three months in August 2007 while it investigated alleged violations of environmental rules. In addition, Eni was accused of breaking fire regulations, and of practising custom irregularities by the Kazakhstani side. Based on all these allegations, Kazakhstan has demanded greater control over Kashagan. The government expressed concern that due to such inadequate management the country's economy could be damaged and its reputation as a reliable global energy supplier questioned. As a solution it was proposed that KazMunaiGaz, the state oil company, would be appointed as cooperator at Kashagan, where ENI had proved 'incapable of fulfilling some of its obligations' (Gorst, 2007a). According to the information from the Kazakhstani banking circle, KMG is hoping to provide a syndicated loan of US$1.05 bln for the development of Kashagan.

According to Kazakh Deputy Finance Minister Daulet Ergozhin, the economic damage to Kazakhstan from delays and overruns of the Kashagan project will be at least US$10 bln. It is obvious that in these circumstances the government will not receive its earnings from Kashagan until Eni and its partners recover their investment costs. In addition, Kazakhstan has to cut its forecast for oil output for 2015 by 13 per cent[93].

It is very difficult to judge who is right and who is wrong in this dispute. However, one thing can be said with certainty: all sides bear some responsibility. Let us start with the KCO consortium. Right from the beginning ENI and its partners set themselves up for trouble by promising Kazakhstan too much when they bid for Kashagan. In private discussions with me, sources close to the KCO consortium highlighted a simple tactic that every oil company uses in negotiations. The logic here is that initially you promise the impossible, but in the future the client (the Kazakhstani government) has no alternative but to accept more realistic conditions and circumstances. It is understandable that five years' delay was a crucial figure for the Kazakhstani government to start to think about changing the terms of the existing contract; it blindly believed (or, at least pretended that it did) that the KCO consortium could fulfil their promises.

There is already in the mass media a strong opinion of resource nationalism in Kazakhstan. The parallel has been drawn with Russia, where behaviour of the Russian government towards the Sakhalin-2 project is compared with the behaviour of the Kazakhstani government towards Kashagan. However, Prime Minister Masimov firmly denied the

---

[93] On 27 August 2007, Kazakhstan appointed Sauat Mynbayev as energy minister to deal with the Kashagan issue, replacing Bakhtykozha Izmukhambetov. Izmukhambetov's replacement reflects government displeasure at the course of talks on Kashagan, observers say. Oil sector sources also expect a management change at KMG, which holds 9.33 per cent of Kashagan (*Argus FSU*, 31 August 2007).

government's involvement as part of a global trend towards increasing state control on mineral resources.

If we consider the situation from the Kazakhstani government point of view, the first conclusion is that either Kazakhstani representatives were highly inexperienced when they signed the deal with the consortium with such unrealistic delivery dates for the first oil, or rent-seeking behaviour prevailed in these negotiations. Cancellation of the project at this stage would have had a significant negative impact on the local economy and the international reputation of Kazakhstan, of course Kazakhstan is just showing political muscle. Some experts thought that President Nazarbayev was hoping to find support from the Italian Prime Minister Romano Prodi in consideration of Kazakhstan's application to chair the OSCE in 2009, and this question was discussed during Romano Prodi's visit to Kazakhstan in September 2007 (Atygayev, 2007; Turmanova, 2007).

Kazakhstan's parliament has passed legislation that would give it the right to cancel oil contracts on 'national security' grounds. This move appears designed to increase pressure on the partners in the 13 bln bbl Eni-led Kashagan project. The Majalis[94] has amended the country's law 'on resources and resources use' to allow Kazakhstan to keep the investors on their toes if their actions are deemed to threaten 'national security'. The Eni case may be resolved by a short-term compromise, but there is a fundamental issue at stake about sanctity of contracts ('good institutions' in the terminology of Chapter 1).

Finally, the dispute was resolved on 14 January 2008 when, on Kazakh TV, the authorities declared country's 'victory' by reducing the Kashagan partners' stakes in favour of KazMunaiGaz, whose share was raised to 16.6 per cent (thus equalling that of the other shareholders). KazMunaiGaz's obligation is to pay $1.78 bln for its increased share. According to S. Munbayev, Minister of Energy and Mineral Resources, ENI and its partners will be obliged to make a payment of $5 bln to the Kazakhstani government over the life of the development as compensation for lost revenue (TV Channel Khabar, 14 January 2008).

The above two cases have been described by critics as forced nationalization. It is premature at this stage to make a firm conclusion whether or not Kazakhstan is attempting to repeat the history of the oil-rich Middle Eastern producers (Marcel, 2005) in its attempt to renegotiate the conditions of the Kashagan oil project. As Helm highlighted, 'in energy markets, spot trading brings the market into instantaneous balance, and the future profile of expected spot prices (the futures market) enables

---

[94] Kazakhstan's lower parliamentary house.

contracting to hedge the price risk' (Helm, 2002: 176). PSAs occupy a significant place in Caspian development. The main incentives for producers in this situation will be negotiating the government–contract split, analysis of the cost recovery and of the profit stream of oil/gas, and mitigation of political and economic risks. To date no liquid futures markets exist if the price risk requires hedging. Therefore the difficulty with PSAs, which are long-term contracts, is to keep them stable, which is not an easy task for the new exploration and development of the oil fields.

However, in order to fully understand the logic of the thinking on the Kazakh side (at least), we should consider this situation from the point of view of the overall oil market environment. Current high oil prices boost profit of all oil companies; however, at the same time they restrict investment opportunities. Countries with significant energy resources (such as Russia or Kazakhstan) are enjoying the results of US$70–90/bbl of oil and do not depend on cash from foreign oil companies as they did in the 1990s. However, high oil prices have added to cost inflation. Since five years ago, when the oil boom had just started and oil prices were increasing steadily, the haste of upstream activity has led to a shortage of manpower and materials, more than doubling costs. So, companies' potential (and the Caspian region is not an exception) is limited by cost inflation and narrowing investment options.

In the early 1990s the Caspian governments signed deals to give oil investors favourable terms. In many cases this means delays with income streams to the host country until all costs had been recovered (see the Azerbaijan case). These projects were as a rule high-profile projects, high on the political agenda at the time. Now the situation is changing. The Caspian economies have turned around and become prosperous through the high oil prices, and the contracts which were signed by the Caspian governments in the 1990s (when the oil price was US$18–20/bbl) are being reviewed by a more confident and enriched political elite. To complete the picture, investment agreements and tax laws are also under scrutiny of governments to add to an 'optimal energy policy' in favour of the host country. The push of KMG as an operator for Kashagan demonstrates the point that the Kazakhstani government is becoming confident that the country could participate in large projects itself. The government is convinced that Eni made a mess of the Kashagan project. Costs soared to US$136 bln from US$57 bln, alarming the Kazakhs, and there will be delays until 2010. However, originally in 2005–2006 it was meant to cost only US$20 bln.[95]

[95] In the case of Sakhalin-2 the budget doubled to US$20 bln.

It would be wrong put all the blame on the IOCs. The situation of escalating prices was not foreseen at the time of bidding for these large-scale projects. However, for the host governments it means that their expected income is shifting further into the future as the cost recovery period becomes longer, and the host governments consider this to be the fault of the IOCs. In addition, the technical complexity of the Kashagan field contributes to greater development delays.

Nevertheless, the IOCs are not entirely blameless. In their enthusiasm to win large contracts, they sometimes underestimated the technical complexities of these projects. Their bids were based on too low cost estimates, a situation often exacerbated by unrealistic timetables. The winners in the current high-oil-price, high-cost environment are host countries with large low-cost reserves, which are not in the Caspian region.

With regard to future markets for gas, the position is no different. To sum up, the investor's risks are political, economic, uncertainty of production, volatility of the commodity price, costs and transit disruption. Energy policies must tackle these problems.

The sceptic might ask why, given the political and other uncertainties, foreign investors are still present in the Caspian Sea region. The reality is that upstream supply in the Caspian region is widely monopolistic (with few exceptions of oligopolistic choices), with the dominant position of big oil international companies (which are usually vertically integrated). The market environment is far from competitive, and as a consequence the development of future markets is restricted. Investors tend to obtain long-term commitments from the national governments to get a timely payback on their investments, to minimize the cost of supply, to have certainty of revenues (volume and pricing), and to secure their supply. The monopolistic nature of the energy sector is one of market failures, which could be an obstacle to cooperation.

In addition to the negative role of the monopolistic structure of upstream supply, Mittra et al. (1995) named other market failures in the energy sector, namely the supply of energy as a *public good* (with the consequence of the 'free-rider problem': the absence of incentives to provide a good to the public); *externalities/environment* (the environmental effect of hydrocarbon exploration and production very familiar in the literature; see IPIECA, 1992, 1993, 2007); *short-termism* (when the players are interested only in short-term returns rather than long-term effects).

The legitimate question for policy is how to avoid or correct the above market failures in the Caspian region. It is not a rhetorical question with an obvious solution. 'In fact, the experience of the UK since the mid-1970s can be taken as an illustration of failed policies ...' (Mittra et al.,

1995: 692). It is clear that the policy instruments will incur costs, where the nature of energy policy will require negotiations with the institutions, the companies and the governments. A final question to explore is the nature of the challenges in each of these three fields – transport, sustainable development and the environment. This represents the 'unfinished agenda' in the field of company–government relations in the region.

7.2   Energy transport policy challenges

One key area for progress in developing a successful energy policy (as an element of sustainable development) is access to the oil and gas international market. At the time of writing, expert discussions are being conducted to define the prospects and conditions for increased participation by both Kazakhstan and Azerbaijan in the EU's internal gas market, taking into account the uncertainty of relations with Russia and Gazprom.

> Concern about over-dependence on Russian gas is leading European governments and the European Commission to examine the possibility of pipeline imports from Caspian sources in Azerbaijan, Kazakhstan and Turkmenistan. Significant imports can probably not be achieved until the late 2010s, but the creation of a new pipeline corridor bringing Caspian gas through Turkey has become a serious objective of European energy security policy. (Interview with Jonathan Stern, Oxford Institute for Energy Studies, Oxford, 17 September 2007).

But the potential scope for official policy involvement is not limited to issues of market access. The technical and geographical challenges in tapping Caspian energy have dimensions that may go well beyond the normal scope of individual company operations.

First and foremost, transport challenges are immense. The future of the region as an energy exporter is critically dependent not only on production infrastructure but also on adequate transport routes. Existing routes are fragile, with distinct security problems, for example, in the Caucasus region. These are risks that may inhibit normal commercial ventures, which do not take policy externalities into account.[96]

---

[96] Existing major pipelines have been discussed in depth in Soligo and Jaffe (2001), and a detailed overview is presented on a weekly basis by CGES 'Pipelines Advisory Service'.

Moreover, unlocking the area's main reserves of natural gas requires the creation of new transport routes. The challenge of ensuring adequate gas pipelines is indeed the clearest – and most daunting – example of public policy challenges in accessing Caspian energy (Box 7.1). There is a pressing need for cooperation between policy-makers in the Caspian region and the companies operating in the region in order to establish frameworks that address legitimate commercial concerns about stable supply and the appropriate sharing of risks and returns.

Box 7.1   Caspian Sea major pipelines – strategic attractions and transport hurdles: companies and governments

The aim of this book so far has been to look at the oil and gas problem of the Caspian Sea region from the governments' and operating companies' points of view. Here we underline the major pipelines projects for which the respective mentioned above parties were involved. The major pipelines were presented in Maps 3.1 and 3.2.

The *CPC pipeline* (see map)   The Caspian Pipeline Consortium was originally started by the three governments of Russia, Kazakhstan and Oman in 1991, without, however, much progress at first. Only after commercial partners (such as Chevron, LukArco, Mobil, Rosneft, etc.) were introduced did the pipeline go ahead. CPC has a complex organizational structure.

> Three Governments and ten companies representing seven countries participate in the project. Two joint stock companies – CPC-R (Russia) and CPC-K (Kazakhstan) – have been created to implement the project. CPC managers and specialists are secondees from shareholder companies. The initial construction of the pipeline was funded by oil producing shareholder companies, combined with the assets provided by the host governments. Future pipeline capacity expansions will be financed from the CPC's revenues. (Official CPC website http://www.cpc.ru/portal/alias!press/lang!en-US/tabID!3357/DesktopDefault.aspx).

The CPC is crucial for the development of major Kazakhstani oil and gas fields such as Tengiz and Karachaganak. Originally the success of CPC put Kazakhstan in direct geopolitical competition with Russia by 'reducing the latter's ability to export its own oil through the Turkish Straits' (Krysiek, 2007: 3). This is why the alliance with China at the later stage of the development of the Caspian Sea region appeared to be a response to such rising competition as a part of President Nazarbayev's multi-pipeline export strategy. Over the years CPC proved to be quite challenging, either in dealing with the Russian government (e.g. in July 2006 the Russian government presented the CPC consortium with a US$253 mln bill for taxes to be paid) or capacity limitations (delays with its expansion). Overall, through CPC Russia proved to be a 'bad' transit state and a significant challenge for the operating companies. Russia wants to exert control through northern export routes, including CPC, and exert leverage at every stage of negotiations.

The *BTC* (Baku–Tbilisi–Ceyhan) pipeline was very much a political pipeline

> that was a critical element in Clinton's US foreign policy for Turkey and the Caspian. In 1998 at the oil celebrations for the completion the first oil project, Washington and Ankara confirmed their exclusive commitment to the BTC project, but without financial commitment. The foreign investors planned to eventually build a pipeline to Ceyhan but only after they had proven bankable oil reserves, not yet discovered. This resulted in a three-year impasse and suspended investment. The foreign shareholders proposed a two-phase approach to the building of BTC but Azerbaijan with Turkey and the US withheld approval. Once a sustainable 1 mmbd export potential was confirmed, the foreign investors immediately agreed to finance a BTC project (Interview with Terry Adams, founding president, AIOC, 25 August 2007, Reading).

Azerbaijan was determined not to have a pipeline through Russia, and the USA was against the pipeline going through Iran.

Concerns have also been raised about the security of the BTC pipeline. It bypasses the border of Armenia, crosses through Georgia (which has two unresolved separatist conflicts) and goes through the edges of the Kurdish region of Turkey. It requires permanent guarding to prevent sabotage. In addition, in economic terms it was one of the most expensive pipelines (see Soligo and Jaffe,

2001: table 5.2, 114), with transportation cost of US$2.52/bbl which is on a lower scale; and other estimates give US$3.5/bbl. At that point, after US pressure on the World Bank and the EBRD, financial support was forthcoming, and these institutions came out in favour of funding the BTC pipeline. This provided critical political risk cover that facilitated private sector financing. 'The madness of this process meant that four years of government and investor revenues were lost through unnecessary political interference.' (interview with Terry Adams, founding president, AIOC, 25 August 2007, Reading).

The building of BTC was strategically crucial to BP's long-term investment in Azerbaijan to service 1 mmbd of crude oil export. Most of the oil for the pipeline I comes from the partners in the AIOC consortium, developing the Azeri, Chirag and Gunashli fields off the coast of Azerbaijan. Oil producers in Kazakhstan are also future users of the BTC pipeline and an intergovernmental agreement on Kazakhstan's participation was signed in 2006. The main idea here is that Kazakhstani oil is shipped in tankers across the Caspian from an oil terminal which should be built at Kuryk; however, this will require more shipping capacity than is now in existence. Obviously BTC represents a more political example of relations between companies and governments, although commercial interests are involved.

The *Kazakhstan–China pipeline* is unique to the Caspian region, in that it is a direct link between producer (Kazakhstan) and consumer (China). There are two state oil companies involved in the project: KazMunaiGaz (from the Kazakhstani side) and the China National Petroleum Corporation (CNCP) (from the Chinese side). Effectively both companies are the arms of their respective governments, which ensures that the national interests of both states are protected.

In August 2007 KazMunaiGaz (KMG) and CNPC signed key agreements on the construction of pipelines in Kazakhstan to carry both oil and gas eastwards to China.

> The oil pipeline agreement covers the expansion and extension of the oil pipeline connecting the two countries, doubling its capacity and creating a pipeline route linking the Caspian Sea to western China. The gas pipeline agreement covers the construction of a section of the planned Turkmenistan–China

gas pipeline across Kazakhstan and paves the way for Kazakhstan to supply its own gas both to China and to its domestic
market in the south of the country, which currently depends
on imports from Uzbekistan. (Lee, 2007b: 2)

The oil agreement envisages doubling the existing capacity of
73.3 mln bbl/year.

Kazakhstan is also looking eastwards with its Atasu–Alashankou
pipeline, linking the country's eastern trunk pipeline to the oil
infrastructure in western China. The pipeline started its operations
in 2006. At the present initial stage, the pipeline has a capacity of
200 000 bbl/day, although this is expected to be doubled by 2015 at
the latest and could be further increased to 1 mln bbl/day at a later
time. CNPC is responsible for finding the oil to fill the line and its
purchase of PetroKazakhstan, if successful, would give it access to
oil from the fields that it operates in central Kazakhstan. There are
plans to extend this pipeline in five years' time across Kazakhstan
to the Caspian Sea.

These challenges notwithstanding, in some respects the EU remains –
from a transport perspective – a natural market for Caspian energy
exports. This is true both geographically and politically. There are, in
fact, quite serious constraints on alternative transit routes. Specifically,
transport via Iran remains problematic, given US sanctions against
Iran;[97] exports via Afghanistan to Pakistan and India also face substantial
hurdles;[98] and exports to China face major cost obstacles due to moun-
tain ranges, as well as the distances to markets in the east of the country.

Reflecting the relative attractions of westward routes, it is notable that
EU-based companies are strongly represented in transport projects
throughout the Caspian Sea region, as well as in the extraction business.
In the Baku–Ceyhan pipeline project, BP has the leading role, with ENI,
Statoil and TotalFinaElf participating as partners. In the CPC pipeline
also, EU companies are involved: Agip, BG, BP (LukArco) and Shell.[99]
This commercial presence provides a motivation for EU policy-makers

[97] However, an oil pipeline from Kazakhstan across Iran is under study by
TotalFinaElf.

[98] Pakistan's gas market is not large enough to support a pipeline from Turkmenistan,
while for India there are evident questions about supply routes via Pakistan.

[99] Currently, US companies would not be able to participate in a project in Iran.

to pay close attention to the appropriate scope for, and limits of, official involvement.

US companies are themselves aware of the marginal nature of the oil and gas operations in the Caspian Sea region, as discussed in Chapter 3. They were also influenced by the significant exasperation and costs incurred by Chevron in the 1990s in the Tengiz field in Kazakhstan. Thus their desire is to protect exit routes.

The Kazakhstan–China pipeline (see Box 7.1) is an important example of the increasing role of the state in Kazakhstan (although this would be strongly denied by anyone in the Kazakhstani government), but less so in both Azerbaijan and Turkmenistan. One explanation could be the significance of an external player (China) for whom getting access to the Caspian resources is the main priority. Kazakhstan realized its unique position in relation to China (producer–consumer link) and exercises its leverage over other players (companies or other Caspian states).

When many of the debates were focused on concerns about the potential western routes, Kazakhstan cleverly played its cards towards eastern interests and eastern routes taking into account China's domestic energy situation. After its unsuccessful attempts to move from the rank of net importers towards a self-sufficient energy state in the early 1990s, China realized the need for a reliable energy partner in the Caspian region and it became imperative for the CNPC to expand abroad, rather than rely completely on the international market. So from 1997 CNPC attempted to break into the Caspian market. The most significant deal was that struck in Kazakhstan, winning the Aktyubinsk field worth some US$4.3 bln. Thereby China opened new horizons for Kazakhstan. First of all, China showed to the rest of the world its interest in the newly established state and thereby gave to Kazakhstan additional leverage over other interests. Second, by entering Kazakhstan, Chinese promised to build a new pipeline to China via Kazakhstan, making Kazakhstan a producer as well as a transit state at the same time.

Economically, from the western perspective such a pipeline does not make much sense. However, for Kazakhstan's geopolitical and energy strategies, as well as for the Chinese economy (in particular for the steel industry), such a project does have a significant impact. If we look at this pipeline in perspective, we can see it as one of the elements of the so-called energy Silk Road, including Turkmenistan. That became feasible, especially with the new Turkmen president, who had already demonstrated a willingness to engage in an energy dialogue (talks between the presidents of Russia, Kazakhstan and Turkmenistan in 2007). The success of the Aktyubinsk deal could be repeated elsewhere in the Caspian, taking into account Chinese growing financial reserves and focus on Caspian energy.

Obviously, China is a special case. Other governments external to the Caspian region ultimately have different aims with regard to the Caspian states. Thus Azerbaijan is seen as a gate to Central Asia as well as an alternative to the Russian or Iranian routes. 'However, Azerbaijan is threatened by unfavourable patterns in its physical, human and economic geography' (Krysiek, 2007: 5) The vital card of Azerbaijan nowadays is the existence of BTC pipeline; however, without the Kazakh input its capacity will not be fully utilized.[100]

In August 2007 Iran proposed a new Caspian export pipeline to link its Caspian Sea terminal at Neka to a port on the Gulf of Oman, raising the volume of Caspian oil exported through Iran to 1 mln bbl/d (Lee, 2007a). At the time of writing, most exports through Iran come from Turkmenistan and Kazakhstan. 'Dragon Oil, operating off Turkmenistan's Cheleken Peninsula, is one company that has switched it export routes to Iran' (ibid.: 2).

Transport issues have been fraught by geopolitics in the past. However, economic and commercial realism will have an increasing role in the years ahead. As Jonathan Stern has pointed out,

> some developments such as Karachaganak in Kazakhstan and Shakh Deniz in Azerbaijan have been able to create a successful blend of CIS and international oil company investors. Others, mainly in Turkmenistan and Uzbekistan, remain more wedded to the Soviet-type model with Gazprom and other Russian companies partnering national oil and gas companies with no significant international participation. (Interview with Jonathan Stern, Oxford Institute for Energy Studies, Reading, 15 October 2007)

7.3   From hydrocarbon-driven development to a diversified economy

Development of oil and gas production has an impact on industrial competitiveness. In addition, as we have shown above, the fiscal regime of the country is affected: the asymmetry on tax exemption for local and imported goods for oil and gas projects; tax overburden in the lower levels of the supply chain raising production costs; uncertainties

---

[100] In 2006 the Kazakh president negotiated Kazakhstan's involvement in the BTC project.

regarding tax exemption at the state government level. On the other hand, development of the oil and gas industry is providing opportunities for all local institutions which are benefiting from the oil and gas projects. Income increases as a result of raising oil and gas revenues, which should lead to higher consumption and investment. It is already possible to see in all three Caspian countries that a booming investment sector provided a boost to the construction industry. Overall development of the economy consists of particular targeted policies, which include energy policy. The fundamental question here is how the governments respond to structural changes in their economies. This response will ultimately have implications with regard to economic stability and the sustainability of economic growth.

It is possible that oil and gas projects can have a double impact on the economy. Over the last decade the oil and gas sector in the Caspian Sea region has been expanding. Employment has increased; new technologies and equipment were deployed in international oil and gas projects. At the same time other sectors were retarded, creating a cause for concern by respective governments and international financial institutions.

In its message the World Bank promoted its Kazakhstani country partnership strategy, underlining its objective to contribute 'to the ultimate goal of increasing diversification and competitiveness of the Kazakhstan economy' (World Bank, 2004: 1). Similar targets were included in the Azeri country partnership strategy, which supports

> the main objective of the government's long-term program to reduce poverty and achieve the Millennium Development Goals (MDGs) by fostering economic diversification and growth, particularly in the non-oil sector, while maintaining macroeconomic stability; improving health, education, and infrastructure services; better targeting social protection; improving gender equality; and achieving environmental sustainability (World Bank, 2006: 2)

So far there is no such broad discussion on diversification in Turkmenistan. However, there has been a sort of diversification strategy (the Turkmenbashi jeans factory, theme hotels in Ashgabat, promotion of wheat – all paid for out of gas revenues) in place for several years.

As discussed in Chapter 1, Turkmenistan was one of the most isolated countries in the world under the rule of President Saparmurat Niyazov. However, since his death in December 2006 the new president, Gurbanguly Berdymukhamedov, has indicated to the rest of the world that Turkmenistan could be more open to foreign investment (already by March 2007 a number of foreign companies had expanded their investments under PSAs) as well as politically more open in future. November 2007 was a very interesting month in the history of Turkmenistan, when many Western government officials and executives from international oil majors joined the race for access to Turkmenistan's natural-gas resources in a two-day annual oil and gas conference held in Ashgabat. I had previously attended a number of similar events and the atmosphere at this conference was strikingly different. There was a seriousness about the event from the investor's point of view, an atmosphere of hope; and investors' expectations seemed to be high. All this indicated that something had changed. Before the conference President Berdymukhamedov stated that Turkmenistan 'is ready for cooperation with well-known companies with experience in production and modern equipment, with global financial organizations, and with banks to implement big oil and natural-gas projects' (Radio Free Europe/Radio Liberty, 14 November 2007).

Could we see this as a solid indicator that there is a positive change towards a more promising market environment in the country? In some sense, yes; there is no doubt that some positive steps have been taken: more openness (including the opening of Internet cafés); pardoning of the people who had been imprisoned under the late President Niyazov; foreign visits by President Berdymukhamedov to the West (including his address to the UN General Assembly); and closer links with neighbouring countries including Kazakhstan, Russia and Azerbaijan.

Nevertheless, Berdymukhamedov has also vowed to stick largely to the course set by the Turkmenbashi, although in 'The President of Turkmenistan G. Berdymukhamedov's policy on a renaissance of the country' it is clearly stated that 'without doubts 2007 became a point of a new count of principally new development period and strengthening of the Turkmen state' (Berdymukhamedov, 2007: 65). Analysing the above-mentioned document, one could say that this is very much the same style as in days of the late Turkmenbashi. The policy would not change much. Berdymukhamedov will probably learn from Nazarbayev how to keep investors on their toes and at the same time to distance Turkmenistan from Russia, although in the short term the country will still be forced to rely on Russian pipelines for its exports.

The sources (ADB, 2002; Havrylyshyn and Al-Atrash 1998) mostly talk about diversification of energy routes, buyers, and suppliers for Turkmenistan, but this would lead directly to the need to diversify the non-oil and gas sector as well. So one could expect that the next logical step in the industrial development of Turkmenistan would be diversification. President Berdymukhamedov has already taken tentative steps to allow the expanded sales of Turkmen energy products and move away from Turkmenbashi's monopoly of the Turkmen energy sector.

The bulk of the academic literature emphasizes the link between institutions and governmental policies in achieving economic diversification in the country (Owusu and Samatar, 1997; Rodrik, 2005; Schrank and Kurtz, 2005; Yeager, 1999; etc.). In the light of this it is understandable why Kazakhstan became particularly engaged in the creation of various development institutions in 2006, including Samruk state holding company and Kazyna[101] fund for sustainable development.[102] (Kazakhstan is the most active of the Caspian states in the implementation of the concept of diversification: in 2003 the Strategy of Innovative Industrial Development of Kazakhstan for 2003–2015 was approved;[103] in 2004 the Kazakhstani government launched its project for 'Diversification of Kazakhstan's economy through cluster development in non-extraction sectors of the economy'; see Box 7.2.) Kazakhstan's diversification policies included the billion-dollar Agriculture and Food Program for 2003–2005. Here we shall concentrate on the experience of Kazakhstan as the most advanced example in pursuing the diversification of its economy.

Box 7.2   Kazakhstan: diversification of the economy through cluster development in non-extraction sectors of the economy

In 2004 the Kazakhstani government first launched the project, inviting leading economist Michael Porter to Kazakhstan. A presidential decree in 2004 mandating the development of Kazakhstan's sources of comparative advantage with the use of cluster theory was the first step in the adaptation of Porter's approach (Porter, 1998).

---

[101] These names are two Kazakh words. *Samruk* is the bird of revival and happiness in ancient Kazakh mythology, equivalent of the Phoenix, and *Kazyna* is a Kazakh word for treasure or treasury.

[102] Other development institutions include Development Bank, Investment Fund, National Innovation Fund and Export Credit and Investment Insurance Corporation.

[103] To ensure stable development of the country on the basis of diversification and modernization of the economy through creation of conditions for production of competitive products and export growth.

The problem is that in theory it might be fine in general, but there is no miraculous way to achieve the formation of these clusters overnight. President Nazarbayev in his address stressed that

> by mid-year [2005], we will need to have a blueprint for the development of at least 5 to 7 of clusters in Kazakhstan in such industries as tourism, oil and gas machine building, food processing and textiles, transport logistics, metallurgy and construction materials. These clusters will determine the long-term economic development beyond the extraction of raw materials. (Nazarbayev, 2005)

Experience has already shown (although it is a very noble desire of the head of the state and the government) that this will be a long-drawn-out process.

The Kazakhstani project is based on the cluster approach, which is treated by the government as an 'efficient instrument for raising competitiveness and promoting economic development of regions and countries' (governmental www: http://en.government.kz/docs/01_claster.doc; Austin Associates, 2004). The heart of the idea is to form

> a certain group of geographically localized interconnected companies, suppliers of equipment, component parts, specialized services, infrastructure, research facilities, higher education facilities and other associated institutions needed to achieve a certain economic effect and amplifying competitive advantages of certain companies, the cluster itself and the country in general. http://en.government.kz/docs/01_claster.doc)

At the time of writing, the various industrial clusters include oil and gas machine-building, a petrochemical cluster, textile industry, metallurgy, food industry, and tourism, among others. The Kazakhstani government is welcoming of foreign investments as an essential ingredient in the process of the country's economic diversification. However, as Zashev and Vahtra pointed out, 'the risk side of the model is more in a long term perspective. The presidential regime is not based on democratic principles and the opportunity for cronyism and mismanagement of governmental funds, programs and initiatives is immense' (Zashev and Vahtra, 2006: 26). On an optimistic note, the government is trying to do everything possible to make sure that the projects selected will produce goods capable of competing at the nationwide, region-scaled and global levels.

One of the dangers that I see here is the attempt to use the NFRK to finance these projects (during the first stage of the Cluster project 55 000 enterprises in 46 branches in 12 regions were studied), which represent high-risk operations for the sustainability of the NFRK. A careful approach is required and certain numerical benchmarks (as for the São Tomé oil revenue fund legislation – Segura, 2006) should be drawn. The mechanism of 'shaping' the revenue inflow into the fund using different rates of return and a mathematical (theoretical) formula should be the basis for the investment decision. Without such a formula there is a great risk that the Kazakhstani authorities will have an open credit line to use as much as they need at this time, attempting to prove that the social rate of return is higher than the LIBOR (London Inter-Bank Offer Rate) or other market interest rate. Kairat Kelimbetov suggests a 'complementary investment strategy for the oil money'. At the time of writing, all relevant revenues go to the NFRK, and then a certain amount is paid as a transfer to the State Central Budget. That amount is only used for development purposes, the so-called Development Budget. With Kazyna involvement, the portion of money that will be allocated to Kazyna will first go as a transfer from the NFRK to the State Budget and then into the capital of Kazyna as an investment by the government.

The purpose of the creation of Samruk was to manage the state's stakes in a number of key firms. It encompassed the oil and gas firm KazMunaiGaz (KMG), Kazakh Railways, KazakhTelecom, KazPost and the national power grid operator Kegoc. The state-owned enterprises (SOEs) are critical for the Kazakhstani economy and have made considerable progress over the years; however, significant performance improvement opportunities remain.

One of the main problems perceived by the Kazakhstani government is the issue of governance; the hope was raised that Samruk would be able to improve it as well as to provide a catalyst for growth in the economy. It was stressed at the beginning of formation that Samruk would be the only governance interface with SOEs, but key decisions should remain within the Kazakhstani government. This means that Samruk will build a consensus within the government every two to three years on SOE high-level objectives. The holding will select, incentivize and develop SOE managers as well as validate and challenge SOE plans and budgets. In addition, it was expected that Samruk would monitor SOEs and ensure corrective actions were taken if needed. Overall, the holding will act as a corporate finance adviser. The Kazakhstani government is fully responsible for the industrial policy and strategic development plans for key sectors. Unilateral decisions are expected on capital allocation and regulatory issues.

Samruk has specific responsibility for oil and gas. In June 2006 KMG's shares were transferred to the holding company Samruk. The vice-president of KMG of that time, Zhaksybek Kulekeyev, in his interview to Argus Media, explained the mechanism of decision-making as well as the role of the government: 'Samruk will defend the rights of the shareholder – the state – but the board of directors will run the company. Samruk will not interfere with their day-to-day work. The government will be involved in setting out basic strategic goals and will also suggest independent directors to the Samruk board of directors' (*Argus FSU*, 22 September 2006). Further development of the role of the state took place in June 2007 when Kazakhstan flagged up the possibility to create a special commission on the development of the oil and gas sector. As Argus Media commented, 'this would help further cement control over the energy sector by Timur Kulibayev, the influential son-in-law of Kazakh president Nursultan Nazarbayev' (*Argus FSU*, 15 June, 2007). The commission is expected to comprise representatives of state bodies, Samruk, large energy firms and KazEnergy.[104]

The government of Kazakhstan has adopted an ambitious programme to become one of the world's 50 most competitive countries. This would be implemented through 'Kazakhstan's 30 Corporate Leaders Programme'. In July 2007, 22 projects were fully ready to be implemented in ten country regions; their total value amounts to KZT 882.2 bln (US$7.2 bln). Overall the project portfolio comprises 183 projects for US$5.2 bln.

The total capital of Kazyna just exceeds US$2 bln. As Kairat Kelimbetov stressed, Kazyna's share in any project that is implemented through its funding should not exceed 30% (interview with Kairat Kelimbetov, chairman of Kazyna, 27 June 2007, London).

---

[104] KazEnergy is a lobby group, chaired by Timur Kulibayev, that was created in November 2005. The mission of the group is to help in the creation of favourable conditions for development of the fuel and energy sectors of Kazakhstan.

So the rest of the funds would be required from private investors. Mobilizing the financial resources is an important task. Will Kazakhstan be able to attract them? Time will tell.

The impact of the implementation of response measures is crucial for the success of the diversification programme. Economic diversification should be a result of the economic development of the country. Caspian economies should aim to create an appropriate institutional framework for entrepreneurship with the business environment competitive enough to have an incentive to invest in the non-oil and -gas sectors. To achieve all this the tax system of the country should assist (and not hinder) the development of the non-oil and -gas sectors. The governments should create a mechanism (transparent and clear) for allocating investment.

In this respect, it remains to be seen whether Kazakhstan will develop a balanced diversification strategy that can serve as an example to the other countries in the region. Such a strategy would have to focus on strengthening the institutional and regulatory framework in ways that will foster a competitive marketplace and encourage the entry, growth and exit of domestic firms. The tax regime and the foreign trade regime are examples of priority areas to tackle. A policy of promoting clusters can play a role in such a strategy, especially in identifying where infrastructure and other network facilities are needed, or where there are educational and training bottlenecks. But an approach of 'picking winners' would be fraught with hazard, and there may be significant risks of non-transparency in allocating official funding for the development of individual companies.

Failures of economic diversification have been very common. 'In Brunei, nearly 30 years after the state prioritised economic diversification as a development objective, the oil sector's contribution to GDP (at constant prices) was still as high as 62.9 per cent in 1990, although it had declined from 83.7 per cent in 1980' (Zhang, 2003: 12). Looney (1994) showed that the impact of the Saudi Arabian programme of economic diversification (one of the largest) has also been limited. Whether or not Caspian economies will achieve a successful diversification remains to be seen.

7.4 Environmental issues

The mosaic of this book would not be complete without a final, but very important, component – the environment. It is exactly this factor that is becoming increasingly the focus of discussions, concerns and disappointments in the relations between companies and governments working in the Caspian Sea region. It is true that environmental goods (as public goods, are i.e. non-rival, non-excludable), are not necessarily valued properly by the market. Much of the literature is based on the assumption that the government wants to achieve a welfare-maximizing objective (see Baumol and Oates, 1988; Beltratti, 1996; Common, 1996; Hartwick and Olewiler, 1986; etc.).

In the Caspian region, however, we cannot see this pattern clearly due to the difficulties of transition issues as well as a lack of experience from the government point of view in dealing with market failure issues in these countries. Of course the governments should act as custodians of their local environment for the benefits of their present and future populations. However, 'the most disappointing fact is that "environmental argument" becoming more and more a political weapon for the state first in Russia and now in Kazakhstan' (interview with Yurii Eidinov, Kazakhstani ecological expert, 6 September 2007, Almaty).

For many years the Chevron-led Tengizchevroil consortium (TCO)[105] was accused as one of the biggest violators of environmental rules in Kazakhstan. In 2006 the authorities fined TCO 235 mln tenge (US$1.99 mln) for breaches of environmental rules. In 2007 Nurlan Iskakov, environmental protection minister, asked the energy ministry to reconsider the consortium's subsoil use contract. In response to governmental criticism, TCO has developed a 40 bln tenge (US$320 mln) environmental protection programme, which includes steps to deal with sulphur disposal, associated gas flaring and waste utilization. This plan is being considered by the environment ministry. Since 1999 the consortium has already spent US$1.23 bln on environmental issues. In an interview with me one Kazakhstani official said that the TCO would rather pay penalties than invest in the protection of the environment.

One of the main concerns of the Kazakhstani authorities is the arrangements by TCO for the disposal of sulphur from the project. Around 9 mln tonnes of sulphur has now accumulated on Kazakhstan's Caspian Sea coast, mostly from Tengiz, the environmental protection ministry says. Kazakhstan's undeveloped offshore fields are estimated to have a sulphur content of up to 40 per cent, making the issue key to future projects in the region.[106]

---

[105] TCO is the largest oil producer in Kazakhstan, with output in 2006 of 97.64 mln bbl (266 000 bbl/day) of crude.

[106] In August 2007 TCO was facing a potential US$1.2 bln penalty from the Kazakhstani authorities over alleged illegal storage of sulphur. The Environmental Protection Agency claims that TCO has stored 2.84 mln tonnes of sulphur in unsanctioned open-air sulphur storage without permission in 2003–2006.

The high sulphur content of Tengiz is a perennial problem, and the same problem will arise in the Kashagan field, so one could expect similar claims from the Kazakhstani government in respect of the Kashagan consortium as well. Sulphur is the expected result of oil production at the highly exploited sub-salted oil fields with a high level of concentration of hydrogen sulphide. TCO has already started to carry out a gas injection project. The Eni-led consortium has also planned to re-inject gas in the next stage of the development of Kashagan. All this is an attempt to reduce the volume of sulphur. However, the government is attempting to use the sulphur problem to extract the maximum benefit from the environmental issue, which in some sense is not very ethical.

It was clear right from the beginning that the problem of sulphur would arise during the extraction of sub-salted oil, and the Kazakhstani government was aware of this. In the Soviet period the Kasgiprograd Institute pursued a territorial scheme of preserving nature in the oil fields in western Kazakhstan. One of the questions asked about the exploration of the Tengiz oil field was related to sulphur utilization. Nobody was able to give a clear answer to what should be done with sulphur, and exploration of Tengiz was stopped by Gosplan (based on an interview with Yurii Eidinov, Kazakhstani ecological expert, 6 September 2007, Almaty). Of course Tengiz was one of the biggest oil fields of the FSU, but not the only big discovery. The situation changed drastically when Kazakhstan became independent and Tengiz became the only real new asset for the oil and gas industry of the young state. Of course there were old oil fields, but Tengiz was the jewel in the crown.

In any discussion of equal responsibilities we should look back to the period of signing contracts for Tengiz and Kashagan. Knowing the history of the postponed Tengiz development, the Kazakhstani government should be particularly vigilant about the provision of sulphur utilization in the contracts. The problem is not trivial and of course TCO is trying to solve it, but the volume of sulphur is huge and nobody in the world yet has come up with the magic solution to this challenge.

The environmental moves by the Kazakhstani authorities form part of a wider campaign against oil companies by the state. However, officials deny that the government is targeting specific private companies. The authorities emphasize that they also have questions for domestic firms, including the state-owned KazMunaiGaz (*Argus FSU*, 14 July 2006). IOCs must play a key role in facilitating environmental cooperation with the Caspian governments. The overall problem resides in a lack of clarity of the domestic environmental regulations and a lack of experience by the Caspian states with mandating environmental regulations.

As a result, international oil companies may incur high liability costs if they generate environmental externalities in the process of oil exploration, as in the case of Tengiz.

We should not forget that the Caspian Sea does not belong to one state, and the impact of one particular part of the Caspian Sea development may become devastating for the rest of the area. This is why the Caspian Environment Programme (CEP), a regional umbrella programme, was developed for and by the five Caspian littoral states: Azerbaijan, I.R. Iran, Kazakhstan, Russia and Turkmenistan, with the main aim to halt the deterioration of environmental conditions of the Caspian Sea and to promote sustainable development in the area.[107] Although every Caspian state will have its own interests and problems, cooperation in protecting the environment is crucial.

Let us take the example of oil spills. CEP published an Azeri, Chirag and Guneshli oil spill assessment for BP Exploration (Caspian Sea); it presents a study of potential accidental oil spills during the lifetime of the ACG Phase 1 project. Although this report has been compiled specifically for Azerbaijan, other Caspian states could benefit from this as 'the likelihood of a spill occurring, and the predicted volume of that spill, has been evaluated based on experience of the oil industry internationally and in the Caspian Sea' (Briggs Marine Environmental Services Ltd, 2001: 1).

The topic of requirements related to oil spill response is very relevant and has been examined in Kazakhstan. To prevent the occurrence of oil spill and to conduct response operations, and given the significance of preserving the Caspian ecological system and internal water bodies, the Resolution of the Government of the Republic of Kazakhstan No. 876, dated 29 June 1999, 'On Drafting National Oil Spill Prevention and Response Plan', instructs appropriate ministries and agencies to develop the Plan. The developed Plan was approved on 6 May 2000 by the Resolution of the Government of the Republic of Kazakhstan No. 676, 'On Approval of National Oil Spill Prevention and Response Plan for Offshore and Internal Water Bodies of the Republic of Kazakhstan' (see materials from the Workshop on Oil Spills Prevention in Astana, 18–20 April 2001). These National Plan requirements are obligatory for all organizations and authorized central and local executive bodies in Kazakhstan. Fortunately these are just plans; there are no records of actual cases.[108]

---

[107] http://www.caspianenvironment.org/newsite/index.htm.

[108] According to the Kazakh Ministry of Emergency Situations, on 29 August 2007 TCO halted crude exports via the CPC after a small oil spill occurred during repairs to the Tengiz–Atyrau section of the CPC (*Argus FSU*, 31 August 2007).

The governmental programme 'Complex Plan on Improving Environmental Conditions for 2006–2010', created by SOCAR, set up a number of environmental aspirational goals in respect of mitigating the current impact of oil and gas production in the Republic of Azerbaijan. In Azerbaijan, most of the wells, offshore as well as onshore, have been left open when abandoned.[109] 'The risks for the environment are many. In 2001, an inspection of 200 abandoned offshore wells and 50 to 60 abandoned platforms indicated that there was no imminent threat to the environment, but the descriptions of some of the wells left open the possibility of future problems' (ECE/CEP, 2004: 142).

Azerbaijan faces problems with removing iron and metal structures which are no longer in use in the oil fields (see Box 3.1, 'Oily Rocks'). 'The shape of the production facilities and the lack of environmental safeguards are very visible when observing the oilfields in and around Baku. The operational fields have been explored for years and the equipment has not been updated' (ibid.: 141).

As Terry Adams has pointed out,

Energy investors in Caspian oil and gas faced a particularly difficult challenge in having to operate in contract areas that were already environmentally contaminated by years of Soviet petroleum operations. Although Soviet environmental laws were the most draconian to be found in any state, if they had been generally applied it would have proved impossible to conduct normal petroleum operations. Consequently during Soviet times these laws were generally ignored with very limited compliance, resulting in widespread environmental damage that would subsequently affect many post-Soviet successor Caspian contract awards. To take protective action AIOC investors in Azerbaijan introduced independent baseline environmental surveys that defined the state of environmental damage extant within their contract area before their petroleum operations commenced. Also it was agreed within their PSA that international environmental standards would apply to AIOC operations (not inherited Soviet environmental laws) based on North Sea and Gulf of Mexico best practice. Other foreign investors elsewhere within the Caspian may not have been so cautious, so that application of successor state environmental laws is now being used for detrimental leverage in contractual disputes between some foreign investors and host governments.

---

[109] The normal practice would be to seal up a well and cut the string at least 10 metres below the seabed, leaving the seabed intact.

(From interview with Terry Adams, founding president, AIOC, 26 August 2007, Reading)

Whether these actions are recoverable or not is a serious issue and affects areas of governmental responsibility.

Very little information is available on Turkmenistan's progress with environmental issues. However, Burren Energy is taking a lead in trying to be environmentally sensitive in Turkmenistan, namely by eliminating gas flaring, cleaning the majority of pollution that was inherited from Soviet times, and putting in a system for oil-based mud. They recover oil from the cutting before disposal.

Another instance is, as Crude Accountability reported, 'Turkmenistan, along with the other Caspian littoral states, faces serious biodiversity threats along the Caspian coast' (Crude Accountability, 2007: 10). This first of all relates to the beluga sturgeon (*Huso huso*), which is at risk not only from overfishing, poaching and increased pollution in the rivers, but also from environmental pressures connected to increased oil pollution. This beluga (as well as stellate and Russian sturgeon) spends the winter in waters of the Cheleken region. 'The area around Ogurchinsky Island, which is approximately twenty kilometres south of the blocks developed by Dragon Oil, is also a known nursery for young Beluga' (ibid.: 11).

Another 'universal' environmental problem for the Caspian Sea (including Turkmenistan and Kazakhstan) is a serious decline in the numbers of the Caspian seal. In 2007 hundreds of seals were found dead in the North Caspian. The Kazakhstani government has blamed Agip KCO in Kashagan. 'A small population of Caspian seals whelp on Ogurchinsky Island, off the coast of Turkmenistan, and are, therefore, especially vulnerable to toxins in the southern Caspian'[110] (ibid.: 18).

Another crucial environmental issue is water quality, which is related to the commercially developable hydrocarbon deposits in the Caspian Sea basin. Such development creates a great deal of traffic, with approximately 10 000 shipping movements annually. In addition, underwater oil and gas pipelines which have already been constructed or proposed may increase environmental threats. All these aspects should be taken into account when the policy is formulated.

In their attempts to mitigate the effects of market failures, the Caspian governments should use the approach of a common set of rules for all

---

[110] For more information on the Caspian Seal Conservation Network, see http://www.caspianseal.org/?option=com_content&view=category&id=22&Itemid=44.

projects with environmental implications. It is important to bring the activity under the control of a single decision-maker. However, it is important not pursue this strategy too far, as happened several times in Kazakhstan. Common rules need to include explicit provision for all major contingencies, including potential oil spills, etc. Another type of approach which is at the disposal of the Caspian governments is tax and saving rules (as we saw in Chapter 6).[111] Overall, all problem cases described in this section could be characterized as incomplete projects which represent one type of market failure. For a collaborative relationship to work between companies and governments, not only financial and technical resources, but also clear rules (which work more easily, the greater the degree of mutual trust) and two-way accountability and transparency are needed.

Transport, environment and diversification are key challenges that now face the region. History gives grounds to hope that these too will be addressed in a cooperative manner, blending the different – but ultimately complementary – interests of governments and international companies engaged in the region. The earlier chapters of this book highlighted how these two parties have worked their way towards arrangements that address the legitimate concerns of each side. The discussion also suggested how some lessons learned in the hydrocarbon industry may be of wider application in attracting direct investment to other sectors, as part of a strategy of broad-based development.

Some recent experience has muddied these issues – for example, by mixing up genuine environmental concerns with less transparent political and economic goals. And the world of pipeline planning has been hostage to many different geopolitical interests. But ultimately these are issues where externalities are important, and where governments have a significant role to play. How they are addressed, and the kinds of solutions that are crafted, will have implications that go far beyond the Caspian region.

---

[111] It should be noted that tax regimes influence the time frame of oil and gas use.

Conclusion

This study has tackled the trajectory of economic relations between oil and gas companies and governments operating in the Caspian Sea region. The topic of energy is widely popular at the present time, with oil prices currently US$125/bbl and rising. A certain amount of research has been done to assess the economic impact of hydrocarbons in the Caspian region (Kalyuzhnova, 2002; Pomfret, 2006; Najman, et al., 2007, etc.) based on macroeconomic or microeconomic analysis. However, there is no single coherent study to date attempting to understand the economics of hydrocarbon wealth from the position of company–government relations. This book aims to fill that gap.

The fundamental issues facing the Caspian economies

These issues are the impact of hydrocarbon resources on the economies and economic development of the Caspian countries, and the management of hydrocarbon wealth. Both these issues are of critical importance to the region, but especially in the light of our emphasis on relations between companies and governments they are the basis of all such relations.

During the last 15 years the experience of economic development in the three countries Azerbaijan, Kazakhstan and Turkmenistan has been both similar and at the same time different. The similarity lies in a strong natural resource dependence (in FDI and export terms) of all the three economies as well as their attempt to manage the resource wealth through resource funds, the establishment of which took place recently. In addition, hydrocarbon wealth became a saviour of the economies of these countries after the collapse of the Soviet economy and transition shock.

All this raises the question of understanding the advantages and disadvantages of the resource-rich economies. Without doubt resource-rich economies are benefiting from natural resource rent, an increase in employment and investment, as well as in boosting a country's capacity to import capital goods, and all this will influence the acceleration of economic growth. At the same time there are difficulties which the resource-rich countries have to overcome. They are related to the concentration on the resource sector of the economy at the expense of others, the raising of employment and investment in the resource-related sectors only, and the ample opportunities for rent-seeking behaviour. All these factors could potentially jeopardize the attainment of sustainable economic growth.

We have also investigated to what extent potential causal links between GDP and oil/gas production as well as GDP and oil/gas consumption are supported by the actual data from the Caspian Sea region. We found that there is no systematic pattern of causality across the three economies, with the exception of causal links between GDP and gas consumption. Overall and as expected, our results point strongly towards causal links between GDP and the energy sector in all three Caspian economies.

As well as similarities, many fundamental differences have been identified in the process of our analysis. These include levels of income and development, with Kazakhstan being richer and more advanced in transition than Azerbaijan and Turkmenistan. As a consequence, the pattern of public expenditure in part reflects these different levels of development. The process of improving living conditions in all three economies is developing slowly.

We concluded that the main challenge which all three Caspian economies are facing is how to sustain economic growth. While development paths differ in all three cases, there are ultimately a small number of common problems that all are facing. These include the challenge of diversification away from the hydrocarbon sector, and indeed the fact that the skilled labour force in the country is concentrated in the resource sector (with the exception of Kazakhstan). Nor can the wider issues of transport links and environmental protection be ignored.

So, as we have demonstrated above, the Caspian governments are facing the challenge of devising optimal economic policies and strategies that can deal with all the issues discussed here. An influential factor in this respect will be a political system type/model that can either help in progressing further or harm the current stage of development. As a result, demand on the countries' resource funds differs as well, reflecting the different priorities and initiatives of their governments. In Kazakhstan, there have been notable efforts to improve the transparency and management principles of the National Fund, and this may in part reflect the relatively more enlightened and accountable nature of its political system.

These funds were created in all three economies, but a long time is still required to achieve and evaluate their full impact. However, as was highlighted in the book, it is of paramount importance in the meantime to continue to enhance the governance and transparency of the oil funds in order to maximize the chances of success. The building of public support for these funds is a big task for the three Caspian governments. They also need to leverage their economic impact through a strong influence on market expectations.

The real players – the real developments

Having described the economic environment in the region as well as the main principle of management of the hydrocarbon wealth, we analysed the main historical steps (projects) in the hydrocarbon development of the Caspian Sea region. The Caspian region had already attracted some attention during the last years of the existence of the USSR, and this increased during the early stages of the establishment of the newly independent states. Companies such as Chevron, BP and Shell looked seriously at the Caspian oil reserves as a potential for market expansion.

Initially, in the early 1990s, oil operators have had to weigh the major challenges typical of the region against the strategic value of access to the reserves, given that oil has high costs of production and transportation. Among the main obstacles that they faced were the decline of the local economies, the rapid rise of corruption, and the difficult investment climate in the region. In addition, reliable information was lacking and reserves were highly overestimated; however, the region represented new fresh potential for the oil majors. In the mid-1990s the oil companies hesitated somewhat when the crude price was US$10/bbl and average costs of production US$12–14/bbl in the Caspian Basin. However, since the rise of the oil price at the beginning of the new century the difference between the cost of production and the sales price has reached a substantial level, and nobody any longer doubts the benefits of the hydrocarbon operations in the Caspian region. Indeed, the last ten years have brought to the Caspian region its own pattern of development, as international oil companies began to announce large-scale projects.

The companies involved in these projects are faced with different strategic issues. The countries of the region have different perceptions and ways of developing hydrocarbon resources. For example, the key Kazakhstani projects such as Tengiz, Karachaganak and Kashagan are significant not only for the country but for the Caspian region as a whole. While Azerbaijan is an example of the exaggeration of Caspian reserves, where the so-called 'Contract of the Century' represents the only significant large-scale project (the Azeri, Chirag and deepwater portion of the Guneshli offshore oil fields) as well as the Shah Deniz gas project, which was the largest discovery for BP since the Prudhoe Bay oil field in the early 1970s.

Since the Soviet era, Turkmenistan had been a medium-sized gas producer (second after the Russian Federation), although estimated oil reserves appeared to be smaller than in Kazakhstan and Azerbaijan. Despite this, the Turkmen gas industry went into a deep recession once the provision of know-how from other parts of the FSU had stopped; equipment was ageing and the infrastructure of the gas pipelines collapsed. The most significant of Turkmenistan's oil and gas fields are five projects with foreign participation under PSA terms. These comprise two onshore projects: Khazar and Nebitdag, and three offshore projects: Cheleken, Block 1 and Block 11–12.

The conclusion of this study is that the impact of the main oil and gas projects on the host countries is already substantial, with the prediction, moreover, of sizeable oil and gas revenues in the future through taxes, royalties and bonuses. However, when we look beyond tax collections to the direct economic impact to date of oil and gas projects on the Caspian economies, the picture is much more mixed.

On the positive side are the creation of employment; investment in local budgets; and, in principle, some purchase of local equipment and services. In terms of externalities, moreover, better access to world markets has the potential to give a positive spin to local content development, expansion and development of private business, and improvement of public services.

On the other hand, the trickle-down from the oil and gas sector to local economic and commercial activities – or more widely to a diversification of economy – seems much more limited. There is also a risk that profits from hydrocarbon activities may not be reinvested in the economies of the region. There is a real challenge of depletion of resources. And there are serious issues of environmental pollution.

Overall, oil and gas projects can lead to a loss or gain of host-country sovereignty. Although the initial relations between host government and foreign investors may be very favourable to the latter, these may be reconsidered later – due to high oil prices, experience with taxes and other benefits of the projects, and in a setting where host-government skills and resources have increased.

Governments may attempt to change, or at least have regrets about, the conditions that were agreed with investors at the beginning. That could make investors quite vulnerable to further government action. On the other hand, such risks or costs may have the effect of deterring future investment – so there is a state of interdependence between governments and companies, even though the features of this evolve over time.

It emerges from the analysis here that the commercial climate of the second generation of investment in the region is characterized by a greater diversity of interests among the Caspian states, but a common theme nonetheless is more assertive market regulation. Moreover, a key issue recurs in all cases: the concern of host governments to improve the capabilities of local companies involved in supply and services.

But it needs to be borne in mind that the Caspian oil and gas industry will continue to require massive capital investment up front, with the expected returns over a long period of 20 years or more, following the initial investment. Therefore, among the key factors that could affect the decision of foreign investors with regard to the new opportunities are: economic stability risk allocation; legal environment; strategic importance of assets; synergies and stable favourable fiscal regime.

The fundamental economic purpose of any oil or gas company is to build shareholder value. Risky investments need to be assured of commensurately high returns to ensure a successful company strategy. Capital budgeting and allocation in a company, to decide what projects to approve, is of great importance.

The system for evaluating projects should be structured as follows: a concept phase; a preliminary evaluation phase; a business evaluation phase; and finally a 'go-ahead or reject' phase. As was demonstrated in the book, capital project portfolios for different companies vary from very diverse (BP, Shell, etc.) to more focused (BG Group, Burren Energy). The factor of risk in the evaluation of any project is evidently important. The crucial challenge for companies is not to avoid all risks but to mitigate them – and diversify them – sufficiently. Companies vary in their strategies, and risk assessments inevitably differ. An example of diverse company strategies in Kazakhstan is presented by BG and, by contrast, ConocoPhillips decided to remain a minority investor in the same country.

The analysis included the specifics of the relations between different types of operating companies. All of them, we found, are likely to pursue different strategies. Three case studies in the text provided insights into this process, with its many complexities and the differing risk preferences and strategies of foreign and domestic oil companies, and it is worth recalling in outline their key messages.

For Azerbaijan the most important business partner is BP – the operator of major projects. As an oil major, BP has an overall group strategy which is the basis for its Azerbaijan exploration and production activities, which are substantial long-term assets. In its long-term business strategy, BP has identified three main areas to which it is committed. These are: supporting targeted learning activities in Azerbaijan; helping to create jobs in the areas of operations; and enabling the Azerbaijani community to gain access to modern energy services. The success of BP in Azerbaijan is defined by the fact that BP had a distinct geological model that reflected reality. This enabled it to identify the location of the best-performing oil fields. In addition, the company took an early lead in commercial negotiation of a PSA, which put it in leading place as a future operator.

Burren Energy is a medium-sized petroleum company whose main exploration and production sites are located in Turkmenistan. Burren Energy originally formed an alliance with Monument, and later Mobil joined the consortium, but both have now left. Through the analysis of the company's strategy I conclude that operational efficiency has been streamlined through the review of all service companies' contracts, and as a consequence Burren manages most of the services. In addition, Burren reorganized its operations into cross-functional exploration. The company assigned a cross-functional team to increase its capacity to react and change more rapidly. All this was made possible by a reduction in coordination and communication problems inherited from Burren's partners; it also reduced operating costs and led to field operations becoming cash-flow positive.

Another interesting example analysed here is the story of JSC NC KazMunaiGaz (KMG) – the Kazakh national oil company. This company is solely owned by the Kazakhstani government with a highly vertically integrated structure of assets. Like any national oil company, KMG espouses three principal objectives on behalf of its respective governments: reduction of dependence on multinationals for oil supplies; provision of the government with an understanding of the oil and gas industry from inside; and finally ensuring continuity of supply at the crude oil producing, refining, and marketing stages within the country.

Without doubt KMG is attempting to become a major offshore player in the long run. However, the main challenge to achieve this aim is a lack of technology, funds and offshore experience. One way to resolve this is through partnerships with international oil, gas and service companies. However, because IOCs are more concerned with short-run profits, this creates an obstacle in NOC–IOC partnerships. Although it is a still big question whether or not KMG will become a fully commercial company, the company clearly demonstrates its international ambitions by looking at different routes to diversification, attempting to expand its geography of acquisition and including in its expansion strategy a retail component.

On the management side KMG lacks skilful experienced managers and in this respect the involvement of international oil companies is very important. Particularly in view of the fact that the future of Kazakhstani oil is offshore, the biggest challenge for KMG is to develop engineering expertise, financing and management skills needed in this sector. In this respect it would be crucial for KMG to take some lessons from the history of the development of other NOCs.

One of the powerful examples of NOCs is Petrobras, which through the years became a truly international player. The factors which could be taken into account by any young NOCs in the Caspian region include the priority given to a strategy based on investing in the development of the company's personnel as well as into relations with the subcontractors. In addition, as José Sergio Gabrielli, CEO of Petrobras, highlighted, the strength of the company is in its very integrated structure (interview, 19 June 2007, London). Petrobras has moved from a very monopolistic company structure to a national company with private interests and corporate strategy based on growth, profitability and social and environmental responsibility. Like any oil company, Petrobras is affected by fluctuations in international commodity prices; this vulnerability is unavoidable and can only be managed by the reduction of operational costs to a certain extent.

One conclusion that deserves to be highlighted here is the extent of national energy companies' autonomy from the state. Taking into account the international experience of such companies as Statoil, Petrobras, etc., the path followed by all of them could be considered as a potential model for KMG. However, both KMG and SOCAR remain in their infant period; although the potential is clearly emerging, nevertheless it will take a long time to find that 'golden middle' place – a suitable balance in the relationship between NOCs and the government.

It is clear that all parties in the Caspian Sea region, companies and governments, want to see the region flourishing. For this, however, key governance issues need to be tackled. On the one hand, governments need to find modalities that secure their legitimate national interests; and at the same time companies need to engage in a dialogue to help arrive at such a governance framework, which balances legitimate interests. In this sense, effective governance is a two-way street, and there needs to be balance between the interests of each side.

There are several levels which successful projects have to include into their foundation: based on the proven reserves and agreement of the partners' best opinions at lowest total cost are put forward together with realistic timetable as well as competitive financing and a sufficient level of local content should be in place.

The issue of corporate governance in the hydrocarbon industry cannot be viewed in isolation; it should shape policies towards the general business environment, which has an important influence on the willingness of foreign companies to set up or expand operations. Also it is crucial for the broader objective of the state to trickle down revenues from the oil industry to the rest of the economy.

The broad shift in the region towards more assertive market regulation has highlighted the common concern of host governments to improve the capabilities of local companies involved in supply and services. There are several strong arguments why the host governments favour local content: it broadens the knowledge base of the local capabilities and, for the companies, local content potentially provides a lower-cost engineering resource, and also facilitates relationship-building with host governments and national oil companies.

It is understandable that the governments of the Caspian region are attempting to create an environment that involves local business wherever possible, and to train the indigenous population. But at the same time there are concerns that the level of local capability development and absorption capacity might not be in the 'right' shape. The concern about local content has found its expression in a range of approaches by Azerbaijan, Kazakhstan and Turkmenistan, as well as a range of regulations.

The book has examined various examples of local content policies and concludes that a badly designed policy may damage growth by consuming wealth rather than creating value, and this may have knock-on effects to other sectors of the economy.

The overall conclusion of the local content implementation is that the Caspian governments should set realistic goals for local content programmes, where a comprehensive Local Content Indicator includes ownership, local content of materials, the percentage of local labour, the percentage of locals in professional and management positions, services (contracts) and local taxes. Only this combination will stimulate substantial growth.

Local Caspian companies face many challenges. These include a lack of knowledge of international standards, as well as inability to provide more than a limited range of products, and other technical problems. All this can sometimes prevent them from become equal partners with international firms.

The corollary is that local content can be a real issue in terms of ensuring a low cost level for oil and gas projects. Sometimes, development of local content might not make commercial sense; therefore it might require a sustainable project workload and clients might have to accept that it could increase a contractor's risks in the early days. The integration of local engineering and project management capability within the company's project management system could be one of the possible solutions to this problem. The importance of achieving acceptable levels of local content in major hydrocarbon projects is becoming increasingly evident in the Caspian Sea region. A key area, in which there have been promising examples of cooperation in the region (and fantastic photo opportunities for me), is a systematic involvement by companies in ensuring facilities for technical training, which can help to remedy a lack of local technical skills.

Overall, it is very important to keep the 'right' balance, and to try to arrive at incentive frameworks that address externalities for both governments and companies, in which respect the area of training is indeed a relevant example. A more confrontational or forced approach, which is not moulded in terms of mutually compatible interests, might also harm prospects for entering the WTO – a goal that at least Azerbaijan and Kazakhstan are now pursuing.

The book emphasizes that for both governments and companies, it is important to realize that increased local content takes time; one must be prepared for risk mitigation and cost-sharing incentives. My conclusion in this respect is that governments can set frameworks that enable the growth of national content via a transparent, self-regulating process, which does not deter companies from expanding their operations. No doubt local content development requires a collaborative approach between clients and contractors to manage resources.

Two important questions discussed in the book relate to the degree to which the oil and gas industry could support the global demand for local content as well as how these demands are to be balanced against project requirements of budget, safety, quality and increasingly shorter schedules. Five elements are presented in the book in order to answer these questions on a country-by-country basis: a set of criteria to evaluate local content impact, which takes into account the specifics of project life-cycles in the industry; the maximization of local content should be based on identifying opportunities to capture local value-added through the selection of specific (not all) goods and services; a clear definition is needed of ways to deliver maximum local value by increasing participation of local nationals in appropriate functions; approaches to subcontracting are needed that increase the scope, over time, to raise the participation of local firms; and a definition is needed of possible additional modalities, including aspects of social responsibility. The local content goals should be realistic, but also ensure ripple effects that benefit the rest of the economy.

'The future is – or could be – bright'?

Maximization of the potential benefits from oil and gas exploitation is the ultimate objective of governments in the Caspian region. In this respect, national energy strategies are of paramount importance. All three Caspian countries have such strategies. They are different as regards the approach in their plans and the specification of ultimate goals. But there is one common feature in all three strategies: the governments are attempting to maximize the effect of hydrocarbon development for their respective countries.

The presence of the state in oil and gas production can be seen in the first instance in a country's licensing regulations and hydrocarbon legislation. Initially, the Caspian governments knew very little about how to conduct negotiations with the companies. This helps to explain why, at this current stage of development, governments may be trying to change some earlier rules, agreements and tax codes – as well as to introduce the new elements (such as the concept of strategic partner in Kazakhstan) into company–government relations.

Logically, any investor is likely to attempt to gain as much freedom as possible to determine the size, characteristics and phasing of plans in hydrocarbon exploration, appraisal, development and production. Ultimately, an investor will want as little governmental interference as possible in the pricing of oil and gas, as well as equipment purchases.

The host government has quite different objectives with regard to oil and gas production. These are mainly to obtain a large share of economic rents from oil exploitation, with the ability to regulate exploration and development as well as the pace of production; and also to enhance local participation in employment and provision of supplies and equipment.

It is, of course, legitimate for a government to extract a share of oil and gas rents for the benefit of the population of the host country. But in this respect the question of spending this rent becomes a very hot issue. How is it possible to make resource-rich governments more accountable for their spending? The main international vehicle for revenue transparency is the Extractive Industries Transparency Initiative. The EITI is a voluntary scheme, which could be very powerful; however, not every country recognizes it. For instance, Turkmenistan is not a member of the EITI; at the same time Azerbaijan made significant progress in the implementation of the EITI and Kazakhstan is only just beginning to do so.

A key conclusion of this book is the need for any resource-rich country (our three countries under consideration here are no exception) to adopt an integrated approach to energy policy, including a clean environment and the sustainable development of the local economy. The book highlights three key elements that should underlie the priorities of an optimal energy policy. These are the energy transport challenge; the nature of instruments to foster oil and gas development, together with the diversification of the national economy; and the need to underpin environmental stability by fostering sustainable growth in the region.

However, some Caspian governments do not necessarily pursue such interests in a consistent manner over time. Current high oil prices have significantly increased the profits of oil companies, but they may also be a factor that influences governments to delay the exploitation of new finds and to change the terms of existing contracts. In current conditions the Caspian economies are becoming prosperous through high oil prices, and it is tempting to review contracts which were signed by the Caspian governments in the 1990s. Indeed, they may use some factors such as the environment, taxes, customs, etc. to justify a significant reverse of the policies. Another side of the same coin is that the companies (IOCs) tried to win large contracts in the early 1990s, promising unrealistically speedy results with the bids based on too low cost estimates and unrealistic timetables. Now, high oil prices have added to cost inflation and companies are squeezed by this; by the high complexity of certain projects; and possibly by a narrowing of investment options being offered by governments.

All in all, there is a need for a balanced evolution in government–company relations, in which tensions can be resolved in a manner that does not raise economic risk and political unpredictability to levels that deter companies from new investment over time.

Other problems are related to transport channels, i.e. the need for adequate transport routes. Existing routes are fragile, with distinct security problems. Unlocking the area's main reserves of natural gas requires new options and new investments. A key constraint affecting costs throughout the region, and constraining export, is that pipelines and port facilities are inadequate. As major Caspian oil fields have been brought to full production, it has become increasingly obvious that oil output from the region has the clear potential to grow rapidly over the next decade. The transport challenge concerns gas as well as oil.

In order to realize the full potential of its gas fields (as well as a more efficient utilization of associated gas reserves), the Caspian region needs additional gas pipelines and infrastructure.

All three Caspian economies will only sustain economic growth if the rest of their non-oil sectors prove competitive. Industrial competitiveness and diversification of the economies are the next steps in the development of the economies of the three countries and in this respect the link between institutions and governmental policies plays a crucial role. The book discussed steps which the Kazakhstani government in particular is attempting to implement at the time of writing (e.g. the creation of Samruk and Kazyna).

Finally, the book addressed a very important issue – the environment. There are real environmental issues connected with the deterioration of environmental conditions of the Caspian Sea as well as with promotion of sustainable development in the area. The Caspian governments have realized the danger of potential accidental oil spills and they are trying to create comprehensive contingency plans in case of accidents. Another environmental problem for the Caspian Sea is a serious decline in the numbers of Caspian seals, as well as the deterioration of water quality, which is related to the commercially developable hydrocarbon deposits in the Caspian Sea Basin. Unfortunately, at the time of writing, this environmental factor is becoming more and more a political weapon in the hands of the governments (e.g. Russia and Kazakhstan).

The Caspian region governments have to mitigate the effects of market failures and develop in the future a common set of rules for all their projects with environmental implications. Overall, a collaborative and successful relationship between companies and governments requires – together with financial and technical resources – clear rules and two-way accountability and transparency.

References

Ades, Alberto and Rafael Di Tella (1999), 'Rents, competition, and corruption', *American Economic Review*, **89**(4): 982–93.

Ahrend, Rudiger (2006), 'How to Sustain Growth in a Resource Based Economy? The Main Concepts and Their Application to the Russian Case', Working Paper No. 478, Paris: OECD.

Aliyev, Heydar (1997), Azerbaijan Oil in the World Policy, Baku: Azerbaijan Publishing House.

The American Society of International Law (2003), *International Law in Brief*, 13 November, http://www.asil.org/ilib/ilib0620.htm#j3.

Argus Media (1997–2007) *Argus FSU*, various issues.

Asafu-Adjaye, John (2000), 'The relationship between energy consumption, energy prices and economic growth: time series evidence from Asian developing countries', *Energy Economics*, **22**: 615–25.

Asian Development Bank (2002), *Board of Directors: The Country Classification Turkmenistan*, R183-2, 17 September. Manila: ADB.

Asian Development Bank (2005a), *Azerbaijan: Country Gender Assessment*, December, Manila: East and Central Asia Regional Department and Regional and Sustainable Development Department, ADB.

Asian Development Bank (2005b), *Asian Development Report, 2005*. Manila: ADB.

Atygayev, Ayan (2007), 'Kazakhstan Khochet zanENIt', in *Kursiv*, 6 September (in Russian).

Austin Associates, Inc. (2004), 'Report on Phase One Analytics and Summary of Other Component Activity. Diversification of Kazakhstan's Economy through Cluster Development in Non-Extracting Economic Sectors', Astana, August.

Auty, Richard (2003), 'Natural resources and "gradual" reform in Uzbekistan and Turkmenistan', *Natural Resources Forum*, **27**: 255–66.

Auty, Richard (2006), 'Transition to mid-income democracies or to failed states?' in *Energy, Wealth and Governance in the Caucasus and Central Asia: Lessons not Learned*, Ed. Richard M. Auty and Indra de Soysa, London and New York: Routledge.

Auty, Richard and Raymond Mikesell (1998), *Sustainable Development in Mineral Economies*, Oxford: Clarendon Press.

Bagirov, Sabit (1996) 'Azerbaijani oil: glimpses of a long history', *Journal of international Affairs*, **1**(2), June–August.

Balassa, Bela (1980), *The Process of Industrial Development and Alternative Development Strategies*, Princeton, NJ: Princeton University Press.

Bandara, Amarakoon, Muhammad Hussain Malik and Eugene Gherman (2004), 'Poverty in countries of Central Asia', in Ahmed Shahid, N.V. Lam, Marin Yari, M.H. Malik, Amarakoon Bandara, John Wong, Djisman S. Simandjuntak, Eugene Gherman, Biswajit Nag and Ron Duncan (eds), *Bulletin on Asia-Pacific Perspectives 2004/05: Asia-Pacific Economies: Living with High Oil prices?*, New York.

Bannon, Ian and Paul Collier (2003), 'Natural resources and conflict: what we can do', in I. Bannon and P. Collier (eds), *Natural Resources and Violent Conflict: Options and Actions*, Washington, DC: World Bank.

Baumol, William and Wallace Oates (1988), *The Theory of Environmental Policy, 2nd edn,* New York: Cambridge University Press.

Beltratti, Andrea (1996), *Models of Economic Growth with Environmental Assets,* Dordrecht, Boston, London: Kluwer Academic Publishers.

Berdymukhamedov, Gurbanguly (2007) *The President of Turkmenistan G. Berdymukhamedov's Policy on a Renaissance of the Country.* Ashgabat, Turkmen dowlet nesiryat gullugy.

BG Group (2006), *Delivering Outstanding Value to Shareholders. Annual Report and Accounts 2005, 2006.* Reading, UK.

Bindemann, Kirsten (2000), 'World development of production sharing agreements', *Petroleum Review,* February: 29–30.

Biswajit, Nag and Ron Duncan (2004), *Bulletin on Asia-Pacific Perspectives 2004/05: Asia-Pacific Economies: Living with High Oil Prices?,* New York: UN.

Blaug, Marc (1978), 'Ricardo's system', in *Economic Theory in Retrospect,* 3rd edn, Cambridge and New York: Cambridge University Press, pp. 91–112.

BP Azerbaijan (2004), *Sustainability Report 2004,* London.

BP Code of Conduct (2005), 'Our Commitment to Integrity', London.

BP (2007), 'Shah Deniz in the Spotlight', *Compass,* 3, March: 12–13.

Briggs Marine Environnemental Services Ltd (2001), 'Final report Azeri, Chirag & Gunashli Oil Spill Risk Assessment for BP Exploration (Caspian Sea) Ltd Baku, Azerbaijan', Ref: 3793R/27527-071-456/R01PV/JW/id. London.

Bunni, Nael G. (2005), *The FIDIC Forms of Contract,* Oxford: International Federation of Consulting Engineers, Blackwell.

Caspian Technical Resources LLP (2006), *A NCCER Accredited Training Unit (ATU). CTR Project Craft Training Information,* March, Atyrau: Caspian Training Centre.

Centre for Global Energy Studies (2006), *Oil in Fifteen Volumes,* Vol. 10, *The Former Soviet Union,* London: CGES.

Chang, Tsangyao, Fang Wenshwo and Wen Li-Fang (2001), 'Energy consumption, employment, output and temporal causality: evidence from Taiwan based on cointegration and error-correction modelling techniques', *Applied Economics,* **33**: 1045–56.

Cheng, Benjamin S. (1997), 'Energy consumption and economic growth in Brazil, Mexico and Venezuela: a time series analysis', *Applied Economics Letters,* **4**: 671–4.

Cheng, Benjamin S. (1999), 'Causality between energy consumption and economic growth in India: an application of cointegration and error-correction modelling', *Indian Economic Review,* **34**: 39–49.

Common, Michael (1996), *Environmental & Resource Economics: An Introduction,* London: Longman.

Corden, W. Max and J. Peter Neary (1982), 'Booming sector and de-industrialisation in a small open economy', *The Economic Journal,* **92** (December): 825–48.

Cornillie, Jan and Samuel Fankhauser (2002), 'The energy intensity of transition countries', EBRD Working Paper EBRD No. 72, London.

Crude Accountability (2007), *Turkmenistan's Environmental Risks in the Era of Investment in the Hydrocarbon Sector. A Report by Crude Accountability,* September. Alexandria, VA: Crude Accountability.

Davis, Graham A. (1995), 'Learning to love the Dutch Disease: evidence from mineral economies', *World Development* **23**(10): 1765–80.

Davis, Jeffrey, Rolando Ossowski, James Daniel and Steven Barnett (2001), 'Stabilisation and saving funds for nonrenewable resources', *IMF Occasional Paper 2005.*

Davis, J.M., R. Ossowski and A. Fedelino (eds) (2003), *Fiscal Policy Formulation and Implementation in Oil-Producing Countries*, Washington, DC: IMF.

Dekmejian, R. Hrair and Hovann H. Simonian (2003), *Troubled Waters – The Geopolitics of the Caspian Region*, London: I.B. Tauris.

DentonWildeSapte (2005), 'Petroleum Regime Changes in Kazakhstan', *AIPN Advisor*, January, Almaty: DentonWildeSapte.

Dobronogov, Anthon (2003), 'Social protection in low income CIS countries', paper prepared for the Lucerne Conference of the CIS-7 Initiative, 20–22 January, http://lnweb18.worldbank.org/ECA/CIS7.nsf.

Downes, John and Jordan Elliot Goodman (1998), *Dictionary of Finance and Investment Terms*, Barron's Financial Guides. Hauppauge, USA: Barron's Educational Series, Inc.

Drake, P. (1972), 'Natural resources versus foreign borrowing in economic development', *The Economic Journal*, 82(327): 951–62.

Dunn, Jonathan (1987), 'Joint ventures in Eastern Europe', in *Multinational Monitor*, Nos 11 & 12, http://multinationalmonitor.org/hyper/issues/1987/11/index.html

Dunning, John (1981), *International Production and Multinational Enterprise*, London: Allen & Unwin.

ECON Centre for Economic Analysis (2002), 'Paradox of plenty: the management of oil wealth', Report No. 12/02, Project No. 25411, Commissioned by Statoil.

Economic Commission for Africa (2007), *Economic Report on Africa 2007: Accelerating Africa's Development*, Addis Ababa, Ethiopia: UN.

Economic Commission for Europe/Committee on Environmental Policy (ECE/CEP) (2000), *Environmental Performance Reviews: Kazakhstan*, New York and Geneva: UN.

Economic Commission for Europe/Committee on Environmental Policy (ECE/CEP) (2004), *Environmental Performance Reviews: Azerbaijan*, New York and Geneva: UN.

Effimoff, Igor (2000), 'The oil and gas resource base of the Caspian region', *Journal of Petroleum Science and Engineering*, 28(4): 157–59.

Eggers, Adrew, Clifford Gaddy and Carol Graham (2006), 'Well-being and unemployment in Russia in the 1990s: can society's suffering be individual solace?', *The Journal of Socio-Economics*, 35: 209–42.

Eifert, Bebb, Alan Gelb and Nils Borje Tallroth (2003), 'Managing oil wealth', *Finance and Development*, 40(1).

Encyclopedia of the Nations: Asia and Oceania (2005), 'Azerbaijan – Foreign Investment', http://www.nationsencyclopedia.com/Asia-and-Oceania/Azerbaijan-FOREIGN-INVESTMENT.html.

Esanov, Akram, Martin Raser and Willem Buiter (2006), 'Nature's blessing or nature's curse?' in Richard M. Auty and Indra de Soysa (eds), *Energy, Wealth and Governance in the Caucasus and Central Asia: Lessons not Learned*, London and New York: Routledge.

European Bank for Reconstruction and Development (2006), *Strategy for Turkmenistan*, London: EBRD.

European Bank for Reconstruction and Development (2007), *Life in Transition Survey*, London: EBRD.

Fasano, Ugo (2000), 'Review of the experience with oil stabilization and savings funds in selected countries', IMF Working Paper WP/00/112.

Fatai, K., Les Oxley and F.G. Scrimgeour (2004), 'Modelling the causal relationship between energy consumption and GDP in New Zealand, Australia, India, Indonesia, the Philippines and Thailand', *Mathematics and Computers in Simulation*, **64**: 431–45.

FitchRatings (2003), *International Credit Analysis: Republic of Kazakhstan*, November.

FitchRatings (2006), 'Tengizchevroil Finance Company SARL (Issuer)', Credit Analysis. London: FitchRatings.

Fowler, Courtney (2005), 'Kazakhstan oil and gas – taxation that always extends', in ITIC Special Report, *The Taxation System, Investment Regulation and Economic Development in Select Countries of Eurasia*, by ITIC in conjunction with Deloitte, Ernst & Young, and PricewaterhouseCoopers, March, Washington, DC: ITIC.

Gelb, Alan H. (1985), 'Adjustment to windfall gains: a comparative analysis of oil-exporting countries', in J. Peter Neary and Sweder van Wijnbergen (eds), *Natural Resources and the Macroeconomy*, Oxford: Basil Blackwell.

Gleason, Gregory (1997), *The Central Asian States: Discovering Independence*, Boulder, CO: Westview Press.

Gleason, Gregory (2002), 'Turkmenistan – Economic System', in *Encyclopedia of Modern Asia*, Vol. 6, New York: Charles Scribner's Sons and Berkshire Publishing Group.

Glennester, Rachel and Yongseokh Shin (2003), *Is Transparency Good For You, and Can the IMF Help?*, IMF Working Paper No. 132, June.

Global Witness (2006), *Funny Business in the Turkmen–Ukraine Gas Trade*, Report, April, Washington DC: Global Witness.

Gorst, Isabel (2007a), 'Profit surge boosts KMG's aspirations for Kazkahstan', *Financial Times*, 18 September.

Gorst, Isabel (2007b), 'Kazakhstan oil tax crackdown', *Financial Times*, 3 December.

Gylfason, Thorvaldur (2001), 'Nature, power, and growth', CESinfo Working Paper No. 413.

Gylfason, Thorvaldur and Gylfi Zoega (2003), 'Inequality theory and policy implications', in Theo Eicher and Stephen Turnovsky (eds), *Inequality and Growth: Theory and Policy Implications*, Cambridge, MA: MIT Press.

Gylfason, Thorvaldur (2004), 'National resources and economic growth: from dependence to diversification', CEPR Discussion Paper No. 4804.

Gylfason, Thorvaldur (2006), 'Natural resources and economic growth: from dependence to diversification' in Harry G. Broadman, Tiiu Paas and Paul J.J. Welfens (eds), *Economic Liberalization and Integration Policy: Options for Eastern Europe and Russia*, Heidelberg and Berlin: Springer.

Gylfason, Thorvaldur (2007), 'International economics of natural resources and growth', CESifo Working Paper No. 1994, May (forthcoming in *Minerals and Energy*).

Hamilton, Tom (1995), 'The Caspian's giant oil potential: a rough road to major producer status', in *New Oil: The World's Oil Map in the Year 2005*, London: Centre for Global Energy Studies, pp. 109–21.

Hannesson, Rognvaldur (1998), *Petroleum Economics. Issues and Strategies of Oil and Natural Gas Production*, Westport, CT and London: Quorum Books.

Hartwick, John and Nancy Olewiler (1986), *The Economics of Natural Resource Use*, New York: Harper & Row.

Havrylyshyn, Oleh and Hassan Al-Atrash (1998), 'Opening up and Geographic Diversion of Trade in Transition economics', IMF working paper No. 98/22.

Havrylyshyn, Oleh and Hassan Al-Atrash (1999), 'Geographic diversification of trade in transition economies', in Mario I. Blejer and Marko Skreb (eds), *Balance of Payments, Exchange Rates, and Competitiveness in Transition Economies*, New York: Springer, pp. 215–38.

Helm, D. (2002), 'Energy policy: security of supply, sustainability and competition', *Energy Policy*, **30**: 173–84.

Higgins, Benjamin (1968), *Economic Development: Problems, Principles, and Policies*, New York: W.W. Norton and Co.

IMF (1999), *Turkmenistan: Recent Economic Developments*, Country Report 99/140, December, Washington, DC: IMF.

IMF (2004) *Republic of Kazakhstan: Selected Issues*, IMF Country Report No. 04/362. Washington, DC: IMF.

International Petroleum Industry Environmental Conservation Association (IPIECA) (various years), *Biological Impacts of Oil Pollution*, http://www.ipieca. org.publications_search.php?crit=full_date.

Isham, Jonathan, Michael Woolcock, Lant Pritchett and Gwen Busby (2002), 'The varieties of rentier experience: how natural resource export structures affect the political economy of economic growth', Worldwide Web document, available at www.middlebury.edu/NR/rdonlyres/23035072-BFD1-43A1-923C-9CF11831F32/0/0308.pdf

Kalyuzhnov, Andrei, Julian Lee and Julia Nanay (2001) 'Domestic use of energy: oil refineries and gas processing' in Yelena Kalyuzhnova, Amy Myers Jaffe, Dov Lynch and Robin Sickles (eds), *Energy in the Caspian Region: Present and Future*, Basingstoke: Palgrave.

Kalyuzhnova, Yelena (2001), 'Economies and energy', in Yelena Kalyuzhnova, Amy Myers Jaffe, Dov Lynch and Robert Sickles (eds), *Energy in the Caspian Region: Present and Future*, Basingstoke: Palgrave.

Kalyuzhnova, Yelena (2005), 'The EU and the Caspian Sea region: an energy partnership?', *Economic Systems*, **29**(1): 59–76.

Kalyuzhnova, Yelena (2006), 'Overcoming the curse of hydrocarbon: goals and governance in the oil funds of Kazakhstan and Azerbaijan', *Comparative Economic Studies*, **48**: 583–613.

Kalyuzhnova, Yelena and Michael Kaser (2006), 'Prudential management of hydrocarbon revenues', *Post-Communist Economies*, **18**(2).

Kalyuzhnova, Yelena and Dov Lynch (eds), (2000), *The Euro-Asian World: a Period of Transition*, Basingstoke: Macmillan.

Kalyuzhnova, Yelena and Uma Kambhampati (2008), 'The determinants of individual happiness in Kazakhstan', *Economic Systems*, forthcoming.

Kalyuzhnova, Yelena, James Pemberton and Bulat Mukhamediev (2004), 'Economic growth in Kazakhstan', in Gur Ofer and Richard Pomfret (eds), The Economic Prospects of the CIS, chettenhan, UK and Northampton MA: Edward Elgar.

Karabalin, Uzakbai (2006), 'Business diversification: trends and outlooks', presentation at the 6th Annual Conference, 'Oil, Gas and Natural Resources in Kazakhstan', London.

Karabalin, Uzakbai (2007), 'JSC NC "KazMunayGas": 5 years of development', presentation at Kazakhstan Economic Growth Forum, London.

Kaser, Michael (1997), *The Economies of Kazakhstan and Uzbekistan*, London: The Royal Institute of International Affairs.

Kaser, Michael (2003), 'The economic and social impact of systemic transition in Central Asia and Azerbaijan', *Perspectives on Global Development and Technology*, 2(3): 459–73.

Karl, Terry Lynn (1997), *The Paradox of Plenty: Oil Booms and Petro-States*, Berkeley, CA: University of California Press.

Kazakhstan Petroleum Association (2006), *2006 Catalogue*, Almaty: KPA Publications.

Kemp, Alexander (1990), 'An assessment of UK North Sea oil and gas policies: twenty-five years on', *Energy Policy*, September: 599–622.

Kornai, Janos (2003), 'Ten years after the road to a free economy: the author's self-evaluation of privatisation', in Yelena Kalyuzhnova and Wladimir Andreff (eds), *Privatisation and Structural Change in Transition Economies*, Basingstoke: Palgrave.

Kostopoulos, Christos (1999), 'Progress in public expenditure management in Africa: evidence from World Bank surveys', Africa Region Working Paper Series No. 1, January, Washington, DC.

Kramer, Andrew (2006), 'Moscow gets further concession on Sakhalin-2', *International Herald Tribune*, 28 December.

Krueger, Anne (1980), 'Trade policy as an input to development', *American Economic Review*, 70(2): 288–92.

Krysiek, Timothy Fenton (2007), 'The CPC, the BTC and the transformation of Caspian Geopolitics', *Geopolitics of Energy*, 29(4): 2–9.

Kutan, Ali M. and Michael L. Wyzan (2005), 'Explaining the real exchange rate in Kazakhstan, 1996–2003: is Kazakhstan vulnerable to the Dutch disease?', *Economic Systems*, 29(2): 242–55.

Lal, Deepak (1995), 'Why growth rates differ. The political economy of social capability in 21 developing countries', in Bon Ho Koo and Dwight H. Perkins (eds), *Social Capability and Long-Term Economic Growth*, New York: St Martin's Press.

Larsson, Thomas (2006), 'Reform, corruption, and growth: why corruption is more devastating in Russia than in China', *Communist and Post-Communist Studies*, 39: 265–81.

Layard, Richard (2005), *Happiness: Lessons from a New Science*, New York: The Penguin Press.

Lee, Julian (1996), *Breaking the Stranglehold*, London: Centre for Global Energy Studies.

Lee, Julian (2007a), *The Future of Caspian Oil Exports*, London: Centre for Global Energy Studies.

Lee, Julian (2007b), 'Iran proposes a new Caspian export pipeline', *FSU Pipeline Advisory*, No. 20, 30 August.

Lee, Julian (2007c), 'Kazakhstan's eastward oil and gas export plans move forward', *FSU Pipeline Advisory*, No. 19, 29 August.

Leite, Carlos and Jens Weidmann (1999), 'Does Mother Nature Corrupt? Natural Resources, Corruption, and, Economic Growth', IMF Working Paper WP/99/85, Washington, DC: IMF.

Lewis, W. Arthur (1955), *The Theory of Economic Growth*, Homewood, IL: R.D. Irwin.

The Long-Term Strategy on the Management of Oil and Gas Revenues. (2004), Baku: Republic of Azerbaijan.

Looney, Robert E. (1994), *Industrial Development and Diversification of the Arabian Gulf Economies*, Greenwich, CT and London: JAI Press.

Lydolph, Paul E. and Theodore Shabad (1960), 'The oil and gas industries in the USSR', *Annals of the Association of American Geographers*, **50**(4): 461–8.

Lynch, Dov (2000), *Russian Peacekeeping Strategies in the CIS*, Basingstoke: Macmillan.

Macleod Dixon (2007), *Kazakhstan Legal Bulletin*, 30 January, Almaty.

Major, John (1997), 'Letter to the President of Azerbaijan on September 18, 1994', in Heidar Alyiev (ed.), *Azerbaijan Oil in the World Policy*, Baku: Azerbaijan Publishing House.

Marcel, Valerie with John V. Mitchell (2005), *Oil Titans: National Oil Companies in the Middle East*, London: Chatham House and Washington, DC: Brookings Institution Press.

Masih, Abul M.M. and Rumi Masih (1996), 'Energy consumption, real income and temporal causality: results from a multi-country study based on cointegration and error-correction modelling techniques', *Energy Economics*, **18**: 165–83.

Mann, Steven (2003), 'the coming phases of Caspian energy', presentation at the International Conference 'Sustainable Development and Social Issues', Centre for Euro-Asian Studies, University of Reading, 14 March.

Mauro, Paolo (1995), 'Corruption and growth', *The Quarterly Journal of Economics*, **110**(3): 681–712.

McKay, John (1984), 'Baku oil trascaucasian pipelines, 1883–1891: a study in tsarist economic Policy', *Slavic Review*, **43**(4): 604–23.

Mehlum, Halvor, Karl Moene and Ragnar Torvik (2006), 'Cursed by resources or institutions?', *The World Economy*, **29**(8): 1117–31.

Mittra, B., N. Lucas and I. Fells (1995), 'European energy. Balancing markets and policy', *Energy Policy*, **23**(8): 689–701.

Morrissey, Oliver (2001), 'Investment and competition policy in the WTO: issues for developing countries', *Development Policy Review*, **20**(1): 63–73.

Najman, Boris, Richard Pomfret and Gaël Raballand (2007), *The Economics and Politics of Oil in the Caspian Basin*, London: Routledge.

Namazie, Ceema and Peter Sanfey (2001), 'Happiness and transition: the case of Kyrgyzstan', *Review of Development Economics*, **5**(3): 392–405.

Nanay, Julia (2000), 'The industry's race for the Caspian oil reserves', in *Caspian Energy Resources. Implications for the Arab Gulf*, Abu Dhabi. UAE: Emirates Center for Strategic Studies and Research.

Nanay, Julia (2005), 'The Transformation of KazMunaiGaz (KMG)'. PFC Energy. Presentation at the 5th Annual Conference, 'Kazakhstan: Oil and Gas', London.

Nazarbayev, Nursultan (2005), 'Kazakhstan on the road to accelerated economic, social and political modernization', Address by President Nursultan Nazarbayev of the Republic of Kazakhstan to the People of Kazakhstan, 18 February.

Nazarbayev, Nursultan (2006), 'Kazakhstan's strategy of joining the world's 50 most competitive countries' Address by the President of the Republic of Kazakhstan to the People of Kazakhstan, 1 March, Astana.

Nazaroff, Alexander (1941), 'The Soviet oil industry', *Russian Review*, **1**(1): 81–9.

Neff, Andrew (2005), 'Caspian nations pursuing oil exports at greatly varying paces', *Oil and Gas Journal*, 13 June: 34–9.

Nelson, Timothy G. (2006), 'BRIDAS v. Government of Turkmenistan: U.S. Courts uphold an arbitrator's power to hold a foreign sovereign liable for the acts of its state-owned enterprise', *ASA Bulletin* 3/2006, September. London: Kluwer Law International, pp. 584–99.

Newendorp, Paul (1975), *Decision Analysis for Petroleum Excploration*, Tulsa, O PennWell Publishing Co.

Olcott, Martha Brill (2002), *Kazakhstan – Unfulfilled Promise*, Washington, DC: Carnegie Endowment for International Peace.

Olcott, Martha Brill (2005), *Central's Asia Second Chance*, Washington, DC: Carnegie Endowment for International Peace.

Owusu, Francis and Abdi Ismail Samatar (1997). 'Industrial strategy and African state: the Botswana experience', *Canadian Journal of African Studies*, **31**(2): 268–99.

Paldam, Martin (1997), 'Dutch Disease and rent seeking: the Greenland model', *European Journal of Political Economy*, **13**, August: 591–614.

Parker Drilling Company (2004), Press Release, 2 July.

Petroleum Encyclopedia of Kazakhstan (2005), Almaty: Munayshy Public Foundation, Vol. 1.

Pomfret, Richard (1995), *The Economies of Central Asia*, Princeton, NJ: Princeton University Press.

Pomfret, Richard (2003), 'Economic performance in Central Asia since 1991: macro and micro evidence', *Comparative Economic Studies*, **43**(4): 442–65.

Pomfret, Richard (2006), *The Central Asian Economies Since Independence*, Princeton, NJ: Princeton University Press.

Porter, Michael (1998), 'Clusters and the new economics of competition', *Harvard Business Review*, **76**(6): 77–90.

Prebisch, Raul (1950), *The Economic Development of Latin America and its Principal Problems*, Lake Success, NY: UN.

Rach, Nina (2004), 'Kazakhs impound Parker's Sunkar barge rig', *Oil and Gas Journal*, 23 August: 44–5.

Ricardo, David (1817), *Principles of Political Economy and Taxation* (3rd edn 1821).

Rodrik, Dani (2005), 'Policies for economic diversification', *CEPAL Review 87*, http://www.cepal.cl/publicaciones/xml/1/25571/G2287iRodrik.pdf.

Rosenberg, Christoph B. and Tapio O. Saavalainen (1998), 'Dealing with Azerbaijan's oil boom', *Finance and Development*, **35**(3).

Sachs, Jeffrey and Andrew Warner (1995), 'Natural resource abundance and economic growth', NBER Working Paper No. 5398, December.

Sachs, Jeffrey D. and Andrew M. Warner (2001), 'The curse of natural resources', *European Economic Review*, **45**: 827–38.

Sala-i-Martin, Xavier and Arvind Subramanian (2003), *Addressing the Natural Resource Curse: An Illustration from Nigeria*, Washington, DC: IMF.

Salameh M.D.G. (2002), 'Caspian oil is no Middle East', *Minerals and Energy: Raw Materials Report*, **17**(2): 33–41.

Sampson, Anthony (1975), *The Seven Sisters: The Great Oil Companies and the World They Made,* London: Hodder & Stoughton.

Sarraf, Maria and Moortaza Jiwanji (2001), 'Beating the resource curse: the case of Botswana', World Bank Environment Department Papers, Environmental Economics Series (October), Washington, DC: World Bank.

Schrank, Andrew and Marcus J. Kurtz (2005), 'Credit where credit is due: open economy industrial policy and economic diversification in Latin America and the Caribbean', *Politics & Society*, **33**(4): 671–702.

Seba, Richard (2003), *Economics of Worldwide Petroleum Production*, Tulsa, OK: OGCI and PetroSkills Publications.

Segura, Alonso (2006), *Management of Oil Wealth Under the Permanent Income Hypothesis: The Case of São Tomé and* Príncipé, IMF Working Paper. WP/06/183. Washington, DC.

Smith, Benjamin (2004), 'Oil wealth and regime survival in the developing world: 1960–1999', *American Journal of Political Science*, **28**(2): 232–47.

Soligo, Ronald and Amy Myers Jaffe (2001), 'The economics of pipeline routes: the conundrum of oil exports from the Caspian Basin', in Yelena Kalyuzhnova, Amy Myers Jaffe, Dov Lynch and Robin Sickles (eds), *Energy in the Caspian Region: Present and Future*, Basingstoke: Palgrave.

Toda, Hiro Y. and Taku Yamamoto (1995), 'Statistical inference in vector autoregressions with possibly integrated process', *Journal of Econometrics*, **66**: 225–50.

Townsend, David and Duncan Rushworth (2001), 'Iran: the Caspian angle', *Petroleum Economist*, September, p. 28.

Turmanova, Asel (2007), '$10 bln. Uzherba ot inostrannykh kompanii', in *Kapital.KZ*, No. 34 (121), 6 September.

United States Court of Appeals For the Fifth Circuit (2006), *Bridas S.A.P.I.C., Bridas Energy International, Ltd., Intercontinental Oil and Gas Ventures, Ltd., and Bridas Corp, Plaintiffs-Appellants, versus Government of Turkmenistan, concern Balkannebitgazsenagat and State Concern Turkmenneft, Defendants-Appellees*. No. 04-20842. 21 April, http://caselaw.lp.findlaw.com/data2/circs/5th/0420842cv0p.pdf.

van der Ploeg, Frederik (2006), 'Challenges and opportunities for resource rich economies', CEPR Discussion Paper 5688, May, London.

Viner, Jacob (1952), *International Trade and Economic Development*, Glencoe, IL: Free Press.

Vologodskii, Victor (2006), 'Zamknutii Krug Dlya Nasosa', *Ekspert Kazakhstana*, No. 34, 18–24 September: 24–6 (In Russian).

Williamson, Hugh (2007), 'Deutsche Bank admits to Turkmen accounts', *Financial Times*, 9 May.

World Bank (2004), 'Civil society and private sector discuss World Bank country partnership strategy for Kazakhstan', News Release No. 2004/004/KZ, Astana.

World Bank (2005), *Republic of Kazakhstan: Getting Competitive, Staying Competitive: The Challenge of Managing Kazakhstan's Oil Boom*, Report No. 30852-KZ, June, Washington, DC: World Bank.

World Bank (2006), 'Country Partnership Strategy for the Republic of Azerbaijan', 8 November. Document FY07-10, Report No. 37812-AZ.

World Bank (2007), 'World Bank launches new partnership strategy with Azerbaijan', News Release No. 2007/167/ECA, Baku.

Wright, David (2002), 'Contract strategy and the contractor selection process', in Nigel J. Smith(ed.) *Engineering Project Management*, Oxford: Blackwell.

Wright, Gavin and Jessie Czelusta (2004), 'The myth of the resource curse', *Challenge*, **47**(2): 6–38.

Yeager, Timothy (1999), *Institutions, Transition Economies, and Economic Development*, Oxford: Westview Press.

Yergin, Daniel (1992), *The Prize*, New York: Simon & Schuster.

Zashev, Peter and Peeter Vahtra (2006), 'Kazakhstan as a business opportunity – industrial clusters and regional development', *Electronic Publications of Pan-European Institute* 6/2006, http://www.tukkk.fi/pei/pub.

Zhang, Le-Yin (2003), Background Paper, UNFCCC Workshop on Economic Diversification. Framework Convention on Climate Change – Secretariat. Teheran, Islamic Republic of Iran.

Other sources

The National Council for Public–Private Ownership: http://ncppp.org/howpart/ppptypes.shtml.

Definitions of contracts were taken from http://www.atkinson-law.com/cases/CasesArticles/Articles/Contract_Strategies.htm.

Workshop on oil spills prevention in Astana, 18–20 April 2001, http://pims.ed.ornl.gov/caspian/Workshops/Astana_bekkaliev.htm.

Index

Note: 'n' after a page reference indicates the number of a note on that page.